Praise for Boomer or Bust

"This book is filled with critically important information and is an essential primer regarding the issues facing our generation. It will be required reading for all of our staff as well as recommended reading for our sandwich generation clients."

—*Joanne R. Wooldridge, R.N., Geriatric Care Manager Clinical Director, Massachusetts General PrimeCare*

"Read this book. It is a great addition to your personal financial arsenal, worth keeping on hand."

—*Rollye James, nationally syndicated radio talk show host*

"As usual, Steve Weisman has the right slant on problems that others just glance over. He takes on all of the government sacred cows and deals with the red tape and regulations that are impossible to understand without help. So here is the help you need. Read this book and get started on the way to helping yourself."

—*Doug Stephan, host of the syndicated* Good Day *radio program, heard in more than 400 markets nationwide*

BOOMER OR BUST

BOOMER OR BUST

YOUR FINANCIAL GUIDE TO RETIREMENT, HEALTH CARE, MEDICARE, AND LONG-TERM CARE

Steve Weisman

Upper Saddle River, NJ•New York•London•San Francisco•Toronto•Sydney
Tokyo•Singapore•Hong Kong•Cape Town•Madrid
Paris•Milan•Munich•Amsterdam

Vice President and Editor-in-Chief: Tim Moore
Executive Editor: Jim Boyd
Editorial Assistant: Susie Abraham
Development Editor: Russ Hall
Associate Editor-in-Chief and Director of Marketing: Amy Neidlinger
Cover Designer: Alan Clements
Managing Editor: Gina Kanouse
Senior Project Editor: Lori Lyons
Copy Editor: Krista Hansing
Senior Indexer: Cheryl Lenser
Compositor: FASTpages
Manufacturing Buyer: Dan Uhrig

Prentice Hall offers excellent discounts on this book when ordered in quantity for bulk purchases or special sales. For more information, please contact U.S. Corporate and Government Sales, 1-800-382-3419, corpsales@pearsontechgroup.com. For sales outside the U.S., please contact International Sales, 1-317-581-3793, international@pearsontechgroup.com.

Second Printing, October 2006

ISBN 0-13-188176-0

Pearson Education LTD.
Pearson Education Australia PTY, Limited.
Pearson Education Singapore, Pte. Ltd.
Pearson Education North Asia, Ltd.
Pearson Education Canada, Ltd.
Pearson Educatión de Mexico, S.A. de C.V.
Pearson Education—Japan
Pearson Education Malaysia, Pte. Ltd.

Library of Congress Cataloging-in-Publication Data
Weisman, Steve.
  Boomer or bust : your financial guide to retirement, health care, medicare, and long-term care / Steve Weisman.
      p. cm.
  Includes bibliographical references and index.
  ISBN 0-13-188176-0 (pbk. : alk. paper) 1. Retirement income—United States—Planning. 2. Older people—Care—United States—Planning. I. Title.
  HG179.W4635 2006
  332.024'014—dc22}   2006004224

To my wife Carole, my love, my life.

As Robert Browning said,
"Grow old with me! The best is yet to be."

CONTENTS

3

ANNUITIES   31

4

INCOME TAXES FOR SENIORS 45

PART II   PLANNING FOR LONG-TERM CARE   97

7

HOME CARE   99

8

CHOOSING A NURSING HOME OR AN ASSISTED-LIVING FACILITY   111

ACKNOWLEDGMENTS

I want to thank some people who have helped make this book happen.

Marc Padellaro, who teaches me so much every day. It is his nature.

Gary Barg, from whom I learned about care giving.

Michael Harrison, a great mentor and a better friend.

Ron Nathan, my great friend and advisor whose knowledge of complex insurance and financial matters was so important to this book.

Joe Newpol, who makes tax matters seem almost logical.

Carole Marks and the people at the *A Touch of Grey* radio show.

Jim Boyd, my editor and guide.

Bing Chen, eminent gerontologist and educator of so many, including myself.

Fran Borek and Gerry Smith, whose constant encouragement is so appreciated.

Ken and Karen Isabelle, whose strong support is always there.

Boppy, who provided the example of a life of great compassion and dignity.

And most of all, as a Sandwich Generation baby boomer, I want to acknowledge the other parts of that sandwich from my parents, Jeanne and Arnie Weisman; to my children (and their spouses), Loren, Roger, Lisa, Hutch, Rick, Julie, Tommy, and Griff; as well as to my grandchildren, Hutcher, Delaney, Taylor, and Chase.

ABOUT THE AUTHOR

Steve Weisman hosts the nationally syndicated radio show *A Touch of Grey,* heard on more than 50 radio stations throughout the country. He has been an award-winning talk show host and commentator for more than 20 years.

A member of the National Academy of Elder Law Attorneys, Weisman is a practicing attorney. He specializes in estate planning, probate, and elder law. He has taught at the University of Massachusetts, Curry College, and Boston University, and is currently an adjunct faculty member at Bentley College. He holds a B.A. degree from the University of Massachusetts at Amherst and a J.D. degree from Boston College Law School, and is admitted to practice before the United States Supreme Court.

Weisman is a legal editor and columnist for *Talkers Magazine* and writes on legal matters for publications from *The Boston Globe* to *Playboy Magazine.* He has earned a Certificate of Merit from the American Bar Association for excellence in legal journalism. His previous books include *A Guide to Elder Planning* (Pearson Education, 2003) and *50 Ways to Protect Your Identity and Your Credit* (Pearson Education, 2005).

INTRODUCTION

I t has always been about us. We are the baby boomers. Between 1946 and 1964, 78 million of us burst onto the American scene. In every stage of our lives, America has been about us. Businesses changed to meet our needs. The Ford Mustang, introduced in 1964, sold 22,000 cars on the first day and 1 million cars in the first 2 years to a population that included large numbers of baby boomers, fresh with their drivers' licenses and looking for sporty cars.

We did not trust anyone over 30. We did not listen to our parents. We were young. We had all the answers.

Now years later, our numbers still dominate the country. Baby boomers represent 27.5 percent of the population. But we are getting old. More than 24 million of us are over 50. Now we do not trust anyone under 30. We are trying to get our parents to listen to us. And we are looking for some answers. Soon we will be retiring, although many of us have not planned sufficiently for that eventuality. Soon we will be dealing with Social Security. Soon we will be dealing with Medicare.

But we are dealing with all of those issues already. For we are not just baby boomers; we are the sandwich generation, with children of our own (who sometimes fail to listen to our collective wisdom) and parents now increasingly dependent upon us for advice and assistance.

Suddenly we are being faced with helping our parents decide about nursing homes, assisted living, and home care. We followed the news and said we never want ourselves or our parents to end up like Terri Schiavo. We are looking into advance-care health directives.

We are concerned about our parents' finances as well as our own. Is their money being invested in the most efficient manner? Is ours? Should they be buying long-term care insurance? Should we? What alternatives are there to long-term care insurance? What about life insurance with accelerated death benefits or reverse mortgages? Is that annuity a good investment for our parents? Is it a good investment for us?

How can we reduce the amount of our income taxes? What advantages in the tax code are just sitting there waiting to save our parents and us money?

What should our parents be doing to meet their financial needs in retirement? What should we be doing now to provide for our own retirement? Will we have to work later in life to meet our own income needs? What do we do when we, the eternally young generation, find ourselves the victims of age discrimination?

How do we deal with all of the questions surrounding Social Security, Medicare, and Medicaid, not just for our parents, but for ourselves? What do we do when our parents ask for our help as they try to understand the complexities and deal with the confusion of the new Medicare Part D prescription drug program?

And what about the even more distant future—the future in which the other side of our sandwich, our children, will live? Will Social Security be there for them? Will Medicare be there for them? Will Medicaid be there for anyone?

We didn't trust anyone over 30. Now, in 2006, our fellow boomers, George W. Bush, Bill Clinton, Cher, and Donald Trump, all turn twice that age.

Now is the time for us to be talking with our parents and helping them with their immediate needs. Now is the time for us to be looking at these complex issues and planning for our own future, which is rapidly approaching. Now is the time for us to deal with issues such as Social Security and Medicare. Otherwise, if left to the whims of politicians, these social programs could be transformed in ways we would not want to see by the time our children face these important issues of aging.

We are all living longer. We need to be informed to make these years the best years of our lives, not a time riddled with fear and want.

This book is about today and tomorrow. It is a guide for baby boomers stepping up to the plate that will empower them with knowledge so that they can help themselves and their parents right now, as well as set the stage for a better situation for their children.

But like just about everything else we baby boomers have done, we are going to have some fun with it. And that is reflected in this book, too. This book is full of helpful information that can make your life better, your parents' lives better, and your children's lives better. This book makes complex material clear and understandable. It lays out a framework upon which you can build a future. But this book is also filled with humor, trivia, and references to movies, music, and television. Why? Because that is the world of baby boomers. We are going to have a little fun while we change the world. Life is entirely too serious to be taken seriously.

This book is also for the parents of the baby boomers, the greatest generation. This book provides them with information to help them sift through the increasing complexities of their lives. It also helps them become better informed to deal with these issues either on their own or with their children as a family.

Finally, this book is even written for the next generation, the children of boomers, because eventually they will have to start dealing with these same issues of Social Security, Medicare and, the rest—not just for their parents, but for themselves as well. You might think you will be young forever, but we know better.

Part I
PLANNING FOR YOUR MONEY

1

IRAs AND 401(k)s

"The question isn't at what age I want to retire,
it's at what income."
—George Foreman

Two of the greatest opportunities for retirement investing are IRAs and 401(k)s. Yet many people fail to take advantage of these gifts from Congress. And many of the people who do avail themselves of IRAs and 401(k)s fail to utilize them as best they can. Knowledge is power. Knowing how to maximize the benefits of these saving graces can help make your retirement so much better.

For Want of a Nail (IRA Style)

According to Benjamin Franklin in *Poor Richard's Almanac,* "For the want of a nail, the shoe was lost. For the want of a shoe, the horse was lost. For the want of a horse, the rider was lost. For the want of a rider, the battle was lost. For the want of a battle, the kingdom was lost. And all for the want of a horseshoe nail." Old Ben certainly had a way with words (and the ladies, too, but that is a subject for another time).

The lesson of this particular quotation is that small details are important. They can be particularly important when dealing with Individual Retirement Accounts. One of the important details that IRA owners neglect is failing to name contingent beneficiaries for their IRAs. A contingent beneficiary is the person designated to receive what is left in the IRA at the owner's death. Neglecting this little detail can dramatically affect the income tax levied on the money distributed from an IRA. Listing your spouse as a beneficiary gives your spouse the ability to roll over your IRA, at your death, into his or her own IRA and then withdraw the IRA funds based upon his or her own IRS determined life expectancy.

Based on the IRS Uniform Lifetime Table, this is 17 years for a 70-year-old. In this instance, then, a 70-year-old surviving spouse could either extend the tax deferral of a traditional IRA or avoid the full tax of a Roth IRA for another 17 years—and that, in turn, results in some considerable tax savings. (By the way, the IRS is even optimistic about the longevity of someone who is 107 years old: The IRS Single Life Expectancy Table gives this person 1.5 more years to take out his or her IRA money.)

Stretch IRA

By naming children or even grandchildren as beneficiaries of your IRA, you enable them to extend the period over which they can withdraw the inherited IRA amounts over their projected lifetimes, as determined by the IRS tables. This could result in tremendous tax savings. For example, a ten-year-old grandchild who inherited a Roth IRA from a grandparent would have 72.8 years to withdraw the money in the inherited Roth IRA tax-free. The money remaining in the Roth IRA would continue to compound during that time.

In a move that allows someone to essentially bet on the race after it is over, you can designate your spouse as the primary beneficiary of your IRA, your children as secondary beneficiaries, and your grandchildren as tertiary beneficiaries. After your death, it then is up to your spouse to decide whether to take all or a portion of the inherited IRA, or disclaim all or a portion of the IRA. Any amount disclaimed passes to the children or, if they disclaimed the money, to the grandchildren. Thus, the benefits of the tax avoidance can be stretched over the lifetimes of your descendants.

Key

However, if you fail to maintain an up-to-date beneficiary designation and your IRA passes to your estate, your family must take out the money over the next five years, translating into a much greater tax burden. Making the best of a bad situation, if you find yourself in this position, IRS rules do not require you to take out the IRA money equally over the five years. The only requirement is that all the money must come out of the IRA within five years. Therefore, if you inherit an IRA through an estate, you at least have the opportunity to leave the money in the IRA until the end of five years, to gain compound interest during that time.

Another Nail

Smokey the Bear always said, "Only you can prevent forest fires." (As a bit of trivia, Smokey's middle name "the" was added in the 1952 song "Smokey, the Bear" for better musical rhythm.) If Smokey had inherited his wife's IRA, he might have warned everyone, "Only spouses can roll over an IRA into their own IRA." This might seem like a small detail, but it's important. Anyone else who inherits an IRA and rolls it over into his or her own IRA risks losing all the tax avoidance and deferral benefits of a stretch IRA. This is because the IRS requires the beneficiary to set up a new IRA with the inheritance that also contains the name of the deceased IRA owner in its title. For example, the title of the new inherited IRA account could read "Smokey the Bear Jr., beneficiary of IRA of Smokey the Bear."

Game, Set, Match

Listen carefully. Gordon Gekko, the character played by Michael Douglas in the 1987 movie *Wall Street,* was wrong when he said, "Greed is good." However, free money is good. The idea of free money might sound too good to be true, but you might have some free money available to you that you are missing. When your employer offers to match your contributions to your 401(k) plan at work, you're essentially getting free money.

According to a 2005 study done by Hewitt Associates, 22 percent of eligible employees in the United States fail to contribute enough to their 401(k) retirement plan at work to get the full company match. This should be a no-brainer. In 2006, the maximum amount that you can contribute to your 401(k) account is $15,000. However, baby boomers who are at least 50 years old are permitted to contribute an additional $5,000, for a total of $20,000 in 2006. It is important to also remember that the money you put into your company 401(k) plan is pre-tax money: You do not pay taxes on it. In addition, any money put into your 401(k) account grows untaxed; you do not pay any tax on the money until you withdraw it at retirement.

Roth 401(k)

The Roth IRA, the relatively new kid on the IRA block because it was introduced in 1998 as a way of saving for a tax-free retirement, now has a new little brother, the Roth 401(k).

In a conventional 401(k) retirement account, a worker contributes some of his or her salary into a tax-deferred retirement account. Any money that is contributed is not subject to income tax when it is put into the account. Instead, the income taxes become due when money is withdrawn from the account. Beginning in 2006, employers can offer a Roth 401(k) that allows employees to put all or some of their 401(k) contributions into a Roth 401(k) account. The amount of the worker's salary that is contributed into the Roth 401(k) is considered as taxable wages in the year in which it is contributed to the Roth 401(k). Once in the account, however, the money grows tax-free and can be withdrawn later without incurring further income tax.

As with the regular 401(k), in 2006 as much as $15,000 can be contributed annually to an employee's Roth 401k account unless the employee is at least 50 years old; in that case, the amount increases to $20,000.

Important Loophole

In 2006, to qualify for a Roth IRA, the adjusted gross income (AGI) of unmarried individuals cannot exceed $110,000, and the adjusted gross income of married taxpayers filing jointly cannot exceed $160,000. However, unlike the regular Roth IRA that is described in detail in my book *A Guide to Elder Planning* (Pearson Education, 2003), there are no income eligibility limitations to qualify for a Roth 401(k).

All or Nothing at All

Besides being the title to a 1939 no. 1 hit by Frank Sinatra, this phrase also refers to the flexibility for workers whose employers offer Roth 401(k) accounts. When both types of 401(k) accounts are offered, the employees get to decide how much, if any, they want to contribute to either type of 401(k) account. For example, a worker over the age of 50 might choose to put $10,000 into a regular 401(k) account so that the amount would not be subject to current income taxes; he then might contribute another $10,000 to his Roth 401(k) account for future tax-free growth, and pay the income tax on that amount of compensation.

The Match Game

Many baby boomers fondly remember *The Match Game,* a daytime quiz show hosted by Gene Rayburn with the familiar voice of Johnny Olson as announcer. Baby boomers are even more fond of the matching employer contributions to their 401(k) accounts. These matching contributions are income-tax-free contributions that employers make to the 401(k) accounts of their employees. Thus, they constitute not just an incentive for employees to contribute to their 401(k) accounts, but they truly can be considered money for nothing. (However, unlike the 1985 song "Money for Nothing" by Dire Straits, you do not get chicks for free.) It is important to note that employer-matching

401(k) contributions may be made only to a regular 401(k). Employer-matching contributions may not be made to an employee's Roth 401(k) account.

For Whom Does a Roth 401(k) Make Sense?

Younger workers who will not be retiring for a long time might choose the advantages of tax-free income in the future over the benefits of deferring present income taxes. Lower-income workers also might find the benefits of future tax-free income to be worth more to them than the present tax deferral. They might anticipate that when they withdraw the money, they will be in a higher tax bracket. Workers who are not eligible for a regular Roth IRA because their adjusted gross income is too high might find that the Roth 401(k) gives them a tax-free retirement option. Finally, baby boomers who are looking at ever-increasing federal deficits might wish to opt for the Roth 401(k) as a hedge against what they might think are future income tax rate increases. And those who still cannot make up their minds can choose to do both: set up a regular 401(k) and a Roth 401(k), and split their contributions. Just remember that the total contributions to 401(k) accounts may not exceed the statutory limits.

Sunrise, Sunset

"Sunrise, Sunset" was the name of a hauntingly beautiful song from the musical *Fiddler on the Roof,* which ran for 3,242 performances on Broadway beginning on September 22, 1964.

Sunset might be beautiful when depicted in a song, but when it refers to the practice of Congress writing laws that quietly wipe out tax advantages previously granted, it is the name of a practice that would make Enron accountants blush. The federal government needs a certain amount of money to operate. When a tax break is granted to the public, Congress often puts a time limit on the availability of that particular tax break. By doing so, Congress can anticipate that future revenues needed to run the government will be restored at the end of a certain period. "Sunsetting" is the term for terminating such a law with a limited shelf life. Of course, this tactic is highly misleading: If there is a large enough public protest over the end of a particular tax break, Congress will make it permanent. That, in turn, could mean that Congress will not have enough money to operate future necessary programs without performing other accounting manipulations that are not drastically dissimilar to the misrepresentative accounting that sent several Enron officials to prison.

A good example of a law with sunset provisions is the federal estate tax. This law provides for the regular increasing of the amounts of assets that are exempt from federal estate taxes through the year 2009 when the exemption amount reaches a peak of 3.5 million dollars. Then in the year 2010, the estate tax will be totally abolished so that no one who dies in that year, regardless of the amount of assets contained in his or her estate, will be responsible for paying a federal estate tax. But then comes December 31, 2010, a day called by some people *Throw Mama From the Train* Day, referring to the 1987 movie directed by Danny DeVito and starring Billy Crystal. Under current law, that is the last day that estates will go untaxed because, on that day, the federal estate tax abolition sunsets. On January 1, 2011, not only does the federal estate tax return, but it does so at the reduced million-dollar exemption level of the year 2002. No one actually expects that scenario to occur, least of all the Congressmen who voted for such a sunset law. Most likely, they will play out the sunset game and either permanently abolish the estate tax (less likely) or pass a new law setting a permanent (or, at least, as permanent as any tax legislation can be) exemption amount.

I tell you all of this interesting information about sunset laws not just for your edification, but also because the Roth 401(k) law has a similar sunset provision. Like the federal estate tax, the Roth 401(k) is set to sunset on December 31, 2010, unless Congress takes further action. However, even if Congress were to permit the Roth 401(k) law to just fade away, such action would only prevent people from putting further money into a Roth 401(k). Funds already put into a Roth 401(k) could most likely be rolled over into a regular Roth IRA and would continue to provide benefits to those people who took advantage of this retirement tax break during the 5 years it was available.

Temptation

Temptation: good when you are talking about the Temptations, one of the greatest of the Motown groups. Temptation: bad when it causes you to take your money out of your 401(k) when you go to a new job, thereby turning an advantage of the 401(k) into a disadvantage. The law permits people to take a 401(k) account with them from one employer to another throughout their working careers. The law also allows three other choices.

The first option, which is less of a choice than just failure to make a decision (which, thereafter, becomes a decision), is merely leaving your 401(k) account with your former employer's plan. This is not necessarily a bad decision, but it does expose you to unnecessary additional management fees if you have 401(k) accounts with multiple employers.

A second option is to roll over your 401(k) from your previous employer into the plan of your next employer. This alternative can be used if you already have another job lined up when you leave your previous job. A key determining factor in deciding to choose this option is the choice of investments in your new employer's 401(k) plan. If the choices do not seem particularly attractive, you might want to take advantage of your third option: rolling over your 401(k) account from your previous employer into your own self-directed IRA.

Rolling over an employer-sponsored 401(k) into an IRA, traditional or Roth, makes a lot of sense for most people. People who leave a job for whatever reason have a right to either leave their retirement money in the company-sponsored 401(k) or have it rolled into an IRA that they themselves control. This enables former employees to invest their retirement money in whatever investments are allowed under IRA rules. The investment choices available to a former employee in a self-directed IRA are far broader than those available when a former employee leaves the money in the company's 401(k) plan. And whether you keep it in the company 401(k) plan or roll over the money into your own IRA, income tax deferral (or complete avoidance, in the case of a company-sponsored Roth 401[k] plan) is fully available to the former employee. There is one major consideration in deciding whether to leave the money in the company 401(k) or take it out and put it into an IRA, however: only workers who take out the money and roll it into their own IRAs can stretch an IRA through multiple generations, as described previously.

Then there is that temptation to just take the money and spend it. This is a lose, lose, lose proposition. You lose the benefit of having the money grow tax deferred in a 401(k) plan. You lose by paying income tax on the money you take out. And you lose by paying a 10 percent penalty for early withdrawal of your 401(k) account unless you are at least 59½ or come within one of the narrow statutory exceptions. Unfortunately, according to a Hewitt Associates study done in 2005, 45 percent of workers cash in their 401(k) accounts when they leave the company.

Know When to Leave

So when does it make sense to leave the money in your company's 401(k) plan? If you want to have the ability to borrow money from your retirement plan, an IRA does not offer that option, whereas a 401(k) does. However, borrowing from a 401(k) is generally not the best choice because even though you are essentially borrowing from yourself, you miss the tax-deferred compounding that is the main reason you have a 401(k) to begin with. In addition, if you leave your job, voluntarily or involuntarily, you must pay back the loan within 60 days—with interest. Otherwise, you must pay not only income tax on the loan amount, but a 10 percent early withdrawal penalty, to boot. Somehow, it does not seem worth the risk.

It might also make sense to leave the money with your employer's 401(k) plan if the fees are considerably less than what you would be responsible for paying with your own self-directed IRA. However, it is important to again do your homework to make sure that the lower costs of your company's 401(k) plan are not limited to participants in the plan who are current employees of the company. Some plans have higher fees for participants in the company 401(k) plan who are no longer employees.

When Should You Take the Money Out and Pay the Taxes?

When you leave your job, you also have the option of neither rolling the money into your own IRA nor leaving it in the company 401(k); you can also just take the money and run. However, although you might run with the money, you cannot hide it from the IRS. When you take a distribution of your 401(k) funds upon leaving the company without rolling the money into an IRA, you are responsible for paying income taxes on the money you withdraw. In addition, you are responsible for paying penalties on the money you withdraw if you are under the age of 59½.

Fortunately, buried within the Internal Revenue Code is a little-known loophole that permits former employees who had their company stock in their 401(k) accounts to transfer that stock into a regular investment account. This is considered an "in-kind distribution" that subjects the former employee to income taxes only on the value of the company stock at the time he or she bought it. This means, for example, that if the stock was worth $5,000 at the time the former employee initially purchased the company stock for the 401(k) and the stock is now worth $50,000, the former employee would pay income taxes only on $5,000 when he takes the money out of the company 401(k) plan. The remainder of the value of the stock could continue to grow. Then when the former employee sold the stock, income taxes would be limited to the lower capital gains rates.

Upside of Anger and Downside of 401(k) Accounts

The Upside of Anger was a terrific movie in 2005 starring Joan Allen and Kevin Costner. Of course, generally we do not think of an upside to anger. Nor do we think of a downside to 401(k) accounts, but there are some as reflected in a number of class actions by employees against employers sponsoring their 401(k) accounts. The biggest problem with 401(k) accounts occurs when the company invests its employees' 401(k) money either exclusively or largely in the company's own stock.

This was the unfortunate situation in which employees in the now-bankrupt Enron and WorldCom found themselves. The problem arises when workers choose from their investment options to put their 401(k) money in their own company's stock, something they know (or think they know, as in the case of Enron and WorldCom). The problem also occurs when a company matches contributions with stock in the company. Often this stock, provided as an employer-matching contribution, has restrictions. In the Enron situation, the matching stock could not be sold until the employee was at least 55 years old.

Even if you work for a good company, failing to diversify your investments puts you at greater risk of a financial downfall if the value of your company's stock goes down; this is true regardless of whether criminal behavior is involved, as in the case of Enron. Remember, just by receiving your salary from your employer, your finances already are tremendously tied to that employer. Spread out the risk. The old adage is correct: "Don't put all your eggs in one basket." Unfortunately, according to a 2005 study by Hewitt Associates, 27 percent of employees hold at least half of their 401(k) investments in their employer's stock.

Another problem that can turn up with some 401(k) plans is a limited number of mutual funds for investing 401(k) money. In addition, in some instances, these mutual funds either have been saddled with particularly high fees that eat into earnings or are poor performers when compared to other funds. The solution to these problems is found in making employees more aware of the choices that are available through the company's 401(k) plan and lobbying company officials for changes in the plan if it is not as investor-friendly as it can be.

What You Don't Know Can Hurt You

According to a 2005 study done by Hewitt Associates of "low savers"— that is, employees who either did not contribute anything to their 401(k) plan or did not contribute enough to meet the requirement for a full company match—a majority of these employees do not have even a basic understanding of how their company 401(k) plan works. In addition, 73 percent do not know the rate at which their company matches employee 401(k) contributions. Most disturbing of all,

54 percent of these low savers do not even know whether their employers offer a matching contribution.

In his song "Kodachrome," released in 1973, Paul Simon sang that his "lack of education did not hurt me none." When it comes to being able to take advantage of your company's 401(k) program, however, ignorance can cost you dearly in lost savings over the years.

2

RETIREMENT INVESTING

"Retirement is like a long vacation in Las Vegas. The goal is to enjoy it to the fullest, but not so fully that you run out of money."
—Jonathan Clements

P lanning for your financial needs in retirement is a complex, daunting task. Perhaps that is the reason so many people procrastinate the planning they know they need to do: They just do not know where to begin, so they get stuck doing nothing, which is the worst decision you can make. The earlier you start planning, the better off you will be. But it is never, ever too late.

How Much Is This Going to Cost Me?

"I've got all the money I'll ever need, if I die by four o'clock."
—Henny Youngman

Unfortunately, for many people, the whole idea of retirement planning and determining what your needs will be in retirement is overwhelming. However, all is not lost. With a little bit of effort and planning, the complexity of this task can be reduced to merely "whelming"—which, by the way, actually is a word, although you hardly ever hear anyone complain about being whelmed.

Predicting your income needs of tomorrow based upon the cost of paying for those needs today is fooling yourself. Inflation erodes the purchasing power of your savings. When computing the amount that you will need to cover your cost of living in the future, it is imperative to factor in inflation. As Yogi Berra said, "A nickel ain't worth a dime anymore."

Then there is the matter of your health-care costs. Medicare will cover many health-care costs, but it does not cover everything. You will need to factor in the costs of so-called Medigap policies that mind the gap left by Medicare patient-pay amounts and deductibles for which you are responsible. You can find a detailed analysis of Medigap policies in my book *A Guide to Elder Planning* (Pearson Education, 2003).

Doctor, Doctor, Give Me the News

In 1979, the late Robert Palmer sang, "Doctor, doctor, give me the news" in the song "Bad Case of Loving You." Palmer died at the relatively young age of 54 in 2003, so he never had to ask his doctor about the cost of health insurance and health care in retirement. For the rest of us, that is the $64,000 question that we fear may cost us $64,000.

The unfortunate trend in business is for companies to reduce or even eliminate health-care benefits for their retired workers. In 2004, a joint survey done by the Kaiser Family Foundation and Hewitt Associates found that companies paying for health benefits for their retired employees experienced an average cost increase of 12.7 percent. The companies and the retirees generally shared this increase in costs. The survey revealed that a typical worker under the age of 65 who retired in 2004 paid $2,244 annually in premiums—$4,644 if that employee included coverage for a spouse. This was 27 percent more than a worker who retired just a year earlier. Workers 65 or older who were eligible for Medicare and retired in 2004 typically paid $1,212 annually in health insurance premiums—$2,508 to cover a spouse. This amounted to a 24 percent increase over the previous year.

The trend toward reducing company payments of health-care benefits for retirees is only expected to increase in the years ahead. This does not bode well for baby boomers who will have a hard time even trying to estimate what they will need to pay for health insurance coverage, let alone find the money to pay for it.

The rule of thumb used to be that you needed to make 70 percent of what you earned before retirement to cover the costs of maintaining the same lifestyle after retirement. But those figures may have gone out the hospital window as the costs of health-care coverage continue to rise. Some financial planners believe you will need to generate as much money in retirement as you do during your working years to get by. Not very comforting, is it?

How Long Will You Live?

Another important factor in determining how much money you will need for retirement is estimating how long you expect to live in retirement. Obviously, the longer you live, the more money you will need. On its Web site www.nmfn.com, the Northwestern Mutual Financial Network has an interactive program it calls "The Longevity Game" that analyzes your particular medical and lifestyle influences on your longevity. When I took the exam, it told me I could expect to live to the age of 93. This both made me feel pretty good and made me wonder where I am going to find the money for all those years. Then just for fun, I took the test again. I started out at my age of 56 and put in information about bad genetics, bad diet, excessive drinking, lack of exercise, excessive drug use, and negative answers to every other question. At the end of the test, my life expectancy was 56 years, the same age as my starting point. Pretty scary. I think if this had been accurate, I might have scared myself into a self-fulfilling heart attack. Still, "The Longevity Game" is a good wake-up call about the many things that we can do to positively influence our life expectancy and the quality of that life.

The 4 Percent Solution

The Seven Percent Solution was a book by Nicholas Meyer, who later adapted it into a 1976 movie. In the movie, Sherlock Holmes and Sigmund Freud join together to fight crime. The title refers to the drug Sherlock Holmes took. It was 7 percent cocaine and 93 percent saline solution.

Sherlock Holmes' 7 percent solution does not solve any problems. In fact, it makes them worse. But the 4 percent solution is something for retirees and potential retirees to consider. This is a rule of thumb for how much money you can withdraw from your portfolio annually and still have enough money to last a lifetime. This number is predicated upon assumptions of a 3 percent inflation rate, taxes of 3 percent, and an average 10 percent return on investments. All of these are variables and will not be consistent, but they at least provide some sort of historical context for determining how much you can spend in retirement as well as how much you need to accumulate to finance your retirement. Of course, a 10 percent return on investment may be historically accurate, but it certainly has not been the rule during the past few years. In dollars and cents, a 4 percent withdrawal rate on a portfolio of a million dollars is $40,000 per year.

Try This

Bankrate.com is a financial Web site that offers a tremendous array of helpful information, along with interactive calculators, one of which assists you in calculating how much money you will need for retirement and offers suggestions on how to meet your goals. A number of other good Web sites have helpful calculators as well.

Baby Steps for Baby Boomers

"Money can't buy happiness, but it can make you awfully comfortable while you're being miserable."
—Clare Boothe Luce

Baby boomers in their 50s and older might find that, with their children having graduated from college, the life insurance they took out to cover their children's educational expenses in case of the parents' deaths is no longer necessary. If so, it could be time to consider re-evaluating life insurance needs and perhaps putting some or all of that money to work in retirement savings. In particular, look at whether you are making the maximum contributions to your tax-sheltered retirement accounts, such as 401(k) accounts and IRAs. Remember, if you are over 50, the law permits you to make additional contributions to those retirement accounts that younger people are not permitted to do. That's yet another advantage of being over 50 (as if that makes up for creaking knees and aching backs).

After you have received that birthday card from AARP on your 50th birthday, you also might want to pay closer attention to what your Social Security benefits are estimated to be. Annually, you should be receiving from the Social Security Administration an estimate of your Social Security benefits in retirement. As you approach retirement, it becomes even more important to make sure that you are credited with all of your earnings throughout your working years. The amount that you receive at retirement is based upon the amount of your earnings averaged over most of your highest-earning 35 years. If the benefits estimate that you receive from the Social Security Administration is missing segments of your working history, the amount of your benefits could be reduced.

Only You

It's a great 1955 hit by the Platters. And it's also your theme song if you find mistakes on your Social Security records that reduce the amount of your benefits check because only you can correct any mistakes that would reduce your Social Security benefits. The Social Security Administration accepts evidence of your past employment, such as copies of pay stubs, W-2s, income tax returns, or even letters from your past employers as proof of your past employment.

Just a Thought

Although you might be in a rush to stop working, if you did not have earnings over 35 years, you might want to keep working for a few more years to make up the difference. Because the amount of your Social Security retirement check is based upon your highest-earning 35 years, if you worked fewer than 35 years, those years in which you did not work are averaged in as $0. So, if you are close to 35 years of work or are able to earn a higher income now than earlier in your working career, then even if you have already worked 35 years, you might want to continue to work for a few more years. The increased Social Security benefit could be well worth it.

Keep on Keeping On

Another incentive for putting off retirement and continuing to work is that the longer you work, the less hard your investments have to work. For many aging baby boomers, continuing to work after typical retirement age might be a matter of necessity because they just have not saved enough. However, many baby boomers do not find the conventional images of retirement that appealing. They might want the mental stimulation and socialization provided by continued employment. And their rich Uncle Sam encourages older Americans to keep on working. A person who has attained the age of full Social Security retirement benefits (that age is being gradually phased up to 67 years for people born in or after 1960—in 2006, that stood at 65 years and 8 months) will still be able to receive full Social Security retirement benefits, regardless of how much money he or she earns through employment.

Now What?

"Why is there so much month left at the end of the money?"
—John Barrymore

When you have determined how much you expect to receive from Social Security, you will be in a better position to determine just how much additional income you will need to have to fund your retirement.

Moving on Up

The Jeffersons was a popular television sitcom that ran on CBS between 1975 and 1985, and was one of a number of successful spin-offs of *All in the Family*. Anyone familiar with the show remembers the catchy theme song, "Movin' On Up." The show began with the Jeffersons enjoying a major business success and moving out of the Queens neighborhood where they had lived near the Bunkers to a more expensive uptown location.

Outside the world of sitcoms, however, many older people choose to move to less expensive housing that costs less to maintain and that perhaps is easier to take care of. They also might want to move to a home that is easier to move around in, with fewer stairs. Many older people find that selling their homes, the value of which has often appreciated significantly over the years, can provide additional cash to not only pay for suitable substitute housing, but also provide much needed additional funds for their retirement.

Some people often seek out a warmer climate in which to live when they retire, for both health and comfort reasons. If you are considering moving to another part of the country, go there for a few weeks and see how the reality of living there compares with the ideal. Do not be in a rush to buy new housing; do not lock yourself into replacement housing too quickly. Try to rent at first so that you can get a good idea of where you might want to live.

Paying Off Your Mortgage

In preparation for retirement, should you pay off your mortgage? The answer is, it depends. The younger you are, the better position you are in to continue to make your monthly mortgage payment, take the tax deduction for the interest payments on your mortgage, and put as much money as you can into tax-sheltered retirement vehicles such as a 401(k) or an IRA. However, if you are older, you might well have been paying on your mortgage for such a long time that the amount of your deduction for the interest is relatively small. In addition, as you near retirement, you are more likely to want to invest more conservatively, so the rate of return that you will get from conservative investments that make sense for you at retirement age or close to it is probably less than the return you would get by paying off your mortgage. And by paying off your mortgage, you eliminate one more regular bill in retirement and gain a little peace of mind.

Hunt for Green October

The Hunt for Red October was a terrific 1990 movie derived from a Tom Clancy novel and starring the charismatic Sean Connery as a Russian submarine captain. Connery, as compelling as ever, manages to have the Russian captain speak with a Scottish brogue, but why quibble?

If, however, you are more concerned about looking for a little more "green" for the October, November, and December of your life, you might want to go back through your work history and see if you are eligible for any retirement benefits from past employers. If your employers have gone out of business, you still might not be out of luck. If the retirement plan of your now-defunct former employer was a defined-benefit plan, the Pension Benefit Guarantee Corp., an organization created by the federal government but funded by private corporations, will help you locate defined-benefit pension benefits to which you could be entitled. Go to its Web site at www.pbgc.gov for assistance.

If you think you might be owed money by a former employer for an old 401(k) account that you had lost track of, PenChecks, Inc., a private company, has established a National Registry of Unclaimed Retirement

Benefits that might be able to help you get that money. This registry is used by both employers trying to locate former employees and employees attempting to find former employers in regard to employer-sponsored retirement plans such as 401(k)s or profit-sharing plans. For employees, the program is free. The Web site is www.unclaimed-retirementbenefits.com.

Bet on the Boomers

Baby boomers comprise a large segment of the country's population. Companies providing for the needs of baby boomers have done well throughout the years, and there is no reason to think that this rule will not continue to apply. The Ford Mustang was a large success, to some extent, because its launch was timed to coincide with the entrance of many baby boomers into the automobile-buying market.

So what kinds of companies are worth considering when it comes to investing in the needs of baby boomers? Travel, leisure, and recreation are industries that will stand to gain from retiring baby boomers with significant amounts of disposable income. Cruises are a popular form of travel for many aging baby boomers. Golf is a sport of choice for many baby boomers. And don't get in the way of a retiree on the way to the slot machines in a casino. You could get trampled. These are just a few types of companies that will stand to profit from the retirement of baby boomers.

Think about what you like to do and what companies meet those needs. Of course, as with any investment, it is necessary to do your homework (even when retired, we are still being told to do our homework) and evaluate these companies carefully, but you might find that meeting the needs of a large segment of the population is a good place to start when considering companies in which you want to invest.

Then there is the matter of the health of us baby boomers. As usual, this large segment of the population does not accept the aches and pains of aging. Baby boomers instead look to pharmaceutical companies and others to meet their health-care needs for relief. The longer we boomers live, the more health care we need. The answer both for now and into the future appears to be to look to the companies that meet the health-care needs of baby boomers. Of course, you can choose individual companies; however, this not only requires a great deal of homework and specialized knowledge, but it also puts you at risk of picking the next pharmaceutical company to take a financial hit for the next Vioxx. A safer way to go is to consider investing in health-care mutual funds, one of the many types of segment funds available. Segment mutual funds limit their investments to companies within a specific segment of the economy, such as technology, gold, or communications. According to Lipper, a financial information provider that is now a part of Reuters, the Fidelity Select Medical Fund led all other health-care funds over the past 5 years, with a total return, including dividends and reinvested gains, of 137 percent. Those are healthy returns.

Of course, for those of you looking for good news in bad news, rumor has it that all of us baby boomers are eventually going to die, regardless of the quantity and quality of the health care we receive. Therefore, macabre investors might want to consider investing in the giants of the funeral industry, such as Service Corporation International, Stewart Enterprises, Alderwoods Group, and Carriage Services, Inc. Again, however, if you choose to invest in individual stocks, it is imperative to do your homework and study the prospects of any company in which you are considering investing. Presently, there is no Herman Munster Fund or any other sector funds for death-related industries, so if you want to make them a part of your portfolio, you will have to invest in individual stocks.

When Life Gives You Lemons

When the stock market is down, you might experience losses in your investment portfolio. That is the time to consider using those losses to offset the taxable gain from your other investments.

Target Funds

For the children of baby boomers, the acronym CD conjures up an image of the latest compact disc of their favorite musical group. But for baby boomers and their parents, *CD* usually refers to certificates of deposit, a favorite and secure form of investment. Unfortunately, with inflation sometimes at a rate actually higher than the rate of return on some certificates of deposit, keeping all of your eggs in this one secure basket can result in your going broke, just at a slower rate. With people living longer, your money has to last longer, too. This means that everyone should have a balanced portfolio of not just secure investments that provide income, such as CDs, bonds, and notes, but also stocks for growth. Of course, with stocks comes risk, as anyone who has watched the stock market in recent years well knows. Spreading the risk with a balanced portfolio of stocks and bonds is the best approach to investing for the long term. The principle is simple. More difficult is determining the ratio of stocks to bonds and other fixed-income instruments. To a great extent, the ratio is determined by your own tolerance for risk. If you are willing to take a greater risk for potentially greater rewards, you will hold more stocks.

A number of rules of thumb can help determine the ratio of stocks to bonds for the portfolios of people as they age. One formula determines the amount of bonds in your portfolio by multiplying your age by 80 percent, with the remainder of your portfolio to be held in stocks. For example, according to this formula, 65-year-olds should have 52 percent of their assets in bonds and 48 percent in stocks.

Another common formula starts by subtracting your age from 100. The resulting figure becomes the percentage of assets that should be allocated to stocks. The rest should go into bonds and other fixed-income securities. According to this formula, a 65-year-old person would have 35 percent of his or her portfolio in stocks and 65 percent in bonds.

But making the initial determination and then readjusting the balance of your portfolio regularly is just too difficult for many people. Recognizing this problem and seeing the opportunity presented, the investment industry came up with target funds. A target fund invests your money based upon when you plan to retire. Your target date is the date of your retirement. Target funds are operated by mutual fund companies that choose the investments based upon the proximity of your retirement. The further you are from retirement, the more of your fund is held in stocks. As with all mutual funds, your investments are managed for you. Target funds offer convenience and the investment acumen of seasoned money managers.

Target funds are not without critics, though. Some believe that they shift too much money to fixed-income investments as the investor more closely approaches retirement. They reason that because people live longer today after retirement than they used to, there is a greater need for growth after a person retires, to have sufficient funds to pay for retirement. One way to still use Target funds and meet this concern is to merely choose a target fund with a target date much later than your actual retirement date. In this way, you will maintain more of your investments in the stocks providing growth.

Fees, If You Please

It's not what you make that counts; it's what you keep. Fees for managing investments can take a significant bite out of the actual return on your investment. Because most target funds are mutual funds that are made up of a mixture of other mutual funds, you might find that this is an expensive way to do your investing. Not only do you pay a management fee to the target fund, but within the fund are buried management fees to each of the mutual funds that make up your target fund. One way to reduce the bite of fees is to consider going with a fund group that generally has lower fees, such as Vanguard.

Risk

Risk is a board game that many baby boomers grew up playing in the 1960s. First sold in 1959, it involves world conquest. Although it does not ever seem to go out of style, Risk has been updated with versions probably unfamiliar to baby boomers, such as Risk 2210 AD, which added underwater and moon territories to be conquered, and, of course, the Lord of the Rings Risk, released in 2002 to capitalize on the renewed interest in J. R. R. Tolkein's stories.

However, when it comes to investing, risk deals with the likelihood of greater investment returns if you take greater chances by buying investments that have the potential to bring you either greater returns or significant loss. Risk can be costly to your fiscal well-being.

Go Long

Go long. It worked for Tom Brady and the New England Patriots, and it can work for you in retirement planning. But unless you are a National Football League quarterback throwing a long pass, this phrase means something very different to most of us. An investment portfolio that emphasizes income-earning investments such as CDs over long-term growth assets such as stocks can leave you without sufficient money in later retirement years. Owning dividend-paying stocks is a good way for many people to meet their needs for both income and growth. Stock dividends range from 2 to 5 percent and also offer the potential for increased value of the stock itself. This obviously compares favorably with CDs and other fixed-income investments. In addition, the income tax on stock dividends is generally at the reduced rate of 15 percent.

However, it should also be emphasized that if you are among the people who actually will have enough money to fund your retirement through conservative fixed-income investments such as CDs and Treasury bills, you don't need to take the risk inherent in even the safest of stocks. On the day Groucho Marx rang the bell at the New York Stock Exchange, he was asked what he invested in, to which he responded Treasury bills. When told that you can't make any money in Treasury bills, he responded that you could, if you had enough of them. So if you are able to meet your retirement goals through conservative investing, that is a good route to travel. Even Tom Brady will hand the ball off to Corey Dillon to achieve his goal through a conservative ground game when he can.

Climb the Ladder of Success

Interest rates change often. If interest rates are going to rise, you are better having your fixed-income investments mature after short periods so that you can purchase new fixed-income investments at higher interest rates in the near future. However, if interest rates are going to fall, you want to lock in your higher-rate fixed-income investments for as long as possible. Unfortunately, unless you are like Carnac the Magnificent, the all-knowing seer and soothsayer character played by the late Johnny Carson on the *Tonight Show,* you will not know at any particular time whether it is best to have your fixed-income investments locked in for a long maturity period or opt for short-term investments. *Laddering* is the name for an investment tactic that can be used with CDs, bonds, and notes to hedge your bet with inevitable interest rate changes.

An example of laddering is buying five CDs, with one maturing after one year, one maturing after two years, and so on. When each matures, you replace it with a new CD that matures in five years. In this way, you have the liquidity of a CD that matures every year, but overall you will be getting investment returns close to the higher rates that are provided at any time when you lock in your money for the longer period of 5 years.

529 Ways to Make Your Retirement Easier and More Fun

It might be a dull name for a college savings plan, but a 529 Plan (named after the applicable section of the Internal Revenue Code) offers significant planning opportunities for retiring baby boomers.

Through a 529 Plan, family members, such as parents or grandparents, can set up an investment account to be used for a child's higher-education needs. The earnings on the 529 Plan are tax-free at withdrawal. In some states, you can even get a tax deduction for contributing to a 529 Plan (a list of those states can be found in my book *A Guide to Elder Planning*).

One major advantage of a 529 Plan is that the parent or grandparent setting up the 529 Plan always controls the money and can get it back at any time (although there are income tax consequences for so doing). Funds spent on education expenses are tax-free. And therein lies the loophole. You can set up a 529 Plan for yourself as the beneficiary, or after your child's or grandchild's educational expenses have been paid, designate yourself as the beneficiary of the 529 Plan that you set up for your child or grandchild, and use the money for your own educational needs.

But why would you want to do that? Well, for starters, keeping your mind sharp through further education is always a good thing. And what qualifies as education for 529 Plan usages might surprise you. Colleges and universities offer courses and programs on cooking, golf, scuba diving, gardening, carpentry, car repair, and tennis, just to name a few of your options. Just about any interest you might have is probably being taught at some college or university. You can tap into the money that has been growing tax-free in a 529 Plan to pay for not just the cost of the program itself. If the institution offering the program in which you are interested is located far from your home, you may also use the 529 Plan funds to pay for the cost of travel and room and board associated with taking a particular program or course.

Bringing Down the Market

Predicting is a scary business. Sometimes it seems that the purpose of many predictions is to scare the fecal matter out of us, which might even be helpful for those of us suffering from constipation.

Dire predictions often have a habit of being wrong. Before January 1, 2000, there was great concern about the Y2k bug. According to the gloom-and-doom predictions of many people, disaster would strike in the year 2000 because early computer programmers had decided to save computer memory by using only two digits to encode the year. When the year 2000 came about, computer programs would interpret the date to be January 1, 1900, and every algorithm that relied upon a date would crash and burn, causing computers worldwide to fail and bringing tremendous destruction of everything from financial records to the computers that operated power plants. New Year's 2000 came and went without much problem. The prediction turned out to be a false alarm.

A current prediction of concern to retiring baby boomers involves the crash of the stock market when baby boomers cash in their stock portfolios to pay for their retirements. The concern is that when the country's largest demographic group begins to retire, baby boomers will all sell their stocks to obtain funds to finance their retirement. According to the law of supply and demand, there will be far more sellers than buyers, so stock prices will plummet. As if we did not have enough about which to be scared.

But the truth is probably a bit less alarming. First, the wealthiest 10 percent of Americans own about 90 percent of all the stock that is owned by individual investors, and all of them are unlikely to be in a rush to cash in their holdings. In addition, finance professor Jeremy Siegel of the University of Pennsylvania writes in his book *The Future for Investors* (Crown Publishing Group, 2005) that when the managers of large pension funds start liquidating funds for retiring baby boomers, foreign investors in developing countries, such as burgeoning economic giant China, will be there to buy up those stocks. Once again, the gloom-and-doomers will be wrong.

3

ANNUITIES

"I advise you to go on living solely to enrage those who are paying your annuities. It is the only pleasure I have left."
—Voltaire

Voltaire, the famous eighteenth-century philosopher and author, apparently was able to derive pleasure from annuities, but today, for many baby boomers and their parents, annuities are a confusing investment that too often bring financial distress to their owners.

Proponents of annuities have simply argued that they are secure investments that provide a guaranteed stream of income. Annuities might be particularly attractive to retirees whose lack of investment knowledge makes them hesitant to invest in the stock market either through direct stock ownership or through mutual funds. The apparent security of a guaranteed source of income is very attractive to some investors. But like everything, it comes at a price, and sometimes the total cost of owning annuities significantly dilutes their advantages. On the other hand, the deservedly bad press about deferred variable annuities as an investment for older people does not necessarily apply to all forms of annuities. As always, the key to determining whether an annuity is a good choice for you is in the details.

Annuities, like ice cream, come in two basic flavors. With ice cream, it's vanilla or chocolate. With annuities, it's deferred annuities and immediate annuities. But, just as with ice cream, those two flavors can be varied considerably by, for instance, adding fudge, chocolate chips, or cookie dough. Deferred annuities and immediate annuities vary tremendously, depending upon other provisions of those basic annuity contract formats.

Fixed Immediate Annuity

An investor buys a fixed immediate annuity with a single lump-sum payment. The fixed immediate annuity then starts making steady monthly payments at a locked-in interest rate. Each payment includes a return of your initial investment along with earnings. The earnings that you receive are subject to income tax. The amount of the monthly payment to you depends on your age and the options that you choose within the annuity. Fixed immediate annuities are often most attractive to older people who are fearful of outliving their savings.

Essentially, a fixed immediate annuity is a bet that you think you will live longer than the insurance company thinks you will. Unlike life insurance, with which you win when you die early because you made few premium payments, with fixed immediate annuities, you win by living longer than some actuary's determination of your life expectancy and having the insurance company pay you for a longer period of time. For some retirees, the combination of the stock market's unpredictability and confusing investment choices makes fixed immediate annuities an attractive choice for older Americans who want a guaranteed source of income for as long as they live and who do not believe that they have the time to weather down periods in the stock market.

As you might well expect, the older you are when you purchase a fixed immediate annuity, the more bang you get for your buck because the insurance company bets that it will not have to pay you much longer. Generally, a fixed immediate annuity stops payments upon your death. If you are concerned about the value of your investment if you die earlier than might be expected, you can add a bell-and-whistle provision to your annuity to guarantee that it will continue to make payments to whomever you name as a beneficiary for a specific period of time—anywhere from 5 to 20 years. An even simpler and less costly option that you can choose is to have the remainder of your original payment for the annuity paid to a beneficiary named by you if you die before you receive back the full amount that you paid into the annuity.

Fixed Can Sometimes Be Broken

Fixed annuity rates are similar to the fixed rates of credit cards. They're essentially fixed only for as long as the insurance company or bank determines. Apparently, the drafters of annuity contracts attended different English classes in school than you or I did. The word *fixed* does not mean the same to them as it does to us. With fixed annuities, the rate that the insurance company says it will pay is often limited for only a year. To avoid surprises, people who depend upon a particular rate of return on their investment should read the fine print of their annuity contract to determine the time period for how long their initial rate of return is indeed guaranteed and establish the true minimum guaranteed rate that the contract must pay. You will find this information buried deep within the contract, but get out your shovel. You need to know this information.

Variable Immediate Annuity

Here your monthly payments vary depending upon the performance of the underlying stock investments that make up your annuity. Unlike the fixed immediate annuity, the amount you receive monthly is not guaranteed at a set amount.

Bells and Whistles of Immediate Annuities

Varying features found in immediate annuities can permit you to find a policy that is more tailored to your particular desires, but they can also confuse you. Comparing policies that do not exactly match up from company to company can be difficult. As always, for every feature, there is a cost.

One option is an increasing life annuity that provides for an annual increase in the monthly payment. This is a hedge against inflation, but it comes at a significant premium cost that must be weighed against the benefit.

A second option is to continue payments after the death of the person who purchased the annuity to named beneficiaries for a specific period, such as 5 or 10 years. Again, this guarantees a better return on the investment if the person buying the annuity has the bad luck of dying early. However, as you can imagine, this provision makes the annuity much more costly to the insurance companies, who, in turn, pass that cost back to us.

Deferred Annuities

Immediate annuities provide instant gratification—you buy the annuity and you immediately begin receiving payments. With a deferred annuity, however, the payments to you do not begin until some time in the future. Deferred annuities are purchased with either a single lump sum payment or paid for through a series of payments over a number of years.

Fixed Deferred Annuity

This form of annuity locks in a specific rate, but only for a guarantee period of between 1 and 5 years. Remember, just as former President Clinton found multiple meanings for the word *is* when he testified to a Grand Jury, the insurance companies that issue annuities have different meanings for the word *fixed*. As you would expect with a deferred annuity, your receipt of payments does not begin until some time after your payment of the premium. Until you begin to take payments, the earnings on this form of annuity accumulate tax-deferred.

Deferred Equity Index Annuities

This form of annuity offers an intriguing combination of a guaranteed minimum interest rate plus a percentage of the increase in the index to which the annuity is tied. A common index used by Equity Index Annuities is the Standard & Poor's 500 Composite Stock Price Index, more commonly referred to as the S&P 500. Like many aspects of annuities, at first blush, the idea looks attractive. Unlike a standard fixed annuity, you get additional interest based upon the performance of the index to which it is tied—yet if the index goes down, you are guaranteed your minimum promised interest rate. It would seem that you get the best of both worlds: a guaranteed rate, but with a no-risk opportunity to participate in a rising stock market.

But once again, as you look more carefully at this annuity, the promises start to look less promising. First and foremost, there generally is a limit to how much you can earn, regardless of how high the index shoots up. In addition, you do not get the full increase in return of the index—you get only a percentage of it, referred to in the annuity as your "participation rate." For example, if your participation rate is 70 percent, as is commonly found in many Equity Index Annuities, and the S&P 500 goes up 9 percent over the applicable period, the interest rate that you get credited is only 6.3 percent (this is calculated by taking 70 percent of 9 percent).

An even more insidious provision is found buried within the fine print of the annuity contract that deprives you of much of the gains of the measuring index. A large part of the investment return in indexes such as the S&P 500 is due to stock dividends. However, in deferred index annuities, dividends are not considered in determining the annuity payment to you. This reduces the return on your investment. As with all annuities, the fees can be exorbitant. Ultimately, although you have the possibility of an increased return on this type of annuity, the potential increase might not be worth the extensive fees that you pay for the privilege.

Variable Deferred Annuities

Fixed annuities are an insurance company product that pays a guaranteed amount on a specified schedule. Variable annuities are touted as being able to bring a greater investment return, but as with all investments that make that promise, they come with more risk. Because variable-annuity payouts depend on the underlying investments (generally, mutual funds) that make up the variable annuity, the amount of the payments varies according to the return (or lack thereof) of the investments that make up the annuity. However, some variable annuities offer an option, for which you pay extra, to guarantee a minimum rate of return. The combination of high surrender charges, large initial fees, and tax drawbacks makes variable annuities generally a poor investment choice for older investors.

Variable annuities are big business. According to the National Association for Variable Annuities in 2004, $130 billion worth of variable annuities were sold in this country. In 2005, the association determined that more than a trillion dollars' worth of assets were held in variable annuities. One reason for these large numbers is that the annuities aggressively sold. A primary reason that they sold so aggressively is that the commissions paid to sellers of variable annuities are among the largest in the investment world, with salespeople making up to 12 percent commissions.

Theory vs. Reality

The theory behind annuities is that they are a retirement investment through which you can annuitize or convert the value of your annuity into regular payments of income over your life in retirement or for a specified period of time. The amount you receive depends on the value of the investments in your annuity, your age, your life expectancy, and whether you want to have the annuity provide income for your heirs. The reality is that only about 1 percent of variable annuities are ever annuitized. Most people just leave the money in the variable annuity and withdraw it as they choose. If you are a betting person, you should generally choose reality over theory.

Theory vs. Reality II: The Sequel

Annuities come with a lot of variations. One option guarantees that if you die while you own the annuity, the insurance company will pay your beneficiaries at least the amount of money you initially invested. Of course, for this option you pay an additional fee, referred to as a mortality and expense risk charge (M&E). The average cost for this option is 1.01 percent of the value of your annuity. This might seem very attractive to many of us baby boomers who saw our stock portfolios take a major hit during recent bear markets. However, the reality is that very few people die holding annuities that are worth less than what they bought them for. This benefit generally is conditioned on a 10-year holding period. Frankly, there are few 10-year periods over which investments have lost money. And these fees to protect you from a risk that is unlikely to occur can really add up.

Theory vs. Reality III: The Quest to Avoid Taxes

Sellers of variable annuities often trumpet the tax benefits of these investments. They tell you that although money that you invest in stocks, bonds, or mutual funds will be subject to income taxes, the money that you invest in your variable annuity will be tax-deferred, like a traditional IRA or a 401(k) account. As with those accounts, you can take the money out when you reach the magic age of 59 1/2 without any penalty. In addition, sellers of annuities will tell you, unlike the limits on the amounts that you can invest in an IRA or 401(k), there is no limit on the amount of money that you can invest in variable annuities.

The reality, however, is that, unlike the money that you invest in stocks, bonds, and mutual funds, the money you take out of your variable annuity is taxed as ordinary income. This could bring an extraordinary income tax of as high as 35 percent, compared to the tax you pay on long-term capital gains and dividends, which is now limited to a maximum rate of 15 percent. Suddenly, these tax advantages of the variable annuity do not seem so advantageous.

Estate Planning

Annuities are sometimes sold as an estate-planning vehicle, but if you do consider them as such, you should think of them as the Edsel of estate-planning vehicles. If you are lucky enough to have value left in your annuity at your death, not only will the annuity's value be subject to estate tax, but as the money is taken out, the money for your heirs will be totally taxed as ordinary income for income tax purposes. Contrast that with the alternative of having bought mutual funds with the money that otherwise would have gone to buy an annuity. Although an inherited mutual fund might still be subject to estate tax, your heirs would receive a step-up in tax basis for the mutual fund. This means that the income tax basis for your heirs will be the value of the mutual fund at the time of your death. This, in turn, means that if they sold the mutual fund at the time that they inherit the mutual fund, they will pay no income tax.

No, No, No!

If the person recommending an annuity to you suggests that you put the annuity in your traditional IRA, follow Nancy Reagan's advice and just say "no"—or if you are feeling particularly polite, just say, "No, thank you." An IRA already defers income tax. You will not get any additional tax benefits from including an annuity in your IRA. Anyone who tells you otherwise is just looking to get at your money with a big commission. Salesmen who are trying to convince you to buy an annuity for your IRA might say that there are other reasons for buying annuities than the tax advantages. They might say that if investors want the guaranteed minimum income benefits provided by an annuity, for example, they should consider purchasing an annuity for their IRA. However, the fees that you pay for these purported benefits of an annuity seem to be particularly out of line when you put the tax-deferred investment into an IRA that is already tax-deferred.

Fewer Fees, Please

"Please, Sir, I want fewer fees" does not have the literary ring of Oliver Twist asking for more gruel by saying, "Please, sir, I want some more," but it could be more meaningful to you than a bowl of thin porridge made from rice, flour, or millet. The fees found in typical variable annuities can be quite high, particularly as they compound over time. The average annual expenses for a variable annuity in 2003 were 2.32 percent of the entire value of the annuity; that compares to typical annual expenses for a stock mutual fund of 1.4 percent.

The costs of variable annuities can take a big bite out of your investment over time. Mortality and Expense Risk Fees (M&E), Administrative Fees, Subaccount Investment Management Fees, and other fees all add up. If you invested $5,000 a year in a mutual fund with annual expenses of 1.5 percent with both the annuity's underlying investment and the mutual fund returning a historically conservative 8 percent, you would end up with $431,874 after 30 years in the mutual fund, but only $362,177 in a variable annuity with annual expenses of 2.5 percent. This is a difference of $69,697.

Surrender Fees

There's no crying in baseball, as we learned in the movie *A League of Their Own,* a 1992 movie directed by Penny Marshall (who would have thought that Laverne Defazio could direct?).

There also are no Mulligans—that is, do-overs—in variable annuities. (By the way, the term *Mulligan* is said to have originated in Canada in 1920 when golfer David Mulligan was given a second try off the first tee because his hands had been so shaken up when he drove his car over the bumpy road to the St. Lambert Country Club.)

When you put money into a variable annuity, you do not get a Mulligan. If you want to get your money out of your variable annuity so you can invest in something else, you are generally required to pay a hefty surrender charge for your do-over. These surrender charges can exist for as long as 10 years, although they're most often for 7 years, and can be as much as 7 percent of the value of the annuity when you take your money out of an annuity in the annuity's first year. Even though these penalties might decline from outrageous (7 percent) in the first year to merely ridiculous (5 percent) in the third year and even less each succeeding year until the surrender charge is no longer charged after the seventh year, this aspect of annuities makes them particularly inappropriate to the elderly.

Of course, remember that baby boomers buying deferred annuities must pay a 10 percent federal tax penalty on money they take out of their deferred annuity before they reach the age of 59 1/2.

Bank of America

When you are being run out of town on a rail, get in front and make it look like you are leading the parade. This would seem to be the public relations tactic used by Bank of America. Under pressure from Massachusetts Secretary of State William Galvin, the bank announced in the summer of 2005 that it would offer refunds to customers throughout the country who were 78 years of age or older when they bought their variable annuities over the previous 2 years. The bank also agreed to conduct a review of the appropriateness of the investment for all of its customers who were between the ages of 75 and 77 when they bought their annuities through the Bank of America.

Bad Citizens

Also in the summer of 2005, Citizens Bank was fined $3 million by the Commonwealth of Massachusetts for unethical and dishonest conduct in its sale of variable annuities to elderly bank customers. Through a settlement with the state, Citizens Bank also agreed to refund the money of Massachusetts's customers who were at least 75 years old when they purchased a variable annuity from Citizens during the last 2 years. According to Galvin, Citizens Bank "pressured elderly bank customers into buying variable annuities without regard for the appropriateness of such an investment."

Don't Buy Any Green Bananas

There's an old joke about a man who asked his doctor how his tests looked. The doctor responded by saying, "Let me put it this way: Don't buy any green bananas." Frankly, many elderly investors are investing for the short term. This is not the kind of person who should probably be buying variable annuities, the investment equivalent of green bananas. Because elderly investors might need to tap into their investments sooner rather than later, a variable annuity might be inappropriate because it incurs large penalties for early access. In addition, because a variable annuity is tied to the stock market, its short-term risk makes it generally a poor investment for someone who is investing over a relatively short time frame.

Class Action

In January 2005, a class-action lawsuit was filed on behalf of about 10,000 senior citizens against Midland National Life Insurance Company regarding the sale of variable deferred annuities. The lead plaintiff was the estate of John Migliaccio, who had been 73 years old when he paid $43,000 for a variable deferred annuity from Midland National Life Insurance Company. According to the class-action complaint, the fine print of John Migliaccio's annuity contract indicated that he would not begin to receive payments from the annuity until he was 115 years old. According to William Shernoff, an attorney for the estate of John Migliaccio, had John Migliaccio tried to withdraw money during the first 13 years he owned the annuity, he would have faced surrender charges of as high as 22% of the amount withdrawn.

So Who Are Variable Annuities Good For?

About the only people who gain from variable annuities are the people who sell them.

In 2004, the North American Securities Administrators Association listed variable annuities as one of its top 10 scams of the year because of the common failure to disclose the large fees and charges involved, as well as because of the unsuitability of annuities as an investment for many older people, who are often sought out by unscrupulous annuity salespeople. According to Ralph Lambiase, the president of the NASAA, variable annuities make sense only for people who do not need to have access to their investment for at least 10 years.

Baby boomers who are wary of the vagaries of the stock market and who are not looking to retire for up to 12 years or more might find the guarantees of a variable annuity comforting. Having gone through the roller-coaster ride of the stock market in recent years—and having felt the effect on their investment portfolios—these people might find the guaranteed payouts of annuities attractive. However, they should be fully aware of the cost of this comfort. It is important to remember the adage that it is not what you make, but what you keep that counts. When it comes to annuities, the fees and commissions that you pay can seriously dilute the value of your investment when compared to other investments such as index mutual funds.

Before even considering a variable annuity, consider maximizing your investments in an IRA, 401(k), or other low-cost way to invest for retirement in a tax-advantaged manner in which you can invest with pre-tax money. There is no tax deduction for your annuity premium payments.

- You should probably not consider investing in an annuity unless you will not need the money before you reach the age of 59 ½.

- Because of the significant surrender fees and other costs, you should probably not invest in an annuity unless you are planning to keep the annuity for 15 to 20 years.

- You should probably not consider investing in an annuity unless you are in a 28 percent or higher income-tax bracket today, and you expect to be in a lower tax bracket at retirement.

- You should probably not consider investing in an annuity if you want to leave your heirs any of the value of your annuity, without their being subject to income tax on the appreciation in value of the investment at the higher ordinary income tax rates.

If after all this you still think that an annuity is for you, remember the wise words of the man Bob Dylan said was America's greatest living poet, Smokey Robinson: "Shop around." Fidelity, Vanguard, T. Rowe Price, Ameritas Life, and TIAA-Cref are among companies that offer annuities at considerably less cost with lower management fees and lower expenses because they do not pay commissions to salespeople. It is also most important to remember that because an annuity is, in the best-case scenario, a very long-range investment, you will want to do business only with the strongest of companies. A terrific annuity contract (using the definition of the word *terrific* to mean "extraordinary") can become a terrific annuity contract (using the definition of the word *terrific* to mean "terrifying") if the company with which you have your annuity goes bankrupt.

Check out the rating of the company you are considering with AM Best, Standard & Poors, Moody's, and Weiss Ratings. Their Web sites are found at www.ambest.com, www.infoinsure.com, www.moodys.com, and www.weissratings.com, respectively. In keeping with the confusion that keeps us on our toes, it is important to note that the ratings of insurance companies by these rating companies are not consistent. A grade of A- is only the fourth-highest rating by AM Best, the third-highest rating for Weiss and, believe it or not, the seventh-highest rating for Standard & Poors. Talk about grade inflation.

4

INCOME TAXES
FOR SENIORS

*"If Thomas Jefferson thought taxation without representation
was bad, he should see how it is with representation."*
—Rush Limbaugh

T he federal income tax was not designed merely to confiscate our
hard-earned money. The Internal Revenue Code was also
designed to encourage certain activities—such as charitable giving, which is deductible—and to discourage other activities, such as
running up credit card debt, which is not. Buried within the Internal
Revenue Code are some tax benefits for older Americans—and their
care-giving children—along with some pitfalls to avoid. So let's get our
shovels and do some digging

Dependents: It All Depends

Turnabout is fair play. Just as baby boomers were once claimed as
dependents on their parents' income tax returns, many baby boomers
are now in a position to claim their parents as dependents on their own
returns. A dependency exemption is worth money to baby boomer

children who are able to claim one or both parents. For the tax year 2006, the tax exemption was worth $3,300.

Under what circumstances can you claim your parent as a dependent on your tax return? Your parent must be an American citizen, resident alien or even just a resident of North America. In addition, your parent may not file a joint income tax return. Your parent's gross income (all of your parent's income, not just the really yucky income, as the term might imply) must have been less than $3,300 for the tax year 2006. This figure changes regularly. Finally, you must have paid for more than half of your parent's expenses for the year.

Although I have been using the example of a baby boomer taking a parent as a dependent for income tax purposes, the person you claim as a dependent does not even have to be your parent. He or she can be a relative or even a member of your household who lives with you.

Reducing Gross Income

At first look, it might appear that your parent or the person you want to claim as a dependent has more than $3,300 in really gross income. However, if you look more closely, much of their income might come from Social Security benefits—and if those benefits are not taxed, they do not count as gross income. In addition, other nontaxable income is not included in the determination of gross income. So, if your parent has gross income of more than $3,300 from bank accounts or certificates of deposit, you might want to consider moving those investments into tax-free municipal bonds or tax-free mutual funds; the income earned from those investments is not used to calculate gross income.

Another way to reduce a parent's income is for the parent to give to the child some of his or her income-producing assets.

Loophole

If you are caring for an aging parent (can you think of any parents who are not aging?) in your own home, you also can count the fair market rental value for the space in your home that you are providing. This could make it much easier to meet the requirement that you must pay more than half of your parent's living expenses. For instance, if your parent's costs total $6,000 for food, clothing, and sundries, and the fair market rent for the room in your home in which your parent lives is $5,000, you must pay only an extra $501 above what you are providing for living space to meet the test.

Multiple Support Agreements

Perhaps you alone do not provide more than half of your parent's support, which is required to take the dependency exemption for your parent on your income tax return. You might have other siblings who, with you, together contribute more than half of your parent's living expenses. In that situation, you might all agree that one sibling may take the dependency exemption. In a multiple-support arrangement, the person making the claim must contribute more than 10 percent of the parent's living expenses. The agreement to allocate the dependency exemption must be documented on IRS Form 2120, "Multiple Support Declaration." (They were going to name it the "Declaration of No Longer Independence," but apparently some descendant of Thomas Jefferson complained.)

Think

"Think" represents a great slogan that was coined by Thomas J. Watson, a founder of IBM. When he moved to Computer-Tabulating Recording Company, the company that morphed into IBM, Watson put this slogan on signs around the company. I wonder how long it took him to think that up—maybe if he'd had the sign when he was trying to do so, he would have come up with the idea sooner. In any event, this is a good slogan, particularly if you are a high-income taxpayer, because the value of the dependency exemption is phased out as adjusted gross income reaches specific levels. In 2006, that is $225,750 for a joint return.

If you are thinking (see, eventually there was a connection), you might determine that a multiple-support agreement will get more bang for the buck if the dependency exemption goes to a sibling with less adjusted gross income, to achieve the maximum financial benefit within the family.

Again, it is important to remember that only one person can take the dependency exemption in any particular year, but the person to whom the dependency exemption is allocated might change from year to year. This means that multiple qualifying siblings can take turns receiving the benefit of the exemption.

Dependent Care Credit

One would think that the dependent care credit on income tax returns might be limited to the cost of care for dependents, but this is the Internal Revenue Code we are talking about (and it is called *code* for a reason). English majors do not write tax regulations. The good news is that even if you do not qualify to claim your parent as a dependent because your parent has more gross income than is allowed, you still might be able to take the dependent care credit if you meet the other dependency conditions.

To qualify for this credit, you must pay someone to provide care for your parent so that you are able to commit your time to your own employment. If you qualify, you can take a 20 percent credit for up to $3,000 worth of care expenses; this translates into a tax credit of as much as $600. And if you are hiring someone to care for both of your parents at a cost of at least $6,000, you can get a tax credit of $1,200. Remember, a tax deduction is used to reduce the amount of income upon which you pay taxes; a tax credit is even more valuable because it comes right off the top of your tax bill, reducing your tax liability dollar for dollar.

Medical Expenses

In determining your itemized medical deductions on your income tax return, you also might be able to add in your parents' medical bills that you pay on their behalf. It is important to remember, though, that you must pay those bills directly to the health care provider for those costs to qualify for the deduction. Giving money to your parents to pay the bills does not qualify.

It is also important to remember that you can do this even if you are not claiming a parent as a dependent. However, as with the dependent care credit, you must meet all of the dependency exemption requirements, except for the limit on your parents' income. As always, medical expenses are deductible only to the extent that they exceed 7.5 percent of the taxpayer's adjusted gross income.

For example, if an adult child has $100,000 of adjusted gross income and $2,500 of his own medical expenses, while his parent has an adjusted gross income of $25,000 and nursing home expenses of $60,000, the adult child would be in a position to deduct $30,000. This is calculated by adding the nursing home expenses of $60,000 to the adult child's medical expenses of $2,500, then deducting the parent's contribution of his own income toward his medical expenses in the amount of $25,000, and finally deducting $7,500 (which is 7.5 percent of the adult child's adjusted gross income). This amounts to a sizeable tax deduction for the adult child of $30,000.

If your parent is living with you, capital improvements to your home could qualify for consideration as medical expenses, as long as a physician has deemed them in writing to be necessary. For example, if your parent's arthritis would benefit from swimming, installing a swimming pool could be partially considered a medical expense. The same goes for that sauna and whirlpool for those achy, breaky joints.

The deductible amount of the cost of home improvements is determined in accordance with IRS regulations by subtracting from the actual cost of the improvement the increase in the value of the property as a result of the improvement. As an example, the IRS cites a home elevator installed to assist a person whose heart disease makes it difficult to climb stairs. According to the IRS, if the installation of the elevator cost $8,000 and the value of the home increases by $4,400, the deductible amount would be $3,600. (I considered adding that a train left Chicago at 9:00 AM because I just had a flashback to dreaded math word problems from my youth, but I decided to spare you that complication.)

But there is good news from the IRS (how about that for an oxy-moron?). Our dear friends at the IRS will permit the deduction of the full cost of some home improvements as capital expenses that qualify for deductibility as medical expenses because the IRS does not consider them to increase the value of the home. These include the following:

- Building entrance ramps
- Widening doorways on the outside or inside of the home
- Installing railings in the bathrooms
- Lowering kitchen cabinets and appliances
- Landscaping to provide easier access

Loophole

Generally, to take a deduction for a medical expense, you must have paid that bill during the tax year for which you will be deducting it. If you used your credit card to charge the payment of the medical expense during the tax year in which you want to deduct the payment, you can take the deduction regardless of when you actually pay the bill.

Senior Citizen's Freedom to Work Act (or the "Do You Want Fries with That?" Act)

It's bad enough that many senior citizens have to work at menial jobs after retirement to make enough money to get by; they shouldn't have to worry about having their Social Security benefits reduced. With the passage of the Senior Citizen's Freedom to Work Act, people of full retirement age who receive benefits will not have their Social Security benefit payments reduced.

However, in 2006, people who elected to take early Social Security benefits before reaching their full retirement age have their benefits reduced by $1 for every $2 they earn over the sum of $12,480. For example, an early retiree who earns an annual salary of $40,000 would lose $13,760 in annual Social Security benefit payments. As you can see, this greatly complicates the decision of whether to keep working. The Social Security Administration adjusts this amount regularly.

Fortunately, regardless of your age, you may receive income in any amount from sources other than employment, such as investments or private pensions, without affecting the amount of your Social Security retirement benefits.

Caution

If you are considering employment after you begin receiving early Social Security retirement benefits (and even though that sounds like another oxymoron, you may elect to receive Social Security retirement benefits while still working), you should consider how much money you will actually end up with after additional federal income tax costs, state and local taxes, and FICA taxes will be levied on your earnings.

Nursing Home Expenses

According to the IRS, nursing home costs can be deducted as medical expenses if the primary purpose for being in the nursing home is for medical care. If someone were in a nursing home strictly for fun, the costs would not be deductible. However, if the reason for being in a nursing home is medical, all costs, including room and board, are deductible.

Long-Term Care Insurance Premiums

Premium payments for qualified long-term care insurance policies may also be deductible as a medical expense. The amount of the premium that may be used for determining the amount of the deduction depends on the age of the insured. In 2006, the maximum deductible premium amount for people 40 years old or under is $280; for people between the ages of 41 and 50, it is $530; for people between the ages of

51 and 60, it is $1,060; for people between the ages of 61 and 70, it is $2,830; and for people ages 71 and over, it is $3,530. The IRS changes these figures periodically. To be considered a qualified long-term care insurance policy for income tax purposes, the policy must be guaranteed renewable and must not have a cash value.

Head of Household

The IRS is big on classifying people. Unmarried people (whom they refer to as single people) who are supporting one or both parents can qualify for the filing status of head of household. This not only sounds much cooler than merely "single," but it also brings with it less income tax than if they were merely classified as "single." Once again, the IRS requires you to pay for more than half of your parent's living expenses. You also must be paying more than half the cost of keeping up the home that is the primary residence for your parent, although this requirement may also be met if you pay half the cost of keeping your parent in elderly housing.

Tax Distributions from Individual Retirement Accounts (IRA)

Roth IRA distributions are generally not subject to income tax. However, distributions made from traditional IRA accounts are subject to income tax in the year in which you receive the distribution. Fortunately, a number of loopholes protect traditional IRA distributions from income taxes.

Amounts that you take as distributions from your IRA before you reach the age of 59½ are not only taxable, but are subject to an additional 10 percent excise tax (except in certain circumstances, which I describe later). By the way, for those of you who have always wondered why Congress chose the rather unusual age of 59½ as a baseline for retirement, the reason goes back to a debate in Congress during the early 1960s when the self-employed retirement plan that has come to be known as the Keogh Plan was enacted into law. At that time, the age of

60 was a common retirement age. However, in actuarial terms used by insurance companies, the age was 59½, so that number was used regardless of how ridiculous it sounds.

Not Too Soon and Not Too Late

Just as it is a no-no (to use the technical legal term) to prematurely withdraw your IRA funds before the age of 59½, it is a no-no to delay beginning your withdrawal of IRA funds beyond April 1 of the year following the year in which you reach the age of 70½. Even if there was a legitimate reason for picking 70½ as a particular age, it is mind-boggling to think that some Congressman actually thought it would make sense to make the date by which you must begin your IRA withdrawals the April Fool's Day after you reach 70½. Failing to celebrate the April Fool's Day (apparently, a Congressional holiday) following age 70½ by withdrawing the appropriately calculated minimum amount of IRA funds can result in as much as a 50 percent excise tax on the amounts that were not distributed correctly.

IRA Withdrawal Tip

If you are lucky enough (or if you planned early enough) to have large amounts of money in your traditional IRA, you are not required to withdraw money from the IRA until you reach the age of 70½. However, you might want to start taking money from the account earlier. If you put off taking withdrawals, the amounts will be larger and could conceivably kick you into a higher tax bracket. Once again, the key is to do the math and see what is best for you in determining when to take IRA distributions.

Exceptions to the Rule

When it comes to avoiding the excise tax penalties for early withdrawals of IRA money, the IRS has a number of regulations that work to your advantage. One exception is that of substantially equal payments to be made over the life expectancy of the IRA owner. However, life expectancy in IRS language (not English, by any stretch of the imagination) means that substantially equal yearly payments must be made either until the person receiving the payments reaches age 59½ or until 5 years have gone by, whichever occurs later.

Another exception to the early withdrawal penalty arises when the money is used to pay for the cost of deductible medical expenses.

A third exception occurs when the money is used to pay for medical insurance premiums after the IRA owner has been receiving unemployment compensation for more than 12 weeks.

Taxability of Social Security Payments

Whether you will have to pay income tax on payments you receive from Social Security depends on your provisional income and your income tax filing status. Provisional income is a concept that exists only in the Internal Revenue Code. It is determined by adding to your taxable income your nontaxable income (such as income from tax-exempt municipal bonds) and half of your net Social Security benefits.

If you are married and filing jointly, none of your net Social Security benefits are taxable if your provisional income is not more than $32,000. If you are single, married filing separately, or filing as head of household, you may have up to $25,000 of provisional income without having any of your Social Security benefits taxed.

Mr. Lucky

Baby boomers who remember the short-lived television show *Mr. Lucky* that was broadcast on CBS in 1959 and 1960 either still have all of their brain cells firing or watched far more television than they should have. Perhaps the show's most notable aspect was another great theme song written by Henry Mancini.

A modern-day Mr. Lucky is Leroy J. Klingaman (who was not a character on the television show *MASH*—you are thinking of Corporal Klinger). In 2001, Klingaman had a good year gambling, taking in $7,340 in lottery and casino winnings. Putting this in perspective, his other income for 2001 consisted of a pension, interest and dividend income of $14,119 and Social Security retirement benefits of $11,088. On his 2001 federal income tax return, Klingaman did not include any of his Social Security benefits or gambling income as taxable income. Ever the spoilsports, the IRS disagreed with Klingaman's interpretation of the Tax Code. They increased Klingaman's taxable adjusted gross income by his gambling winnings. That, in turn, triggered the taxability of some of his Social Security benefits because it pushed his provisional income over $25,000. Klingaman argued that his gambling winnings should not have been counted because he had gambling losses for the year that totally offset his winnings. However, the Tax Court agreed with the IRS that gambling losses do not directly offset gambling winnings; instead, they are allowed as an itemized deduction. Ultimately, our Mr. Lucky not only had a net loss for his gambling for the year, but he also gambled himself into making some of his Social Security benefits taxable.

Loophole

You can strengthen your position for avoiding tax on your Social Security benefits by investing in growth assets rather than investments that pay dividends or interest. Series EE savings bonds are a particularly good choice in this situation because the interest on these bonds is not taxed until the bonds are actually redeemed.

Yet Another Loophole

Supplemental security benefits are not subject to income tax, nor are they considered in determining your provisional income.

Taxability of Accident or Health Insurance Policy Benefits or Life Insurance Proceeds

If you receive payments under the terms of an accident insurance or health insurance policy, these benefits are not subject to income tax if either you paid the premiums for the policies, or your employer paid the premiums but you included the premium amounts in your gross income.

Life insurance proceeds on life insurance policies of which you are the beneficiary are not subject to income tax.

Taxability of Long-Term Care Insurance Policies Proceeds

Money you receive from a qualified long-term care insurance policy is not subject to income tax as long as any amounts you receive per day over $240 are applied toward your actual cost of long-term care in a nursing home. So if your policy pays you $245 per day and your daily rate at the nursing home is $250, none of the amount that you receive from the insurance company that you use to pay for your nursing home costs will be taxable.

Taxability of Disability Payments

If you paid for the premiums for your disability insurance policy, any payments that you receive through the policy are not subject to income tax. If your employer paid for the entire amount of the premiums for a disability policy for you, payments made to you through the policy are subject to income tax. If both you and your employer both contributed to the payment of the policy premiums, a portion of the amount you receive will be subject to tax. Your employer can provide you with the amount that will be taxable to you.

Taxability of Accelerated Death Benefits

Accelerated death benefits does sound like something of an oxymoron, but more people are tapping into their own life insurance policies, either with the company that sold them the policy or with a viatical company that buys the policy from the policyholder who gets money for present needs. Viatical settlement companies buy your life insurance policy while you are alive. The company then becomes the beneficiary of your policy and continues to pay the premiums. Upon your death, the viatical settlement company collects the insurance proceeds. Some people use the money they get from a viatical settlement company to pay for long-term care needs in a nursing home. If the person receiving this money is terminally or chronically ill, the payments do not constitute taxable income. The IRS considers people to be "terminally ill" who have an illness that reasonably can be expected to result in their death within 2 years from when a physician so certifies. A "chronically ill" person is a person who is not deemed terminally ill, but rather has been certified by a physician within the last year either as someone who cannot perform at least two activities of daily living for a period of 90 days or more because of a loss of functional capacity, or someone who requires substantial supervision to protect him or herself from danger to health and safety due to severe cognitive impairment.

Sale of Home

For many older Americans, a home represents their largest asset. The tax ramifications of selling a home are very important. Individuals can exclude up to $250,000 of the gain from the sale of their home when determining their income taxes. Husbands and wives filing a joint tax return can exclude a gain of up to $500,000. It is also important to remember that when we talk about excluding the gain, we are not talking about the sales price, but rather, essentially the difference between what you paid for the home and the price for which you sold it. So, for example, if you and your spouse bought your home for $100,000 and sold it for $600,000, you would generally be able to exclude the entire gain on the sale of your home from income taxes.

Some conditions apply (don't they always?), but they are not particularly onerous. During the 5 years before the sale of the house, you must have owned and lived in the home for at least 2 years. Even if you did not live in the home for at least 2 years, you still might be able to exclude some of the gain if you pass the Internal Revenue Service's "unforeseen circumstances test." Among the unforeseen circumstances that the IRS specifically recognizes are death and divorce. Multiple births also qualify as unforeseen circumstances; in the case of a couple in their 80s, this might be properly classified as improbable more than merely an unforeseen circumstance. Going into a nursing home or assisted-living center also qualifies as an unforeseen circumstance.

Loophole

Even if you own your home in a living revocable trust (also sometimes called an "intervivos trust"—of course, if your trust really is called an intervivos trust, you probably paid more for it because the more Latin you find in your documents, the greater the fee usually is), you can still use the $250,000/$500,000 exclusion from capital gains income taxes. The term "living revocable trust" describes a trust created for you while you were alive, as compared to a trust that is made a part of your will. It also is a form of trust that you totally control and can revoke or change at any time. A living revocable trust is often used to keep the assets contained in the trust from having to go through probate. A living revocable trust enables you to control the property during your lifetime but then have the trust property pass to whomever you indicate in your trust directly upon your death, without having to involve the probate courts. Married couples filing joint income tax returns can take the full $500,000 exemption from capital gains taxes even if only one of them owns the home. Unmarried couples who own a home in both of their names can each get a $250,000 exemption from capital gains taxes when the house is sold.

The Fly in the Ointment

This is a rather disgusting image, but it's a good metaphor for a problem that some people encounter. Under prior tax law, if you bought a home that cost more than your previous home, you could defer payment of the capital gains tax that related to the tax on the sale of your previous home by rolling that gain into your new home. This would reduce the basis of your new home so that when you sold your new home, you would be subject to the income tax on the gain of the first home. This applies to gains from the sales of homes before May 7, 1997, that you postponed declaring. This basis reduction will increase the possible taxable gain on the sale of your current home.

Record Collection

Like many baby boomers, I love my record collection of real vinyl records the way God intended music to be recorded, with all its glorious scratches. Digitally remastered compact discs of the music of bands of the 1960s just do not sound right. However, I am fighting a losing battle. Records as we knew them are history. But tax records are very important. The question is, what records do you keep?

There are two kinds of people in this world. People like me save everything and people like my wife, Carole, who just cannot wait to throw things out. My wife calls me a packrat and says that she just does not like clutter. I adore clutter. But when it comes to tax records, what records should you keep and for how long?

The starting point for maintaining your records is 3 years, which is the period of time after you have filed your income tax return that the IRS has to audit that return. However, we packrats point out that the IRS has up to 6 years in which to audit your tax return if they allege that you underreported your income by at least 25 percent. And when it comes to receipts and records for capital improvements to your home, such as that remodeled kitchen with the island in the middle or that expanded family room with a television screen larger than a billboard (a personal favorite of mine), as a packrat, I am thrilled to tell you that you should keep those records for as long as you own your home. They will be useful in determining the adjusted basis of your home when it comes to establishing the amount of taxable capital gain to which you could be subject when you sell your home.

Also, as a packrat, I am ecstatic to tell you that you should forever hold on to the records pertaining to the purchase of stocks and other investments. You will need these to properly compute your gains or losses when you sell these investments. Monthly or quarterly statements from brokerage houses or mutual funds should be kept only until you receive your annual statement, I am sad to say. However, keep those annual reports permanently. They might be needed to aid in the preparation of later tax returns. Monthly or quarterly statements from retirement plans need also be kept only until you have received your annual report, but once again, you should permanently tuck away those yearly reports because either you or your estate might need them later.

Once and for All

Everyone has opinions, but not all opinions are valid. Just because someone tells you that you are not required to pay income taxes, does not make that statement anything more than that particular misguided person's opinion. For years, the IRS has been plagued by a number of people, some merely deluded, others downright frauds, who try to avoid paying taxes, citing various frivolous purported legal arguments. Not long ago, the IRS announced that it was changing its internal auditing procedures in an effort to speed up the prosecution of people who file frivolous claims in an effort to avoid paying federal income taxes. A common tactic used in the past by tax protestors to postpone the inevitable (taxes, not death) was to request a technical advice ruling that tied up an audit for months or even years. The IRS no longer honors such requests when the legal status of the questions presented has been established as frivolous.

It is important to note that, despite what you might have heard from self-proclaimed tax experts, the IRS has never lost a single court case on the issue of whether income is subject to tax or whether the federal income tax system itself is constitutional. In 2005, notorious professional tax resister Irwin Schiff was convicted of income tax evasion and aiding in the preparation of false income tax returns. Some of the arguments tax protestors use include the argument that filing a tax return is an unreasonable search and seizure in violation of the Fourth

Amendment to the Constitution. It has also been unsuccessfully argued that the federal income tax violates the Thirteenth Amendment prohibition of involuntary servitude. Another favorite tax-avoidance argument is that paying income taxes is purely voluntary and that, in any event, the term *income* is not defined in the tax laws. None of these arguments has ever been successful in court, and they never will be. Failure to pay income taxes is a serious matter that can result in civil or even criminal penalties.

5

AGE DISCRIMINATION

"The years teach much which the days never knew."
—Ralph Waldo Emerson

I t's bad enough getting old, although it certainly beats the alternative. Being discriminated against on the basis of your age somehow seems like adding insult to injury. Fortunately, your fellow aging baby boomers in Congress have seen fit to pass laws protecting people from age discrimination in employment. It is interesting to note that in a culture that still seems to worship youth, the threshold for age discrimination is a mere 40. Of course, for a generation that once did not trust anyone over 30 but now hardly trusts anyone *under* 30, this should not seem so young. According to Victor Hugo, "Forty is the old age of youth; fifty the youth of old age."

Even the Supreme Court has weighed in on the issue of age discrimination and has been somewhat protective of the rights of older people faced with age discrimination. That should come as little surprise: The youngest Supreme Court Justice, Clarence Thomas, was born in 1948. I say "somewhat protective" because although headlines in 2005 trumpeted a landmark case, Smith vs. City of Jackson, Mississippi[1] indicating the court's strong endorsement of the laws against age discrimination, the loopholes of that decision make the law quite a bit less user-friendly for older Americans.

Issues with age discrimination in the workplace are of great concern to baby boomers who are not only aging, but also planning to continue working even after they reach the traditional retirement age of 65. According to the General Accounting Office, by 2008, one of every six workers in America will be over the age of 55.[2] Some older workers will continue to work because they want the stimulation and the challenge; others might prolong their working careers because they have not saved and invested sufficiently for their retirement. Whatever the reason, there will be a much greater number of older workers in the years ahead.

The ADEA

Age discrimination in the workplace is an unfortunate fact of life. In 2003, 23.5 percent of the discrimination claims filed with the Equal Employment Opportunity Commission involved age discrimination. This number is expected to rise. The federal Age Discrimination in Employment Act (ADEA) prohibits age discrimination in employment.

It is important to note that the ADEA applies to cases in which age is not even the sole factor for the action taken by an employer against an employee. However, for the ADEA to apply, age must be a significant contributing factor.[3]

Exceptions to the Rule

Exceptions arise for every rule except this one. Under an exception to the ADEA, older workers are not protected from age discrimination in employment in the fields of law enforcement and firefighting. In addition, if age is a "bona fide occupational qualification" (known by yet another acronym, BFOQ) that is reasonably necessary for the normal operation of the particular business, the ADEA does not apply. For example, Burt Reynolds could not sue because a considerably younger Adam Sandler got

---

the leading role of Paul Crewe in the 2005 remake of the movie *The Longest Yard,* a role Reynolds played in the original 1974 version of the movie.

Fortunately, the courts have chosen to interpret the BFOQ rule in a strict fashion, to limit its use as an easy excuse for companies to gloss over blatant age discrimination. In the 1985 case *Western Airlines v. Criswell,* the Supreme Court refused to recognize a BFOQ defense when an airline tried to use it to defend its rule compelling flight engineers to retire at 60 years of age.[4]

Reduction in Force

Sometimes it is necessary for businesses to downsize to survive, and the ADEA does not give any special consideration to older workers in avoiding layoffs. As the court said in *Wilson v. Firestone Tire & Rubber Company,*[5] "The ADEA only bars discrimination on account of age; it does not place on employers an affirmative obligation to retain older workers whenever a reduction in staff becomes necessary."

However, it is equally clear that downsizing may not be used as a pretext for getting rid of older workers because of their age. Age discrimination charges commonly follow reductions in force. In those situations, the workers claiming age discrimination have the initial burden of showing that age was a substantial motivating factor in the decision to let them go.

Beast of Burden

"Beast of Burden" was a 1978 hit for the Rolling Stones, a group of baby boomers (and older—Mick Jagger was born in 1943) still performing.

When a worker has presented evidence in a court case that supports his or her allegations of age discrimination, the worker is deemed to have met his or her initial burden of proof. The burden of proof shifts to the employer to prove a legitimate reason for terminating the older employee that is unrelated to the employee's age, such as sheer economic necessity. The dance then continues: The burden of proof shifts back to the terminated worker, who must then show that the employer's reason is merely a pretext for the true reason of age discrimination. Reductions in workforce cannot be used to cover up age discrimination. In the case of *Burger v. New York Institute of Technology*,[6] evidence emerged that shortly before the layoff of the oldest worker in the department, the company transferred into that department a much younger employee, fully aware that adding the new, younger employee to the department would necessitate a reduction in workforce and eliminate one position in that department. The Appeals Court concluded that this action indicated that the company's layoff of the older worker, Betty Jane Burger, was improperly motivated by age discrimination.

Statistics Don't Lie

Sometimes numbers tell the story. In the case of *Benson v. Tocco, Inc.*,[7] the federal court noted that, during a time of layoffs, the termination rate of Tocco employees who were over 40 years of age was five times greater than the termination rate of employees younger than 40.

Not everyone trusts statistics: The cynical Benjamin Disraeli once observed, "There are three kinds of lies: lies, damned lies, and statistics." Still, statistics can provide compelling evidence of age discrimination. In the reduction in workforce case of *Blum v. Witco Chemical Corporation*, the court was convinced that age discrimination had occurred when statistics revealed that all chemists less than 40 years old had kept their jobs, whereas about two-thirds of the chemists over 40 had been fired. According to the testimony of a statistician, the probability that this would have occurred for a reason other than the age of the workers was only 8 in 1,000.[8]

Disparate Treatment

Disparate treatment is one of two types of age discrimination claims. In this instance, the employer displays intentional discrimination.

Obviously, a victim of such discrimination usually will not be able to point to a letter from the company stating that he or she was fired, not hired, or otherwise badly treated because of age. However, you do not have to be Lieutenant Columbo (extra points if you remember his first name, although this is a trick question because in all the years the show ran, beginning in 1968, he never had a first name) to prove that your company is guilty of age discrimination. Indications that similarly situated younger workers were treated better or that company management personnel made age-discriminatory remarks can be used as evidence of disparate treatment constituting age discrimination.

Disparate Impact

Unlike the 1998 science-fiction movie *Deep Impact*, which, despite its name, did not leave much of a lasting impression other than that Morgan Freeman would probably make a good President of the United States, disparate impact is an important aspect of an age discrimination claim. Under the theory of disparate impact, age discrimination can be shown through actions taken by an employer that, although not done specifically to discriminate against older workers, disproportionately and negatively affect older employees. The United States Supreme Court approved the theory of disparate impact in age discrimination cases in 2005 in what was considered a startling and important recognition of the rights of older workers. Unfortunately, the reality of the Supreme Court's decision was not quite as advantageous to older workers as headline writers led many to believe.

The case, known as *Smith v. City of Jackson, Mississippi*, involved the policy of the city of Jackson, Mississippi.[9] To both attract and keep qualified police officers, the city had granted pay raises to all of the city's present police officers. However, under the city's plan, officers with fewer than 5 years of service received proportionately higher raises than more senior officers. Most of the police officers who were at least 40 years old had more than 5 years of service. Those senior police officers sued the city under the ADEA, claiming that the city had both intentionally discriminated against them (a disparate treatment claim) and that they were adversely affected by the plan, regardless of its intent (a disparate impact claim).

Even though the evidence was clear that the city had increased the wages of younger officers by a higher percentage than the wage increases granted to the more senior officers, the city explained that the wages of the more junior officers had to be increased more to make the wages of these junior positions more competitive with the wages of junior officers in nearby cities. Therefore, the city argued, it did not discriminate by age under either the theory of disparate treatment or disparate impact.

What Do Words Mean?

"'When I use a word,' Humpty Dumpty said in a
rather scornful tone, 'it means just what I choose
it to mean—neither more nor less.'"
—Lewis Carroll

The language Congress used to outlaw age discrimination in the ADEA is the same language it used previously in Title VII of the Civil Rights Act of 1964 to prohibit discrimination based upon race, sex, religion, or national origin. The courts had already interpreted Title VII to permit claims based upon disparate impact, but there was some disagreement over whether the same words in the ADEA would also permit claims based upon disparate impact. In a victory for the older Jackson police officers, a five-justice majority of the Supreme Court agreed that the ADEA permitted claims based upon disparate impact. Unfortunately, for these apparently victorious officers, theirs was a Pyrrhic victory.

By the way, the term "Pyrrhic victory" comes from the Greek King Pyrrhus who lost so many troops in his defeat of the Romans in a 279 B.C. battle that, when congratulated on his victory, he responded "Another such victory over the Romans and we are undone."

Although five justices agreed that the officers could bring an age discrimination claim based upon the theory of disparate impact, all eight justices who participated in the decision concluded that there was no disparate impact in this particular case. The Supreme Court ruled that the officers failed in their burden to identify a specific business practice that adversely affected the older officers and was responsible for the statistical disparity. To make things worse, the court further indicated that even if there were a specific business practice that caused the disparity, the city would still be constitutionally permitted to utilize that practice if it was able to show that the practice was based upon reasonable factors.

In this case, the city had made the reasonable business decision that it needed to increase the wages of its more junior police officers to make the city's police force more competitive with comparable jobs in other cities. The Supreme Court also did a little fancy verbal footwork when it said that this business decision was not only reasonable, but also was not based on age. This defense is referred to by the acronym RFOA, which stands for Reasonable Factors Other Than Age. Here the court distinguished age from seniority, a distinction that would have made Humpty Dumpty proud. In essence, it stated that a business decision based upon seniority is not the same thing as a decision based upon the age of the affected individuals.

Ultimately, the older police officers of Jackson, Mississippi won the battle; disparate impact was now recognized as an indication of age discrimination, but they lost the war when the court ruled that in their particular case, no disparate impact was present.

Who Are You Calling Old?

In 2005, a Los Angeles jury awarded 85-year-old Dr. Robert Johnson $20 million when he claimed that he was forced to retire as chief physician and surgeon at the Lancaster State Prison because of his age. Dr. Johnson had been the chief medical officer for the California Department of Corrections since 1993. Then in 2001, he was informed that his position as chief medical officer was being eliminated; instead, he was given the position of chief physician and surgeon. However, a short time later, a younger physician was hired as chief medical officer, the same position that Dr. Johnson had held. That same year, Dr. Johnson said, pressure was put on him to retire. When he refused to retire, he was forced to take a fitness exam, which he passed with flying colors. His supervisors then filed a complaint with the Medical Board of California alleging that he had memory loss and that his performance as a physician might be impaired.

After an investigation, the board exonerated Dr. Johnson of all charges. Frustrated with harassment that he believed was due to his age, Dr. Johnson sued the California Department of Corrections. During the trial, an expert testified on Dr. Johnson's behalf that he could have worked effectively until he was 96. Ultimately, the jury believed that the capable physician was the victim of age discrimination.

In 2003, 53-year-old Delta flight attendant Joyce Ziegler (and for all you baby boomers accustomed to saying "stewardess," the term is "flight attendant"—I know because I have a daughter who is one) was awarded a $770,000 age discrimination judgment in federal court in Kentucky based upon her firing despite her 27 years of exemplary service to Delta.

You Can't Always Get What You Want

This great Rolling Stones song was picked by *Rolling Stone* as the 100th greatest rock 'n roll song of all time. It also is memorable for its atypical rock and roll use of the London Bach Choir in the background.

At 51 years old, Ralph Williams was fired from Raytheon as director of internal communications for insubordination. According to Williams, his supervisor wanted to get rid of "old white men." So Ralph Williams filed an age discrimination lawsuit against Raytheon. Unfortunately, for Ralph Williams, he came to learn that indeed you can't always get what you want when the court ruled that because Williams's replacement was only 3 years younger than he was, there was no evidence of age discrimination.

Reverse Age Discrimination

We know that the law prohibits favoring younger workers to the detriment of older workers, but what if a company has a policy that works to the benefit of older workers over the interests of younger workers? To complicate things even further, what if the younger workers who are discriminated against are themselves over the age of 40? Is that reverse age discrimination? Is that the equivalent of the "double secret probation" that the Delta House was put on in the 1978 movie *National Lampoon's Animal House*? Believe it or not, this was the exact dilemma facing the United States Supreme Court in the case of *Cline v. General Dynamics Land Systems, Inc.*[10]

The lawsuit was prompted by a new collective bargaining agreement between General Dynamics and the United Auto Workers Union. According to the terms of this agreement, General Dynamics would no longer offer retiree health benefits to employees. However, employees who were 50 or older on July 1, 1997, were grandfathered in and were able to receive retiree health benefits according to the terms of the previous agreement. A number of employees between the ages of 40 and 49 sued, alleging that they were the victims of age discrimination.

Initially, the courts ruled in their favor, indicating that they had indeed been the victims of age discrimination and were over the threshold age of 40. However, in February 2004, by a vote of 6 to 3, the United States Supreme Court ruled that the plan did not amount to age discrimination. Writing for the court, Justice David Souter indicated that the ADEA was "manifestly intended to protect the older from arbitrary favor for the younger." Justice Souter went on to say that "the enemy of 40 is 30, not 50." He reasoned, "If Congress had been worrying about protecting the younger against the older worker, it would not likely have ignored everyone under 40. The youthful deficiencies of inexperience and unsteadiness invite stereotypical and discriminatory thinking about those a lot younger than 40, and prejudice suffered by a 40-year-old is not typically owing to youth, as 40-year-olds sadly tend to find out."

Oldster vs. Codger

It would seem pretty clear that replacing a worker over 40 years of age with a younger worker brings up the possibility of age discrimination. But what if the new worker is also over 40? This was the question that faced the Supreme Court in the case of *O'Connor v. Consolidated Coin Caterers Corp.*[11] In that case, the court ruled that a 56-year-old employee could still be the victim of age discrimination even if his or her replacement was over 40. Justice Antonin Scalia wrote the unanimous opinion in which he said, "The fact that one person in the protected class lost out to another in the protected age class is . . . irrelevant, so long as he has lost out because of his age." However, the court did say that the replacement worker had to be "substantially" younger for the ADEA to apply.

It would seem, then, that if another worker who was even older replaced the worker, there could be no claim of age discrimination. But that was not the conclusion reached by the Federal Court in the case of *Greene v. Safeway Stores,*[12] in which 52-year-old employee Robert Greene successfully claimed age discrimination even though he had been replaced by an employee who was actually 5 years older than him.

Greene had worked his way up in the grocery chain from company clerk to produce manager to finally manager of Safeway's Denver division. He was fired 28 months before he was to become vested in the company pension plan. His replacement was a 57-year-old manager from another division within the company. The company said Greene had been fired because he was a poor merchandiser, that sales had flattened or declined at stores in his Denver division, and that he was intimidating to his employees and pessimistic about competing with another supermarket chain in the Denver area. Greene said that these reasons were just a pretext for age discrimination. Testimony during the trial indicated that none of the company's concerns about Greene had ever been discussed with him before his firing. In addition, internal memoranda praising Greene's work and the performance of the Denver region were entered into evidence at his trial. Greene's attorneys pointed out that the new company president, who had fired Greene, replaced eight high-level executives who were over the age of 50 with younger workers in his first year. The jury believed Greene and awarded him $6.7 million, which will buy a great deal of groceries.

California Sets Record

In 1995, Ron Arnett, a Fremont, California, police officer who was injured during on-the-job training along with six other disabled public safety officers, sued the California Public Employees' Retirement System, alleging age discrimination in disability payments. Because Arnett was 43 at the time he was hired, his disability payments under California law were limited to 32 percent of his salary. A 1980 California law tied disability payments to the age of the public employee at the time of his or her hiring. Some disabled employees received as little as 12 percent of their salaries; employees hired at age 30 received 50 percent of their salaries.

After 8 years of litigation, California settled with Arnett and the class of more than 1,700 public safety officers affected by the lawsuit, and agreed to pay approximately $250 million in disability payments to the affected officers. In addition, the state agreed to abandon the system that used an employee's age in determining disability payments.

Not So Simple

In 2000, the Federal Third Circuit Court of Appeals ruled in the case of *Erie County Retirees Association v. County of Erie*[13] that providing lesser health-care benefits to retired employees age 65 years of age or older than those provided to younger retirees constituted illegal age discrimination. On its face, this seems to be a victory for older retired workers. But it might not have been because the effect of this ruling was to actually discourage employers from providing any health-care benefits to retired workers: Many companies have deemed the requirement that all retired workers must be treated equally in regard to health-care benefits too expensive to provide. Because no law requires employers to provide health insurance for retirees, the simplest and least costly way of avoiding an age discrimination problem for employers has been to merely refuse to provide health insurance benefits for any of their retirees.

The initial reasoning behind some companies' decisions to treat their retirees differently in regard to health-care benefits was not to discriminate against their older retired workers, but rather to maximize the benefits to all of their retirees. Retirees at least 65 years old have the opportunity to receive Medicare benefits and, therefore, are not in as dire a need for the same health insurance coverage as younger retirees who do not have that option.

Following the Erie decision, the EEOC, which initially had been in support of the court's position, found that the unfortunate result of the ruling was to reduce health insurance coverage for retired workers. Consequently, the EEOC enacted a regulation that created an exemption permitting employers to reduce or even eliminate health insurance benefits for retired workers eligible for Medicare.

The State of Age Discrimination

Along with the federal ADEA, just about every state has its own age discrimination laws that might provide greater protections to affected individuals. For instance, the ADEA applies only to companies that have 20 or more employees, whereas the great majority of states cover age discrimination in companies with fewer employees. Ohio's law applies to companies with as few as four employees. As indicated by Sen. Ralph Yarborough of Texas in 1967, the ADEA provides a floor of protection from age discrimination, not a ceiling.

The provisions of the ADEA require people who believe that they have been the victims of age discrimination to file not just with the EEOC, but also with their own appropriate state agency that deals with age discrimination laws.

What Should You Do If You Believe You Are a Victim of Age Discrimination?

The more evidence you have, the better. And don't trust your memory. As many of us age, many of us tend to suffer from CRS disease (an acronym for Can't Remember Stuff or something like that). Write it down. Keep a written log of anything that happens that you think indicates age discrimination at work, whether it is statements or actions of management. In the case of *Tennes v. Commonwealth of Massachusetts Department of Revenue*,[14] comments made by a supervisor about a 58-year-old employee that suggested senility, lack of sexual ability, and a mind too old to remember department procedures were used to show the supervisor's state of mind and intent to discriminate on the basis of age. Also keep copies of any e-mails or memoranda that substantiate claims of age discrimination.

So who do you call if you believe you have been the victim of age discrimination? Calling baby boomer Bill Murray (born in 1950), the star of the 1984 movie *Ghostbusters,* will not help much, but calling the Equal Employment Opportunity Commission might work. This federal agency deals with enforcement of the ADEA. You can get information about filing a claim from the EEOC's Web site, www.eeoc.gov, although actual claims must be filed either in person or by mail.

Private Actions

A person who believes he or she has been a victim of age discrimination must generally file a complaint with the EEOC before a private lawsuit may be filed in court on behalf of the victim. The complaint with the EEOC must be filed within 180 days of the date of the alleged age discrimination, although this deadline for filing a complaint is extended to 300 days if state age discrimination laws also apply.

If the EEOC finds after investigation that there is "no reasonable cause" to conclude that actionable age discrimination has occurred, the EEOC will inform the complainant of its decision not to do anything further in the case. At this point, the person complaining of age discrimination has 90 days to bring a private lawsuit alleging age discrimination. However, a private lawsuit also may be filed as early as 60 days after filing a charge of age discrimination with the EEOC.

EEOC Action

If the EEOC determines after its investigation that age discrimination has likely occurred, it will then attempt to settle the case through a process of "informal methods of conference, conciliation, and persuasion." If those actions fail, the EEOC must decide whether to bring a lawsuit in federal court. If the EEOC does file a lawsuit, the complaining party is not permitted to file his or her own private lawsuit.

A Look into the Future

The combination of an aging workforce and still prevalent stereotypes of aging seems to guarantee that we will see the number of age discrimination cases increase. Unfortunately, as in the case of Dr. Robert Johnson, some employers will continue to see just the number of a person's age rather than a person. Perhaps these employers should pay more heed to the words of former baseball great Satchel Paige: "How old would you be if you didn't know how old you were?"

Endnotes

1. *Smith v. City of Jackson, Mississippi*, 125 S. Ct. 1536 (2005).

2. General Accounting Office, "Older Workers: Demographic Trends Pose Challenges for Employers and Workers," 32 (GAO-02-85. November 16, 2001).

3. *Boyle v. McCann-Erickson, Inc.*, 949 F. Supp. 1095 (SDNY 1997).

4. *Western Airlines v. Criswell*, 472 U.S. 400 (1985).

5. *Wilson v. Firestone Tire & Rubber Company*, 932 F. 2d 510, 514 (6th Cir. 1991).

6. *Burger v. New York Institute of Technology*, 4 F. 3d 830 (2d Cir. 1966).

7. *Benson v. Tocco, Inc.*, 113 F 3d 1203 (11th Cir. 1997).

8. *Blum v. Witco Chemical Corporation*, 829 F 2d 367 (3d Cir. 1987).

9. *Smith v. City of Jackson, Mississippi,* 125 S. Ct. 1536 (2005).

10. *Cline v. General Dynamics Land Systems, Inc.,* 124 S. Ct. 1236 (2004).

11. *O'Connor v. Consolidated Coin Caterers Corp.,* 517 U.S. 308 (1996).

12. *Greene v. Safeway Stores,* 98 F. 3d 554 (10th Cir. 1996).

13. *Erie County Retirees Association v. County of Erie,* 200 F. 3d 193 (3d Cir. 2000).

14. *Tennes v. Commonwealth of Massachusetts Department of Revenue,* 745 F. Supp. 1352, aff'd 944 F. 2d 372 (7th Cir. 1991).

6

REVERSE MORTGAGES

"Home Is Where the Heart Is."
—Pliney the Elder

"Home Is Where the Cash Is."
—Steve Weisman

Throwing it in reverse is a way of getting out of trouble if your car gets stuck in a snow bank. It also could be a way of getting the money to pay for necessary repairs or everyday bills by tapping into the equity of your home. After all, your home is an asset that very well may have grown tremendously in value since you first bought it.

A *reverse mortgage* is a loan that uses your home as security for a loan, just like a conventional mortgage arrangement. However, with a reverse mortgage, you generally do not have to pay back the loan for as long as you live in the home. This allows you to take the equity out of your home and turn it into cash to meet your daily needs, without having to be concerned about making a monthly mortgage payment. The loan is repaid with interest generally when the borrower sells the home, moves out of the home, or dies, whichever comes first. With some reverse mortgages, however, the total loan with interest is due after a specific number of years.

Reverse mortgages are particularly attractive to wealthier seniors. To avoid capital gains taxes from the sale of their stock portfolios, these people might be more inclined to tap into their home's equity for regular income. But this is no panacea. In fiscal year 2004, homeowners took out 37,829 HECMs (the FHA's Home Equity Conversion Mortgage, the most popular reverse mortgage), which was an increase of 109 percent over the previous year. The states with the greatest number of HECMs were, in order, California, Florida, and Texas.

Origin

Although reverse mortgages have been available in some form for many years, their popularity dramatically increased following the enactment of the federal Alternative Mortgage Transaction Parity Act, a law also known by the equally catchy title of Title VII of the Garn-St. Germaine Depository Institutions Act of 1982. Sounds like the title to a classical music composition. This law authorized banks and mortgage companies to make "alternative" real estate loans that might not have been allowed under state laws.

Uncle Sam Likes Reverse Mortgages

The National Council on Aging received a $295,000 grant from the Centers for Medicare and Medicaid Services to encourage reverse mortgages. The motivation for the grant was simple: Nursing home costs paid by Medicaid are extremely costly to state and federal governments. If people could be encouraged to use their homes to finance their long-term care in nursing homes, it would be better for the government. But would it be better for you? Not necessarily. Once you go into a nursing home, you must pay back the reverse mortgage, which could mean losing your home; if you employ other forms of planning, you might be able to preserve that home as a legacy to your family.

Not Exactly a Good Match

Ham and eggs is a good match. Starsky and Hutch was a good match. But as desirable as it might seem to link long-term care insurance and reverse mortgages, there are some problems. Presently, the average age of a person buying long-term care insurance is 64, whereas the average age of a person getting a reverse mortgage is 75. The best time to get long-term care insurance is when people are in their 40s and 50s. However, the optimum time for getting a reverse mortgage is when homeowners are in their 70s. This discrepancy creates a potential problem because a person who waits until his or her 70s to buy long-term care insurance could have a more difficult time passing the medical tests necessary to qualify for long-term care insurance.

Another potential problem with tying long-term care insurance to reverse mortgages is indicated by a 2000 study done by the Department of Housing and Urban Development (HUD): Homeowners using reverse mortgages were most often unmarried people with little income and few assets other than their homes. These people still might not be able to afford long-term care insurance even with the money they would get from their reverse mortgages, and they might be less inclined to bother with long-term care insurance than a person concerned about the needs of a spouse. These people could well be more inclined to merely depend on Medicaid to meet their long-term care needs, with little concern about protecting their other assets.

Conventional Mortgage vs. Reverse Mortgage

With a conventional mortgage loan, you borrow money from a lender and pay back the money on a monthly basis. However, with a reverse mortgage, the bank pays you each month. What a deal! Reverse mortgages are not bad or good in and of themselves; they are sort of like carbohydrates. When used appropriately, they can be beneficial. When used inappropriately, you can get into trouble.

Reverse mortgages provide distinct advantages for many people seeking to tap into the equity of their homes. Unlike selling the home, you continue to be able to live in your home and do not have to be concerned about any capital gains income taxes. You can borrow just the money you need to supplement your other sources of income to meet your needs; you don't need a conventional mortgage or a sale-and-lease agreement of your home.

But there are drawbacks. The magic of compound interest is a wonderful thing when you have an investment that increases in value as you get interest on the interest that your investment accumulates. The flipside of that coin is that when you have a loan upon which you are not making payments, such as a reverse mortgage, the interest on interest grows tremendously. The eventual cost to you (or your heirs, if you want to leave something to them) is tremendous.

FHA-Insured Reverse Mortgages

FHA-insured reverse mortgages can provide you with regular monthly payments for a specific period of time or for as long as you occupy your home. The loan can also be constructed as a line of credit that you can choose to tap into at any time: In such a case, until you actually activate the line of credit, the interest does not start to accumulate; it builds only on the amounts you actually borrow. You also can choose, just like I often do from the frozen yogurt machine, to get the twist: in this case, regular monthly payments along with a backup line of credit. With an FHA-insured reverse mortgage, even if the lender goes under and becomes insolvent, the federal government guarantees that you will receive your regular reverse mortgage payments.

However, as good as this sounds (and it is good), don't think for a minute that you are not paying for this benefit. Directly or indirectly, you are paying for the cost of this insurance. An advantage of an FHA-insured loan is that the federal government backs it. A disadvantage is that the amount available for an FHA-insured loan is less than that available through lender-insured plans.

Lender-Insured Reverse Mortgages

Lender-insured reverse mortgage plans also offer regular monthly payments to homeowners, or lines of credit, or combinations of both, as long as the homeowner lives in the home. The interest rates of the loans can be either fixed or variable, and, of course, there are the fees, which include mortgage insurance premiums to be paid by the homeowner.

You might be able to borrow more through a private lender-insured mortgage than an FHA-insured mortgage, but the costs of the loan are generally more than what you will pay with an FHA-insured mortgage.

Bells and Whistles

A particularly helpful option found with some private lender-insured reverse mortgage programs is a tie-in of an annuity that makes regular monthly payments to the homeowner even if he or she has to move out of the home. But nothing comes without a cost, and it is important to know just what the cost of purchasing this particular benefit will be to you.

Other people buy an annuity with a lump-sum payment they get from a reverse mortgage. However you tie your reverse mortgage to an annuity, you should make sure that you are buying an annuity that will provide enough money to offset the costs involved with the reverse mortgage. It can end up costing you 8 to 10 percent to get an annuity that pays you 3 to 4 percent.

Uninsured Reverse Mortgages

Uninsured reverse mortgages provide regular monthly reverse mortgage payments for only a specific, fixed period of time. At the end of that time period, all bets are off: The payments to the homeowner cease, and the full amount of the reverse mortgage, along with all of the accumulated compounded interest and fees that you built into the loan, become immediately due and payable. This could mean selling your home. If there is any good news here, it is that the interest rate is generally fixed, so it does not go up during the period of the loan even if interest rates increase. Nor are you responsible for any mortgage insurance premiums during the loan period.

Another advantage of the uninsured reverse mortgage is that it offers more bang for the buck. You can receive a larger loan with an uninsured reverse mortgage than you would with other forms of reverse mortgages. More money sounds good, but before you leap, it is important to remember that with more money comes more risk. If you are receiving monthly reverse mortgage payments from a lender that declares bankruptcy, your payments are in serious jeopardy (as in, I'll take Financial Ruin for $500, Alex).

Open-End Reverse Mortgage

Another form of reverse mortgage is the open-end reverse mortgage. This is a reverse mortgage loan that does not have a set maturity date (come to think of it, neither do I). Open-end reverse mortgages are offered as FHA-insured loans. The loans are made by FHA-approved lenders, and the repayment requirement is totally limited to the mortgaged property. You will never owe more than the value of your home. To qualify for such a loan, a homeowner need only be at least 62 years of age and own a home used as a primary residence. In addition, the property must be either mortgage free or close to it. There are no income requirements.

To the Max

There are limits to just about everything. The maximum amount of an FHA-insured reverse mortgage amount or HECM (Home Equity Conversion Mortgage) varies from locale to locale. For example, it is $239,250 in the Boston area, regardless of the fact that the fair market value of the home could be significantly greater.

Size is important when it comes to determining the payment that you will be receiving from a reverse mortgage lender. The amount of your monthly payment or the size of your reverse mortgage credit line depends on your age, the interest rate, the type of reverse mortgage plan you take, and the value of the property. Logically, the older you are and the more valuable your property is, the more money you will generally be able to get. The interest rate plays a particularly important role in determining how much money will be loaned to you. The lender calculates the amount of the loan to cover the amount loaned plus interest, plus any other fees included in the loan. This is calculated so that it will not be more than the projected value of the home at the time the loan is expected to become due.

In 2005, borrowers using the HECM for the first time were able to lock in their interest rate at the time they applied for a HECM reverse mortgage. For anyone concerned with the cost of borrowing money in an environment of rapidly changing interest rates, being able to lock in an interest rate is important. However, for someone borrowing money through a reverse mortgage, the ability to lock an interest rate is even more critical because the interest rate has a direct effect on the amount of money that can be borrowed. Under the provisions of the 2005 interest lock regulations, an applicant for a HECM receives a guaranteed interest rate for 60 days from the time of application.

Of further benefit to HECM borrowers is the fact that if interest rates decline between the time of the HECM reverse mortgage application and the closing of the loan, the borrower gets the new lower rate; this means that he or she will be able to borrow more money. Previously, reverse mortgage borrowers were given only an estimate of the amount of money that they could borrow at the time of application. If interest rates rose before the closing of the loan, they ended up receiving less than the original estimate. HUD approved this rate-lock provision in 2003, but it was not implemented until 2005. This only applies to HECMs.

Home Keeper

Fannie Mae, the largest purchaser of home mortgages, offers a reverse mortgage product called the Home Keeper. The Home Keeper mortgage has a higher interest rate than the HECM, but if you're looking to borrow as much as possible, the program allows you to borrow more than the maximum value limit of a HECM. In 2006, the maximum amount that could be borrowed through a Home Keeper reverse mortgage was $362,790.

An interesting bit of trivia is that Fannie Mae originated from the way the acronym FNMA (for Federal National Mortgage Association) was pronounced. With a name like that, you would expect that the organization would be a federal agency, but you would be wrong. In any event, in 1997, FNMA became Fannie Mae, which now stands for nothing. (Although doesn't that name just beg for a "Clampett" to be affixed to the end? If you are a baby boomer, you know I am referring to the *Beverly Hillbillies*.)

Payment Plans

A number of different payment plan options are available for an open-end reverse mortgage:

- Monthly payments for the fixed term of years of the mortgage
- A tenure plan by which the homeowner receives a specific monthly payment for life
- An option to utilize the reverse mortgage as a line of credit through which the homeowner may access the line of credit whenever he or she needs money
- An option to receive a lump-sum payment from the lender
- The lifetime payments option combined with a line of credit

Indecisive homeowners can change the payment option they select as often as monthly for a small fee. Someone with an increased need for more money to pay regular bills might switch to a fixed-term payment option because the monthly payments are greater.

Very Interesting

The interest rate for the open-end reverse mortgage is often a variable one, although some reverse mortgages provide for fixed interest rates. It is important to note that regardless of which plan you choose, you will not be required by the lender to vacate your home at any time during your lifetime. In addition, the lender cannot foreclose on the mortgage, even if the maximum allowable limit of the reverse mortgage has been reached.

Reverse Mortgage Fees

Then there are the fees. It is not unusual for the fees associated with a reverse mortgage to reach between $6,000 and $12,000. Lenders are allowed to charge up to two points on each loan. Points are an interesting concept. They represent money you pay the lender, in addition to the interest on the loan, just for the privilege of doing business with that bank. They bear no relation to any cost of processing the loan. Each point—or origination fee, as they are also called—is equal to 1 percent of the loan amount. As an example, a $100,000 loan with two points would translate into $2,000 that you pay the bank. You really do not get anything in return, which, to me, is the classic definition of extortion, but the courts have seen fit to disagree with me on this one.

Origination fees (points in disguise) are limited under HECMs to 2 percent of your home's appraised value or 2 percent of the FHA loan limits for your geographical area, whichever is less. However, lenders are allowed to hit you with a minimum origination fee of $2,000. This is negotiable. Although some lenders charge the maximum they are allowed to charge by law, others are willing to negotiate these fees.

Mortgage insurance is another closing cost for which you are responsible. This works to the benefit of both you and the lender. It guarantees that you will receive payments even if your bank goes bankrupt, and it also ensures that if you are unable to pay back the loan when it becomes due, the bank will get what it is owed. Unfortunately although both you and the bank benefit from mortgage insurance, guess who pays the bill? Those of you who said we do get a gold star. Remember, all financial institutions essentially follow their version of the golden rule: They have the gold, so they make the rules.

The initial premium for reverse mortgage insurance can be steep. It is limited to the lesser of no more than 2 percent of the appraised value of your home or 2 percent of the FHA maximum loan amount for your geographical area. And don't forget to add on an annual insurance premium of up to .5 percent of the loan balance, to the interest rate charged on the loan. In an attempt to encourage the use of reverse mortgages to provide funds for the purchase of long-term care insurance policies, Congress eliminated the up-front mortgage insurance premium for HECMs if the entire amount of the reverse mortgage is used to purchase long-term care insurance.

The bank or other lender can also charge you a monthly fee for servicing your account. Service fees are limited by the FHA to $30 per month if your loan interest rate is adjusted annually, and $35 if your loan interest rate is adjusted monthly.

Also among the fees for a reverse mortgage with a private lender are appraisal fees to evaluate the worth of the property (usually between $300 and $400), credit report fees to evaluate your creditworthiness (usually about $20), flood-certification fees (usually around $20), title-examination fees (costs vary), document-preparation fees (usually between $75 and $150), recording fees (usually between $50 and $150), title-insurance fees (varies depending upon the amount of the mortgage), and survey costs (usually around $250). There is no *i* in *team*, and there definitely is no *r* in *fee*. Fees represent a tremendous expense to the borrower. It is not unusual for your costs of closing the loan to reach 4 to 5 percent of the loan amount—and that does not even include your compound interest costs. Because the fees are so substantial, the cost of obtaining a reverse mortgage for short-term needs probably does not make sense.

Consider this example on reverse mortgages given by the National Center for Home Equity Conversion, from the AARP Web site (www.aarp.org). A single woman who is age 75 gets a $150,000 HECM, financing her $6,500 up-front costs as part of the loan. She begins taking monthly advances of $562 that will continue as long as she lives in the home. If this reverse mortgage is paid off 2 years later, the loan's effective interest cost is 49.5 percent. This is because the up-front costs and fees of $6,500 and the accrued interest are high in relation to the $13,488 in advances she receives over 2 years. If she stays in the home and receives the monthly advances for 12 years, she would receive $80,928 and the effective cost of borrowing would be a more reasonable 10.8 percent. Whenever a reverse mortgage matures early due to the death of the homeowner or a move to a nursing home or an assisted-living facility, the lender ends up receiving a tremendous amount of payments for loaning a relatively small amount of money.

The good news about fees (and there is little) is that you might be able to roll these fees into your loan so that you do not have to come up with cash to pay them at the closing. The bad news is that if you do this, you are just adding more to your loan balance, upon which compound interest will accumulate. And the magic of compound interest quickly becomes voodoo to you.

A good place to go to get an estimate of the various fees you might encounter is the Web site of the National Reverse Mortgage Lender's Association (www.reversemortgage.org). You'll find a handy, dandy calculator you can use. Another good interactive calculator for determining the financial viability of a reverse mortgage can be found at AARP's reverse mortgage Web site (www.rmaarp.com).

Picky Little Detail

People who borrow mortgage money from a bank are used to the concept of points: Each point represents 1 percent of the loan amount. A tricky detail that can be quite costly to reverse mortgage borrowers is that with a reverse mortgage, the points are tied not to the amount of money you are borrowing, but rather to the value of the home, which represents a much greater figure.

Particularly when the loan ends up being for a short period of time (such as when the borrower dies shortly after borrowing the money), the fees make the loan a very expensive way to borrow money when compared to other types of loans. Therefore, it is my advice to live beyond your life expectancy. Drive your creditors and the actuaries who calculate life expectancies crazy.

Some Good News

Just like the Wicked Witch of the West proclaimed in the musical *The Wiz*, "Don't bring me no bad news," there is some good news to offset some of the bad news about reverse mortgages. Reverse mortgage payments that you receive are not subject to income tax. But wait—there is more (sounds like an infomercial). If you are also receiving payments through Supplemental Security Income (SSI), the amount that you receive through your reverse mortgage will not affect the amount of your monthly SSI payment as long as you exhaust the payment during the month you receive it. But hold on—believe it or not, there is even more! Social Security payments and Medicare payments also will be unaffected by any money you receive through a reverse mortgage.

Repayment

Eventually, everyone has to pay the piper although I must admit, I have never paid a piper in my life. In any event, all good things must come to an end (even my list of clichés), and the money borrowed through a reverse mortgage must be repaid. For closed-end reverse mortgages, payment in full is due at the end of the fixed period of the reverse mortgage. Other reverse mortgage programs provide for payments when you either permanently move out of the home (to another home, a nursing home, or an assisted-living center, for example) or die. Although the lender has a mortgage to secure the payment of the reverse mortgage funds, the bank or other mortgage lender is not very interested in taking your home. But it certainly is interested in being able to auction off the property to cover the debt that is owed to it if you or your heirs are unable to pay the reverse mortgage loan amount plus all of the interest that has accumulated on the loan when the loan becomes due. If there is sufficient equity in the home, heirs of a deceased reverse mortgage homeowner—or the homeowner himself or herself, in a closed-end reverse mortgage—might seek to refinance the property to obtain the money necessary to pay off the reverse mortgage loan.

Another advantage of a reverse mortgage is that generally the amount that you must pay back is limited by the value of your home at the time of the repayment of the loan. However, it is important to remember that buried within the fine print of your reverse mortgage loan is a provision that, in determining the fair market value of your home, the value is determined as of the time the reverse mortgage is due, not the time you took out the loan.

The Catch

According to the lawyer joke, a new client comes to see his lawyer and, while he is sitting in the young lawyer's office recounting his story, the lawyer cannot keep from staring at the top of the man's head. Noticing this, the client says, "Okay, let's be candid. Yes, those are horns coming through my hair on the top of my head. I am the Devil, and I have a proposal to make to you. I will make you the most powerful lawyer in the world; you will be fantastically successful and rich beyond your wildest dreams." The lawyer then interrupts by saying, "But what do you want in return?" The Devil responds, "Your immortal soul, the soul of your wife, the souls of your children, and the souls of your children's children." The lawyer responds, "What is the catch?"

The catch, when it comes to reverse mortgages, is the conditions. Breaching them is considered defaulting on the reverse mortgage, which makes the entire amount of the loan due (at least they don't require your soul). You must maintain the property in good condition, keep your real estate taxes up-to-date, and keep your home covered by homeowner's insurance. In addition, if you add the name of someone else to the title of your home as a co-owner, rent the property to a tenant, take out another mortgage, or use your home for commercial purposes, you will be required to pay back the mortgage at that time. However, these conditions should not pose too much of a problem to most people.

For Whom the Reverse Mortgage Tolls

So, for whom are reverse mortgages advisable? Reverse mortgages made for a fixed number of years are useful for people who are particularly old, whose life expectancies are not long, and whose income needs are great. If you are on a fixed income that feels more broken than fixed, and your primary asset is your home (which you do not plan to leave to your children), a reverse mortgage just might be for you. Closed-end reverse mortgages also make sense for "younger-oldsters" who may have serious and chronic medical problems that require continuing care, but who may be able to receive this care in their own home.

Obviously, caretakers to provide this at-home care must be available either through professional health-care agencies or through family members.

The typical person who chooses an open-ended reverse mortgage has a house that has appreciated considerably in value but does not have many liquid assets to support him- or herself or maintain the home. According to HUD, around 70 percent of older Americans own their homes, and 80 percent of these older homeowners own their homes outright, having paid off their mortgages.

Home might be where the heart is, but it also is where many of the largest expenses can be found for older people. It is particularly important to remember that, just as with a conventional mortgage, you are still responsible for all of the maintenance costs, homeowner insurance costs, and real estate taxes when you take out a reverse mortgage. Often, however, people are quite aware of this and, in fact, take out reverse mortgages to pay for these very costs.

Reverse mortgages should not be a first choice because of their expense. A homeowner might be eligible for various state or federal aid programs that can reduce or defer real estate taxes or pay for other costly expenses such as medical expenses. A simple, free, and confidential way to see what benefit programs you might be eligible for is to go to the Web site www.benefitscheckup.org, sponsored by the National Council on Aging, and fill in the online questionnaire.

Caution

Do not pass go, do not collect $200, and absolutely do not use a reverse mortgage to obtain money to invest in the stock market. To do so would be risky business beyond what even Tom Cruise could imagine.

Counseling

Because of the complexity of these loans, FHA rules require mandatory counseling before an FHA-insured reverse mortgage may be issued.

However, the counseling may consist of nothing more than a phone call from a HUD-approved agency that involves a discussion of alternative methods the homeowner might use to obtain necessary funds. The counseling session also will include consideration of the tax consequences of a reverse mortgage and the effect of a reverse mortgage on the ability to pass the home on to heirs.

Change Your Mind

An unusual aspect of a reverse mortgage is that you can change your mind within 3 days of closing the loan and signing the loan documents. In this situation, you are permitted by law to rescind the transaction at no cost. Imagine if marriage contracts came with a 3-day right of rescission.

Legacy for the Next Generation

If it is important to the elderly homeowner to leave his or her home as a legacy to children, a reverse mortgage might not be the way to go. Speaking of children, let them pitch in. Why should the elderly parent jump through financial hoops to protect an asset if children are unwilling to help their parents? They should be involved in the process. The elderly parent should let them know that he or she is considering getting a reverse mortgage that could reduce or even eliminate what they inherit. The children could well help contribute to the parent's financial needs by buying the home, buying long-term care insurance for the elderly parent, or otherwise acting in a manner to meet the elderly parent's needs as well as their own in the long run.

One way for adult children to benefit themselves as well as their parents is to buy their parents' home and lease it back to them. The parents selling the home get the capital gains exclusion of $500,000 for married couples and $250,000 for single people. The children can rent the home to their parents and get deductions for depreciation and other costs of maintaining the property. The children could buy the home from their parents through a lump sum that they can obtain through mortgaging the property themselves, through conventional mortgage sources such as a bank. Alternatively, the parents could finance the home sale themselves. By loaning the money to the children to buy the property, they could provide themselves with a steady income and a secure investment return on the money. In addition, if estate taxes are an issue, by selling the property to the children, the parents remove the appreciating asset from their estates.

Another way that parents might consider accessing the equity in their home while protecting a legacy for their children is to have their children purchase a remainder interest in the property. In this scenario, the parents keep a "life estate" in the property, which means that they retain the right to live in the property and control the property during their lifetimes. The parents are responsible for all costs of maintaining the property and paying all other attendant costs, such as real estate taxes. The children buy a "remainder interest"—that is, they buy the right to inherit the property directly and outside of probate upon the death of their parents. The value of the remainder interest is calculated using IRS charts that consider the age of the parent in determining when the children will likely receive full ownership of the home.

For example, an 80-year-old parent's interest in a home whose fair market value is $200,000 would be $168,000. The remainder interest that the children would be purchasing at that time would be valued at $32,000. Once again, the parents can receive the money either in a lump sum or paid over time with interest from the children. This compares favorably with what parents would be able to receive through a reverse mortgage, and it enables parents to pass the home to the children at the parent's death.

At-Home Care

Current Medicaid laws permit a homeowner to have $500,000 worth of equity in his or her home and still qualify for Medicaid payment of nursing home bills. The law also permits individual states to increase this figure to $750,000. In addition, this figure is tied to inflation and will increase accordingly. The Deficit Reduction Act enacted by Congress in 2006 also specifically permits reverse mortgages to be used to reduce the equity value of a home to help reach the $500,000 exempt figure.

However, although all states have Medicaid programs that will pay for nursing home care, few states have Medicaid programs that pay for at-home care, so a reverse mortgage could be an effective way of obtaining funds to keep seniors in their preferred place of residence: their own home.

It has been shown that, when medically possible, it is actually more cost-effective (a fancy way of saying cheaper) to care for seniors in their own homes than to place them in a nursing home, which is generally not a place most people desire to go anyway. Think about it: Was there ever a Superbowl at which the Most Valuable Player, when asked where he wanted to go now that he had won the Superbowl, answered, "I want to go to a nursing home"? I rest my case. In any event, it is cheaper and more accommodating to use Medicaid funds to care for seniors at home than to force them into nursing homes to get the care they need. Unfortunately, few states have the wisdom to use Medicaid funds in this manner.

Scams

Everything is an opportunity to a scam artist, and reverse mort-gages are no exception. Some older homeowners have been con-tacted by people offering to help them find a lender to provide them with a reverse mortgage for just a small percentage of the loan. The only problem is that what they are offering to sell you, you can easily get for free from the Department of Housing and Urban Development at www.hud.gov.

Shared Equity and Appreciation Fees

One of the great lessons in the book *All I Really Need to Know I Learned in Kindergarten* (Random House, 2003), by Robert Fulghum, is the benefit of sharing. However, sharing is not always such a good thing to do. When it comes to reverse mortgages, sharing could be more akin to being financially taken advantage of. With a shared equity fee, the fine print in the reverse mortgage indicates that at the time the loan becomes due, you are required to pay an additional amount that is equal to a specified percentage of the value of your home at the time of the loan's maturity. The Fannie Mae Equity Share plan offers somewhat higher monthly payments to reverse mortgage borrowers who choose this option, but they must pay an additional fee equal to 10 percent of the home's value at the time of maturity. This could be a steep price to pay. If your home is worth $300,000, this provision will cost you an additional $30,000 on top of the interest you are paying on your loan.

In the case of a shared appreciation fee, a share of the home's appreciation in value from the time of the origination of the loan to the time the loan becomes due is payable to the lender. This fee can reach 50 percent. Yikes! Tony Soprano does not even get rates like that. An increase in value of a home by $75,000 would result in an extra fee of $37,500 at the time of the loan's maturity when the reverse mortgage loan carries a 50 percent shared appreciation fee. The danger of both shared equity fees and shared appreciation fees is that if a borrower dies or must leave his home because of health reasons or other circumstances within a few years of the loan being made, the fees could actually be larger than the reverse mortgage payments received.

Stay away from reverse mortgages with equity appreciation and equity share provisions that will provide you with somewhat higher monthly payments but can end up costing your heirs much more money. With these, the amount the lender ultimately receives is increased by a percentage of the value of your home when the loan is paid back with a shared equity or a shared appreciation fee.

The Bottom Line

The bottom line is that rarely should a reverse mortgage be the first choice when it comes to obtaining necessary funds for elderly homeowners. However, in some circumstances they could be the best option available. As always, the best thing you can do is to educate yourself about reverse mortgages and their alternatives.

Part II
PLANNING FOR LONG-TERM CARE

7

HOME CARE

"We are all here on earth to help others; what on earth the others are here for I don't know."
—W.H. Auden

When physical or mental deterioration takes away the independence of older people, these seniors and their families are faced with a profound choice of either seeking institutionalized care or having care provided at home. Elders who require less help might find that an assisted-living facility adequately and comfortably meets their needs. But for others, the choice could come down to going to a nursing home or receiving care in their own home. Providing care at home can be costly if it is done entirely by hired professionals.

According to the *MetLife Market Survey of Nursing Home & Home Care Costs,* published in September 2004, the average hourly rate for Home Health Aides provided by a home-care agency is $18 per hour. This figure varies throughout the country, from a high of $27 per hour in Alaska to a low of $13 per hour in Shreveport, Louisiana. It is easy to see how the cost of home health care, if needed around the clock or close to it, would be more expensive than nursing home placement.

Family members often are put in charge of taking care of their relatives, to reduce the cost and become more personally involved with their care. According to the General Accounting Office, about 80 percent of home-care services are provided by family caregivers.[1] Gary Barg, the editor in chief of Caregiver.com and *Today's Caregiver Magazine,* both valuable resources for caregivers, says, "Caring for a family member at home is a cherished duty, but one that comes at a cost." According to Barg, many caregivers lose their jobs as a result of the time they must devote to caring for a relative at home. In addition, Barg estimates that the average caregiver loses $600,000 in income over the duration of his or her working career, factoring in the loss of promotions and other job benefits. The cost of caring for an elderly person at home can also increase—the living area must be modified, such as to accommodate a wheelchair. Caregiving for a family member truly is a labor of love.

How About a Sandwich?

Not surprisingly, the invention of the sandwich is usually attributed to John Montagu, the fourth Earl of Sandwich. (I had always thought he was also the Duke of Deli, but apparently this is incorrect.) Scurrilous rumors say that the Earl of Sandwich invented what we call the sandwich in 1765 so that he could dine more quickly and, thereby, leave more time for gambling. Others believe that Montagu might have been an early workaholic who invented the sandwich so he could eat at his desk and continue working. In any event, baby boomers also are often called the sandwich generation, not because of an affinity for such fare, but rather to describe their position as being caught between children who still require some care or financial assistance and aging parents who also are in need of care.

One way for baby boomers to perhaps put their generational position to good use is to enlist the assistance of their children to help care for the aging parents. This could make a positive thing out of what could be a taxing situation. The children of baby boomers can help in many ways with the care of their own grandparents, not only relieving their parents of some time-consuming responsibilities, but also advancing their own relationships with their grandparents.

A Statistical Look at Caregiving

According to the 2004 study *Caregiving in the U.S.*, done by the National Alliance for Caregiving and AARP, there are 44.4 million unpaid family caregivers in this country. The typical caregiver is a 46-year-old woman with some college education who has a job and still spends more than 20 hours per week providing care to a family member. Female caregivers outnumber male caregivers at 61 to 39 percent (is anyone surprised by that?). Sixty-two percent of caregivers adjust their work schedules as a result of their caregiving duties.

The value of the unpaid services provided by family caregivers is approximately $257 billion annually.[2] American businesses lose between $11 billion and $29 billion of business productivity as a result of employee-caregivers caring for older family members.

Home Health Agencies

This is the commonly used designation for a Medicare-certified agency that is approved to provide Medicare and Medicaid home health services. Services are usually provided though doctors, nurses, therapists, social workers, and homemakers. According to the MetLife study, more than 1.3 million people receive various home health-care services from 7,200 different agencies throughout the country. Home Health Aides provide assistance with what are referred to as activities of daily life, such as bathing and dressing. Under the supervision of a professional nurse, the Home Health Aide might also provide more complex care.

Medicare

Medicare covers the cost of home health services when the particular services are deemed to be "reasonable and necessary," when the person needing the services is homebound, and when the person's physician prescribes the care and periodically reviews the home health services needs of that person. In addition, to qualify for Medicare coverage, the services required must qualify as intermittent skilled nursing services, physical therapy, or speech therapy.

For Medicare purposes, **homebound** means that a person's condition limits his or her ability to leave home except with the assistance of someone or through the aid of a wheelchair, a walker, or some other supportive device. The person does not have to be bedridden, but, according to the law, it must require a "considerable and taxing effort by the individual" to leave the home. It should be noted that leaving the home for a short period to attend a family matter such as a graduation or even to regularly go to adult day care does not disqualify a person from being considered homebound for Medicare purposes.

To qualify for Medicare coverage of home health-care expenses, the patient must provide a certification signed by a physician indicating that the home health services are needed because the patient is homebound; that the patient needs either skilled nursing services on an intermittent basis, physical therapy, or speech/language pathology services; that a plan of care has been established with the physician and is periodically reviewed by the physician; and finally that the services are being furnished while the patient is under the care of a physician.

In the past, a Centers for Medicare & Medicaid Services Form 485 was used to document these matters. However, since 2003, use of this form has been discontinued. Now all that is required is a letter signed and dated by the treating physician that provides the necessary information described in the preceding paragraph.

Homemaker Agencies

These agencies provide less medically oriented, but still important home care services such as meal preparation, housekeeping, and even assistance with activities such as bathing, eating, and grooming. The cost of these services is generally privately paid.

It's a Family Affair

Family Affair was a number 1 hit for Sly and the Family Stone in 1971. More trivia for music fans: Sly's real name was Sylvester Stewart. Sly sounds a lot better, unless you are a cat or Sylvester Stallone.

Caregiving is a family affair, although most often it seems that one person within the family takes over the role of primary caregiver for aging parents. It usually doesn't make sense to have too many people making decisions—as the old Australian proverb says, "A Platypus is a duck made by committee." However, helpful it might be to have all the family members share in the work and decision making regarding the care of aging parents although, it makes sense to ultimately place someone in charge.

Sharing responsibility also keeps caregivers from burning out, which is a significant problem for caregivers. It also can help the other adult children feel involved.

Lines of communication are important. Didn't we all learn that in the 1967 movie *Cool Hand Luke,* when Strother Martin, who is described in the script merely as "Captain, Road Prison 36," says, "What we've got here is failure to communicate"? Caretaking is not a static activity. All family members should regularly discuss the various issues involved in the care of their aging relatives. These matters might include health-care questions, legal questions, financial questions, and housing matters. These items should be revisited often to make sure that the plan reached and the implementation of that plan still meets the needs of the elderly relative. Even when some of the children live a great distance away from their relatives, they can still help research the sources of assistance that could be available. The Internet is a tremendous source for obtaining such information, as you will find later in this chapter.

Respect My Authority

Okay, it is not a baby boomer reference, but if you have Generation X children or a juvenile sense of humor yourself (a charge to which I plead guilty), you will be familiar with the Comedy Central series "South Park." The Cartman character in the series has the catchphrase "Respect my authority." To be a proper caregiver for an aging parent or grandparent or other relative, you must have the proper authority to make decisions on his or her behalf of your relative; that person might not be in a position to make decisions on his or her own.

Obtaining this authority is best done ahead of time, when your aging relative is still competent and able to choose the person to make decisions when he or she is unable to do so. This is accomplished through a durable power of attorney and an advance-care health directive. Both of these documents are discussed in great detail in my book *A Guide to Elder Planning* (Pearson Education, 2003). These documents will enable the caregiver to make the necessary financial, health-care, and basic life decisions for the aging relative without having to go through the delay and expense of obtaining authority to make such decisions through a guardianship proceeding in court. These documents also are preferable to obtaining authority by way of a court-ordered guardianship because they permit the older person to designate the desired person to make decisions on his or her behalf. The elder can even place limitations or restrictions on that power.

Long-Distance Information

"Long-distance information, give me Memphis, Tennessee" is the first line of the 1958 hit "Memphis, Tennessee," by Chuck Berry (later sung by Johnny Rivers). For many family members, trying to be involved in the care of their family members in cities and towns far away is a difficult and guilt-ridden task. But if you're a long-distant caregiver, you can take steps to make things better.

First, find out what local agencies and services are available to provide assistance to your aging relative. After you have established contact with these agencies, maintain that communication. A good resource for getting information on the elder services available throughout the country is found on the Eldercare Locator, maintained by the U.S. Department of Health and Human Services Administration on Aging. Its easy-to-use, interactive Web site at www.eldercare.gov provides information on local support resources.

The Boy Scouts were right. Be prepared: Have a list of all of the telephone numbers and contact information for the various professionals involved with the care of your aging relatives. It also is helpful to have the names and numbers of neighbors who might be able to help in a pinch.

Another simple thing that you can do from a distance is arrange for the direct deposit of Social Security, pension, and other regular checks into your family member's bank account. Conversely, you can arrange for automatic payments from his or her account to regular creditors for such things as mortgage, rent, utility payments, and health insurance premiums.

Just the Facts, Ma'am

The fact is that Jack Webb, the star of the television show *Dragnet* in the 1950s, never did say, "Just the facts, Ma'am," although he did say similar phrases. If you are going to be a caregiver, however, you do need to know some facts.

In particular, you need to know the facts about the financial situation of the person for whom you will be caring. A detailed financial statement is important. What are the sources of income, and how is that income accessed? You need to know the answers to these important questions so you can care for the person's needs. What are the expenses? What kind of insurance coverage (particularly medical insurance) does the person have? You must also be familiar with the person's medical situations and relevant medical professionals.

Among the first things you need to know are the facts about any particular illnesses of the person for whom you are caring. You should learn as much as you can about a disease from the many online medical information Web sites. You also should get specific information from your loved one's physician regarding his or her particular situation. To do so, you must have an advance-care health directive authorizing you to receive this information, as discussed earlier in this book.

Who Can I Turn To?

"Who Can I Turn To?" is one of my favorite songs. It was sung by Anthony Newley and written by Newley and his writing partner, Leslie Bricusse for the 1965 Broadway show *The Roar of the Greasepaint—The*

Smell of the Crowd. The full title of the song is "Who Can I Turn To (When Nobody Needs Me)?" For family caretakers, the question is changed to "Who Can I Turn To (When Somebody Needs Me Very Much?"

The daunting task of caring for a relative when one is hardly trained in social work, geriatrics, medicine, law, or finance begs the obvious solution: Contact professionals in these disciplines for guidance in what to do for your aging relative. Speak with doctors, nurses, pharmacists, social workers, lawyers, financial planners, and anyone else whose services will enhance the health and security of your aging parents or grandparents.

Adult day-care centers are found throughout the country and can provide a safe and secure setting for social interaction. These programs can also give the caregiver a little "time out" to regenerate his or her own batteries. Services that might be provided in an adult day care setting include health screening, meals, and recreation. Adult day-care centers are generally open during regular working hours. The staff there might also monitor medication during the day. Costs vary considerably, from around $25 per day to more than $100 per day. Generally, the cost of adult day care is paid privately and is not covered by insurance. Adult day-care centers are not regulated or licensed in all states, so you will probably want to thoroughly check out any adult day-care center you are considering before you entrust your loved one to their care.

Meals on Wheels programs found in communities throughout the country will provide nutritious meals for your loved one. Any time you can get help meeting the ordinary and not-so-ordinary needs of the person for whom you are caring, you should consider using them: Trying to do everything for your loved one is a good way to ensure that you will get burned out.

Thank God for the Internet (although wasn't it former Vice President Al Gore who invented it?). The Internet provides myriad resources for caregivers. As I indicated earlier, one of the first places to go for information is the Eldercare Locator of the U.S. Administration on Aging, which was established in 1991. The interactive Web site of the Eldercare Locator, at www.eldercare.gov, permits you to access reliable information on senior services in your state, city, or town. In addition to giving information on the providers of specific elder services, the Eldercare Locator supplies contact information on local, regional, and state agencies on aging.

If you are caring for a family member in his or her own home, you might want to consider the physical condition of the home and determine whether repairs are needed to make the home environment safer and more user-friendly. Widening doorways and adding ramps are examples of modifications that might be helpful. Often there are state or federal grants to pay for those costs.

Geriatric Care Managers

Many caregivers are able to successfully maneuver on their own through the maze of organizations and services necessary to put together a plan for caring for their loved one. Many others find the use of a guide—in this case, a geriatric care manager—to be extremely helpful. For costs that range from approximately $300 to $800 for an initial evaluation and at hourly rates of between $50 and $150 for services thereafter, a geriatric care manager can help you determine just what organizations and services might help meet your loved one's many health-care, financial, and social needs.

Geriatric care managers are generalists, but usually they also have specialized knowledge as a nurse, social worker, or financial professional. They leverage their specialized knowledge to help you determine the best course of action to meet your loved one's many needs. One of the biggest benefits of using a geriatric care manager is being able to rely on the person's knowledge of not just determining your family member's needs, but also evaluating who and what organizations are best suited to assist you in meeting those needs.

Who Takes Care of the Caretaker?

Taking care of an elderly relative is an extremely stressful job. And that stress can lead to the physical and mental deterioration of the caregiver. The 2004 "Caregiving in the U.S." study by the National Alliance for Caregiving and AARP found that the biggest unmet need of caregivers was finding time for themselves, managing emotional and physical stress, and balancing work and family responsibilities. Sixty-one percent of family caregivers providing at least 21 hours of care per week have suffered from depression.[3] According to Gary Barg, 36 percent of caregivers die before the person for whom they are caring.

Consequently, it is very important for caregivers to be conscious of their own needs. Finding the time to take a break from this difficult and consuming job is very important. Barg suggests taking vacations when you can, but also just getting a break during the day is important. Dana Reeve, the wife and caretaker for her husband, the late Christopher Reeve, used to speak about taking a mental bubble bath. The prescription is one that we all know, but it is worth repeating: Eat well, get regular exercise, get enough sleep, and try to maintain a positive attitude.

Caregiver.com

This very helpful Web site provides information for family and professional caregivers. Along with a helpful Web site and magazine, *Today's Caregiver,* Caregiver.com provides chat rooms and information for support groups for caregivers who too often find themselves isolated. According to Caregiver.com's editor in chief, Gary Barg, caregivers need to connect with others who are similarly situated so they can realize that they are not alone. Barg points out that some caregivers initially avoid support groups, thinking they're for people who are merely whining about their situation. When they finally give support groups a try, they find them filled with people like themselves who are actually in the trenches; together, they give each other practical advice, wisdom, and love.

Barg says those who are hesitant about going to a support group should take a leap of faith: Try it three times before deciding whether a support group works for them. Caregiver.com maintains a nationwide list of support groups and even provides teleconference support groups in rural areas of the country.

Other Resources for Caregivers

Surf's up! Surfing the Internet can help caregivers find information to help them be better caregivers as well as locate care providers. I recommend the following sites:

National Family Caregivers Association: www.nfcacares.org

National Alliance for Caregiving: www.caregiving.org

Family Caregiver Alliance: www.caregiver.org

Eldercare Locator: www.eldercare.gov

National Adult Day Services Association: www.nadsa.org

National Association for Home Care: www.nahc.org

Visiting Nurse Association: www.vnaa.org

Some Final Thoughts

Caring for a loved one is a difficult job fraught with emotional pitfalls, but it is also is a tremendously rewarding time to connect with family members during their later years. There are no second chances when it comes to caring for an elderly family member. The trick to being an effective caregiver is that there is no trick. It is a difficult job that requires you to get as much information and assistance as you can to make your job easier and your performance more effective.

Endnotes

1. General Accounting Office, "Long Term Care: Diverse, Growing Population Includes Millions of Americans of All Ages" (GAO/HEHS 95-26, 1994).

2. Peter S. Arno, "Economic Value of Informal Caregiving" presented at the American Association of Geriatric Psychiatry, 24 February 2002.

3. National Family Caregivers Association/Fortis Long Term Care, "Caregiving Across the Life cycle," 1998.

8

CHOOSING A NURSING HOME OR AN ASSISTED-LIVING FACILITY

"Be good to your children—they pick your nursing home."
—Bumper sticker

hoosing a nursing home for a parent or grandparent is a difficult and emotional experience. However, it is a very important task and should be done with much preparation and thought.

For Information, Go Right to the Source

It is as true now as it was then when Mr. Ed told us in his theme song "Go right to the source and ask the horse." Unfortunately, Mr. Ed—that is, Bamboo Harvester, the horse who played him—died in 1970 at the age of 19.

But it still makes sense to go right to the source when you need information. One good source on how to choose a nursing home is the "Nursing Home" section of www.medicare.gov, the official federal government site for Medicare information. An interactive section of the Web site, "Nursing Home Compare," maintains information on more than 17,000 Medicare- and Medicaid-certified nursing homes throughout the country, including the number of beds, whether the nursing home is affiliated with Medicare or Medicaid, information about the nursing home's most recent state inspection, and information on the number of nurses and nursing assistants in the nursing home.

These details come from two sources. The first is the Center for Medicare Service's own Online Survey, Certification, and Reporting database, referred to by the acronym OSCAR. This database includes information from the three most recent state inspections, as well as information from any recent complaint investigations. OSCAR is updated monthly (if it were FELIX, I'll bet it would be updated more frequently).

The second source of information is a database known as the Minimum Data Set (MDS) Repository. This database contains information on the nursing home residents' health: physical functioning, mental status, and general well-being. This profile is gathered by the nursing homes themselves, which also used the information to develop individual care plans for individual residents. MDS information is updated quarterly.

Who Can Help?

Hospital discharge workers, social workers, geriatric managers, and social service agency workers can all suggest nursing homes for you to consider. In addition, as always, you might talk to someone whose family member has had a good experience with a particular nursing home. When you are considering a list of nursing homes, go to the "Nursing Home Compare" section of the Medicare Web site to gather further information. When you have narrowed your choice, make arrangements to personally visit the nursing homes. It's sort of like the trips you made to pick a college to attend.

Have a nursing home employee give you a tour of the place. Get an idea of how the nursing home operates. Then go back to visit it again on a different day of the week and at a different time of day. The staffing of nursing homes can be quite different at different times of day or on weekends.

Don't talk just to staff, either: Also speak with residents of the nursing home. When you speak with the residents, pay attention to their grooming and manner of dress. These little things will tell you much in the way of how the nursing home cares for its residents. Also observe whether the residents tend to be aware of their surroundings. Such a general impression could indicate that the nursing home is overusing drugs to maintain order.

Meals are important, too. Check out not just the dining room for the more self-sufficient residents, but also the dining room for the residents who need more assistance. Finally, check out the manner in which residents who are unable to leave their rooms are fed. Consider the food also: Would you eat it? Is it fresh? What would Emeril or Wolfgang Puck say?

The Basics

How many beds are there in the nursing home? How much staff? What is the ratio of staff to residents? Does the nursing home provide the level of care necessary for your family member? For some people, this means a special Alzheimer's unit.

Fees, Fie, Foe, Fum

Fies, foes, and fums might not be that important (well, I suppose foes could be significant), but fees are definitely a prime consideration when choosing a nursing home. The fee schedule of the nursing home should indicate what services are provided for the regular monthly fee and which services require you to pay extra.

Security

How secure is the facility? This is particularly important if you have a parent or grandparent with a mind disorder, such as Alzheimer's disease, which results in wandering. Does the nursing home have employees who are responsible for the security of residents who could become confused while walking the hallways? Is the facility sufficiently locked, to keep residents in and unauthorized people out?

Hospitals

Where is the closest hospital, and what is the nursing home's relationship with that hospital for handling emergencies?

The Smell Test

Too often the first thing that you notice when you enter a nursing home is the smell. If the place does not please your nose, turn around and leave.

Location, Location, Location

"Location, location, location," is the clever answer to the question of the three most important considerations in real estate. However, location is also an important consideration when choosing a nursing home. Interaction with family and friends is important to the health and well-being of nursing home residents. Visits are important and meaningful. Having a nursing home in easy proximity to friends and family is an important consideration.

Bingo

Many older people are fond of the game Bingo. The game goes back to an Italian lottery game entitled "Lo Giucco del Lotto D'Italia," first played in 1530 and still played every Saturday in Italy. As much as Bingo has been the butt of many jokes for its association with older people, it provides a great opportunity for social interaction among people, some of whom might otherwise avoid such socialization. Bingo also is good brain exercise. You can even win prizes. Does it get any better than that?

Bingo and other activities should form an integral part of daily life at a nursing home. Check out what the nursing home has to offer for physical and mental activities, classes, and social events, and see if it has a library. What is the availability of community social and cultural events?

Roommates

Were you nervous before meeting your college roommate? Imagine if you were going to spend the rest of your life with that person: That is the situation for many people entering nursing homes. Find out how the nursing home determines who will be rooming together and how roommates are changed.

Care Plans

Every nursing home resident has a specialized care plan. Find out how often that plan is reviewed and revised.

Nursing Home Workers

Problems have arisen with nursing home employees harming or stealing from nursing home residents. Find out how nursing home workers are screened prior to employment.

Doctor, My Eyes

Jackson Browne's hit song "Doctor, My Eyes" first appeared on his 1972 album *Jackson Browne*. In that song, Browne sang, "Doctor, my eyes have seen the years and the slow parade of fears without crying; now I want to understand." (Admit it, you are singing along.) When it comes to picking a nursing home, you want to know about the eyes of the doctor who will be caring for your family member. Does a doctor serve as the resident physician for many of the people at the nursing home?

How often is the doctor on the premises, and what is his or her bedside manner like?

Transportation

If your family member requires routine medical care, such as dialysis, that cannot be provided at the nursing home, how is transportation arranged and at what cost? Is transportation readily available for other purposes?

Smoking!

(Imagine Jim Carrey saying this in the movie *The Mask,* and it sounds much more entertaining.)

"That's our policy." This justification can be used for just about anything, so it is important to know the policies of the nursing home where you are placing Mom or Dad. For example, the nursing home might not allow smoking, and although that is a very understandable and laudable policy, it could have a significant effect on your decision. After all, your dad could be a chain-smoker with good genes who has managed to avoid respiratory illnesses despite smoking for 65 years. If Dad is happy smoking, as the Beatles would say, "Let it be"—in this case, find a nursing home that provides a convenient place for Dad to smoke to his heart's (if not his lungs') content.

Licensing, Certification, and Accreditation

Nursing homes are licensed by state. Check out the nursing home's license and its file with your state's licensing authority.

Particularly if you anticipate that Medicaid will at some time help pay for the cost of a nursing home, you will want to make sure that the institution you select is Medicare- and Medicaid-certified. This certification tells you that the nursing home has passed a state survey to achieve that status.

Is the nursing home accredited by the Joint Commission on the Accreditation of Healthcare Organizations (JCAHO)? Although the organization does not have a cool acronym such as OSCAR, it is an important nonprofit organization that can help you evaluate a nursing home. The JCAHO sets standards and evaluates health-care organizations, including nursing homes. You can access the commission's wealth of material at www.jcaho.org.

Identity Theft

Identity theft is both the biggest and the fastest-growing consumer crime in America today. Identity thieves steal your personal information and access your accounts, or buy things using your name. They can ruin your credit. In the summer of 2005, a security guard at a New York nursing home was sentenced to three years in prison for stealing the identity of Mildred Shonts, a resident of the nursing home, and using the stolen identity to rack up large credit card debts in her name. The guard had obtained Shonts' Social Security number through records at the nursing home and used that along with other information to apply for credit cards in her name. The scam went on unnoticed for two years before Shonts' son found collection notices from a credit card company addressed to his mother.

Unfortunately, identity theft that results from stolen personal information such as Social Security numbers from hospitals, doctors' offices, and nursing homes is an increasingly common occurrence. Many institutions do not do enough to protect the security of this important information. It is always prudent to ask any business with which you do business about its personal information security policies. However, it is even more important to be satisfied that personal information about a vulnerable elderly parent or grandparent in a nursing home is protected.

Assisted-Living Facilities

Alf, the television comedy about a furry visitor from another planet (Melmac), used the acronym for Alien Life Form as the name of the main character. For the four years that it was broadcast (1986–1990), Alf was a cultural icon. People who remember little else from the series might remember his loud laugh—it was always good for a laugh. (Extra points for you if you remember that although he was referred to as Alf, his name on Melmac was Gordon Shumway.) It was always hard to determine just exactly what Alf was. So it is only fitting that *Alf* is also an acronym for *assisted-living facilities:* As much as the term is bandied about there is no precise definition of what an assisted-living facility is. In a way, it is like Supreme Court Justice Potter Stewart's attempt at defining the term *hard-core pornography* by saying that although he could not define it, he knew it when he saw it.

One unfortunate result of the lack of precision in the term *assisted-living facility* is the lack of regulation. Even where there are regulations, they are not particularly vigorously enforced. This means that when it comes to choosing an assisted-living facility, the best place to find a helping hand is at the end of your own arm. The responsibility is yours. Although many of us are always a bit cynical when we hear the phrase "I'm from the government and I am here to help you," at times you would like to rely on government regulations for at least minimal protection of your interests.

So what is an assisted-living facility? The generally understood meaning is that it is a facility that provides housing, some level of personal care, and some form of health center for people who need some assistance with activities of daily life such as bathing, dressing, eating, mobility, and personal hygiene, but who do not require the level of services provided in a nursing home.

What's in a Name?

Exacerbating the problem of choosing an assisted-living facility is the fact that assisted living is so undefined. In fact, not only are there more than 17 different designations for what most often can be called assisted-living facilities, but in some states, such as New Hampshire, more than one term is used to refer to assisted-living facilities.

According to a study commissioned by the Senate Special Committee on Aging, assisted-living facilities should have written disclosures of all costs, services provided, and facility policies, including a policy for minimum notice for evicting residents. The study also recommends that the facilities have rules that guarantee that "trained and awake staff are on duty" at all times. I find this recommendation particularly troubling. James Martin, my high school social studies teacher, always said that society's strongest rules are the unwritten rules that everyone just knows and accepts. The fact that the Senate's study found it actually necessary to say that the staff should be "awake" is something that Mr. Martin would have found amusing.

Which Is Better—No Regulation or Little Regulation?

Although the federal government offers no direct regulation of assisted-living facilities, the regulations found in the individual states most often leave much to be desired. A mere half of the states require a nurse to be employed by or independently contracted with the facility. And to make things even worse, in most of those states, the nurse does not have to even actually be available at the facility.

The state requirements for the training of direct-care workers are also pretty slim. Just 19 states have any minimum hourly training requirements for direct-care workers; five states require a mere 12 hours or less of training. Four states require between 13 and 24 hours of training, and 10 states require 25 or more hours of training—all the training they ever need, in just over a half a week.

Another little tidbit: Although only a nurse can administer medication in a nursing home, 28 states permit assisted-living workers with little training to perform that function.

Minimum staffing ratios are required by only 18 states, with Alabama's one staff member to every eight residents during the day shift the best. Oregon's regulations require only "sufficient staff," whatever that means. Also, take what they tell you at the assisted-living facility with a grain of salt: Some assisted-living facilities mislead families by including janitors, cooks, administrators, and even gardeners when computing the staff-to-resident ratio. Your concern should be the ratio of people actually available to assist your family member entering an assisted-living facility.

Accreditation

Approximately a million people now live in assisted-living facilities, according to the National Center on Assisted Living, an association of assisted-living facilities. Although the federal government does not regulate assisted-living facilities and the state regulations are generally somewhat lacking, some help is provided by the nongovernment Joint Commission on Accreditation of Healthcare Organizations (JCAHO), which evaluates and accredits assisted-living facilities as it does with nursing homes. Its Web site, www.jcaho.org, can be quite helpful.

But, on the Other Hand, the Pictures Are Pretty

A 2004 study by the federal Government Accountability Office (formerly known as the General Accounting Office for 83 years, I wonder how much tax money they spent to determine that they should change the name of an organization that is most commonly referred to by its acronym GAO in any event) found, to no one's surprise, that in the information and glossy brochures routinely provided to prospective residents of assisted-living facilities, important information about residents evictions, staff training, and qualifications of facility workers had been omitted. The GAO report indicated that even where states have instituted regulations of assisted-living facilities, many facilities do not meet the standards mandated.[1]

Oral Contracts

According to early Hollywood movie producer Sam Goldwyn, oral contracts are not worth the paper they are not written on. A bit puzzling, but the essential truth is that oral contracts in general are not particularly worthwhile. Yet when it comes to assisted-living facilities, some states do not even require a written contract for an assisted-living facility agreement with a resident.

Warning: Negotiated Risk

I have always believed that life would be much better if we had background music as exists in the movies. Up-tempo, light music would enhance our enjoyment of happy times, and more intense music would alert us to impending danger. It is for this reason I have little sympathy for anyone who was eaten by the shark in the movie *Jaws*. The shark consistently never attacked anyone until it had given ample warning through the theme music that built up to a crescendo just as it finally attacked.

If life had background music, we would be so much better off. Unfortunately, it does not. Therefore, I want you to imagine the theme from *Jaws* whenever you see a negotiated risk provision in an assisted-living facility contract. A negotiated risk provision releases the assisted-living facility from any legal responsibility if it fails to provide adequate care.

Because this provision might not be immediately apparent to you, it is important to employ your own shark, a lawyer, to review your contract with an assisted-living facility before signing anything.

Judge Judy

What is the policy of the assisted-living facility for resolving disputes? Do you have any right to appeal the decision?

Just How Much Assistance Does a Resident Get at an Assisted-Living Facility?

Asking how many angels can fit on the head of a pin could be an easier question to answer. The answer is a consistent one: It depends. Among the basic services generally provided at an assisted-living facility are light housekeeping (not to be confused with lighthouse keeping), two or three meals per day, social activities, and some manner of assistance with activities of daily living. According to a survey released by MetLife in 2004, the cost of these basic services ranges from a low of $1,340 per month in Miami to a high of $4,327 in Stamford, Connecticut; the average monthly cost is $2,524. Troubling indeed is the fact that an assisted-living facility can raise its rates any time it wants, which makes it somewhat hard to plan for future costs. Most assisted-living facilities require an initial entrance deposit as well as monthly fees that can vary considerably, depending upon the services available. Some measure of medical care might also be provided through services sometimes managed by a nurse. However, many facilities have no on-site nursing staff; physicians are generally not part of the package.

Things to Ponder When Choosing an Assisted-Living Facility

Help! Although the federal government does not regulate assisted-living facilities, it does at least offer a good Web site, www.eldercare.gov, which was developed by the Department of Health and Human Services. This Web site can help you find assisted-living facilities in your area.

You can also look for help from your state's long-term care ombudsman. Each state has one, and you don't even have to be able to pronounce the word to be able to avail yourself of this person's services. Your state's ombudsman might also be able to assist you in locating inspection reports and records of complaints that have been lodged against the facilities you are considering. An easy place to find your state's long-term care ombudsman is www.ltcombudsman.org.

Geriatric care managers also can help you in both gathering and analyzing information on particular assisted-living facilities. *Geriatric care manager* is the term for health and human services professionals such as social workers, gerontologists, or nurses who specialize in issues facing older people. They can aid you in constructing a plan for your older family member. A good place to start your search for a geriatric care manager is at the Web site of the National Association of Professional Geriatric Care Managers: www.caremanager.org.

A Word of Warning

When you are considering hiring a geriatric care manager, make sure that the person you are considering hiring has total allegiance to you. The assisted-care facilities pay some geriatric care managers for placing people with them. Obviously, this is a conflict of interest that you want to avoid.

Location, Yada, Yada

Just as when buying a home or picking a nursing home, location is an important factor in choosing an assisted-living facility for a loved one. If the location is inconvenient for family members and friends, visits that are so important might be lessened.

Check It Out

Go to facilities you are considering and check them out for yourself. Go beyond the fancy lobby in some facilities and look for the building adaptations that are so important to seniors, such as elevator access, ramps for wheelchairs, accessible bathrooms, and emergency call buttons.

Go right to the source. The spirit of Mr. Ed does not exist just in nursing homes, but also in assisted-living facilities. Talk to the residents and get their take on what life is like in the particular assisted-living facility.

Observe the buzz. What are the residents doing? Are they watching Oprah, Maury, and *The View* every waking hour, or are they involved in activities that stimulate their minds and bodies? Study after study has shown that combining physical and mental exercises helps preserve cognitive function. Check out the exercise room, the computer room (if there is one), the craft facilities, and the library.

Bring your family member with you. Make this person a part of the decision-making process—and listen.

Pet Policy

Pets are important to many people because they provide companionship and affection. If your family member has a pet, find out the facility's policy regarding pets. Many are quite understanding, although few, I imagine, would be too thrilled to see my llama or horse coming through the front door.

Transportation

Transportation is a critical aspect of life in an assisted-living facility. Unlike in a nursing home, many routine medical services are not provided onsite, so the availability of transportation to and from medical appointments is of major importance. In addition, because assisted-living facility residents could be quite active and self-sufficient in many ways, transportation to shopping and social engagements is of major importance. Find out whether the transportation costs are included in the basic package at the assisted-living facility you are considering and, if not, what those costs are.

Do You Get Fries with That?

It is very important to know precisely what services are included with your basic monthly payment. You also should have a complete fee schedule for services that are not included in your basic monthly payment.

You will want to know the facility's policy on changing its fees. How much advance notice will you receive? How much may it raise fees?

Is a security deposit or other fee required upon entering the assisted-living facility? If so, are any of those fees refundable, and under what circumstances? Preferably, the policy should state that if residents must leave the facility, for whatever reason, they can get a proportionate refund of any entrance fee, depending upon how long they were there.

What Would Tim Russert Ask?

Tim Russert of *Meet the Press* always manages to ask probing questions without appearing hostile. You need to ask probing questions to evaluate the assisted-living facility. You need to know how long they have been in business, how strong the parent company is financially, whether complaints or lawsuits have been filed against the facility, and whether the facility is accredited by the Joint Commission on Accreditation of Healthcare Organizations.

The financial stability of the assisted-living facility is of supreme importance, and it makes sense to have your attorney or accountant review the facility's financial statement to ensure that there are sufficient financial reserves to operate the facility in a secure manner.

The Fine Print

There is nothing particularly fine about fine print. Actually, fine print often should be described as "really small print containing confusing language that describes rules that work against you." However, that is quite a mouthful, so I guess we are stuck with "fine print."

A report entitled *Critical Issues in Assisted Living: Who's in, Who's Out, and Who's Providing the Care,* by the National Senior Citizens Law Center in 2005, showed that not only may assisted-living facilities in 39 states evict residents when they no longer meet the residents' needs, but the determination of this is generally left up to the facility itself, with little right of appeal by residents. Many assisted-living facilities are aligned with nursing homes within the same complex and might be a good choice: If your family member is no longer able to function in the assisted-living facility setting, he or she may be able to merely transfer within the complex to the company's nursing home.

How Do You Pay

How do most people pay for assisted living? Simple. They pay out of their pocket. A few long-term care policies also cover the cost of assisted living, making it very important to look into this when you consider purchasing a long-term care insurance policy. Medicaid generally does not pay for assisted living, nor does Medicare care much about paying for the cost of assisted living. When the resident's funds are exhausted, some assisted-living facilities have programs that will pay for continuing care, but most do not. This means that the person might have to go to a nursing home where Medicaid will, in appropriate circumstances, pick up the cost.

Final Words

The lack of federal regulation and comprehensive state regulations places a great deal more responsibility on people who are considering moving to an assisted-living facility and their family. There is great variance in the cost and quality of entities calling themselves assisted-living facilities. The bad news is that it will take much more effort and questioning to ensure that you are making the best decision for your family member. The good news is that there are some wonderful assisted-living facilities that provide a life-enhancing experience. The trick is making sure you get one of those.

Endnotes

1. U.S. Government Accountability Office, "Assisted Living: Examples of State Efforts to Improve Consumer Protections" (GAO- 04-684, 2004).

9

LONG-TERM CARE
INSURANCE

"I will gladly pay you a dollar Tuesday for a hamburger today."
—Wimpy from Popeye

W hen it comes to paying for the cost of long-term care in a nursing home, the option of paying later is not a good option. Arranging your finances now so that you will have the resources to pay for long-term care when it is needed is an important consideration for baby boomers and their parents. Evolving to meet that growing need is long-term care insurance. Much has changed in the last few years in regard to long-term care insurance. This chapter gives you the most up-to-date information you need to determine whether long-term care insurance makes sense for you and, if so, what you should consider in making that purchase.

The good news is that we are all living longer. At age 65, a man today has a life expectancy of another 10.3 years, and a woman that age has a life expectancy of 12.4 years (and that does not even factor in a woman lying about her age). As Oscar Wilde said, "One should never trust a woman who tells one her real age. A woman who would tell one that, would tell one anything."

Baby boomers can expect to live longer lives than their parents and grandparents. The bad news is that, for many of us, those latter years may be spent in a nursing home. The worse news is that the cost for that care will be extraordinary.

A 2003 study by the Kaiser Family Foundation predicts that 44 percent of people over the age of 65 will require some nursing-home care during their lifetimes, with the average stay being 2.4 years. Playing the odds is problematic, however: According to the Kaiser study, although 50 percent of those who go into a nursing home stay there for less than a year, 20 percent stay there for 5 years or more.

Rule of Thumb

If you have the cash, you can self-insure. If you have no cash, Medicaid should foot the bill. But what if you fall in the middle of these two extremes? A rule of thumb is that people with assets (not including the value of their home) of between $250,000 and $1.5 million should consider buying long-term care insurance. Another factor in determining whether your assets are sufficient to self-insure is whether you want to leave a legacy to the next generation.

Of course, the main problem with self-insuring is that there are too many unknowns. Although you might need long-term care in a nursing home in the future, it is difficult to estimate now what the cost of that care will be and how long you will need that care.

We are all familiar with people who personally live unhealthful lives, eating less-than-nutritious meals, exercising just enough to get off the couch to go to the kitchen for another doughnut or cigarette, and perhaps drinking a bit more than they should. Yet despite these shortcomings, some of these people live to ripe old ages because they have chosen their parents well. Genes are important. Conversely, people whose family histories contain Alzheimer's disease, dementia, Parkinson's disease, or other genetically linked diseases might find that the odds are not in their favor when it comes to predicting the possibilities of long-term care in the future. These people should well consider buying long-term care insurance.

Why Get Long-Term Care Insurance?

Medical insurance will not cover long-term care needs for people with either a physical or a mental condition that makes them unable to care for themselves. Medical insurance will still cover medical needs, but for the everyday care required by someone who needs assistance with activities of daily living such as feeding and personal hygiene, medical insurance will not cover the costs of assisted living, adult day care, in-home care, or nursing-home care. Long-term care insurance will.

Medicare pays for only a maximum of 100 days of long-term care in a nursing home, and Medicaid has serious qualification issues. Paying for the cost of long-term care privately can destroy a person's finances, leaving long-term care insurance as an option to be considered.

Long-term care insurance coverage does not automatically cover all three possible long-term care possibilities—namely, assisted living, at-home care, and nursing-home care—so it is important to buy a policy that reflects your desires and your needs.

The Early Days of Long-Term Care Insurance

About 20 years ago, long-term care insurance first hit the market as a way to help people pay for the cost of long-term care both at a nursing home and, as many people would prefer, in their own homes.

When long-term care insurance was first introduced to the public, the insurance company actuaries, who help set the premiums for these policies, had little information to go on. Many of the assumptions upon which the premiums for the early policies were based have turned out to be inaccurate. As a result, the insurance companies have raised the premiums for policyholders of these early policies.

Long-term care insurance has evolved, as have the needs of a graying (and sometimes balding) population. The first wave of long-term care policies neglected to recognize the need and value of home health care coverage. In the 1980s, coverage for this as well as for adult day care and assisted-living care first became available.

When you buy a life insurance policy, you generally know what your premium will be. Many purchasers of long-term care insurance policies thought they knew what their premiums were going to be as well. Precision in language is critical. The exact meanings of words are important. Unfortunately, sometimes what we think we hear is not exactly what was said. Specifically, what some insurance agents told their clients when selling them long-term care insurance policies was, "You will never be singled out for a policy increase due to your increased age or deteriorating health." What the prospective policy buyers might have thought they heard was, "Your premium will never go up as you get older." But that is not what the salesmen said. What few salesmen probably said was, "Although you may not be singled out for a premium increase as you get older, all policy holders may be subject to policy increases if the company determines that it priced the policies too low."

And that is just what happened. Why? There are many answers. Some companies probably purposefully underpriced their policies so they could sell more policies and get a greater market share. Or, the insurance company's investments in stocks and bonds might not have been as good in recent years as they were in the past, so the companies have less money to meet their needs. In addition, the company might have miscalculated the number of people who would abandon their long-term care insurance policies before ever making a claim. Ten years ago, 10 percent of long-term care insurance policyholders just let their policies lapse, compared to about 1 percent today, according to Peter Goldstein, executive vice president of Long Term Care Group, a consulting firm. That translates into more claims and greater payouts for the insurance companies. Finally, many insurance companies failed to accurately predict the large increases in the costs of nursing home care over the years.

Just how dramatic are the premium increases facing policyholders? CNA policyholders in some states found themselves facing premium increases of as much as 50 percent. Individual state insurance commissioners must approve premium increases for long-term care insurance policies before they become effective. Some states granted the full 50 percent increase the CNA sought, while others authorized somewhat less but still significant increases in annual premiums.

Dropout Rate

> *"Turn on, tune in, drop out."*
> —Timothy Leary

I do not know if there is any turning on or tuning in going on in the major insurance companies, but faced with increased payouts, a number of them have dropped out of the market for long-term care insurance policies. Among those companies are some big names such as CNA and TIAA-CREF that are no longer writing new long-term care insurance policies. According to America's Health Insurance Plans, a trade organization, the number of companies now selling long-term care insurance policies dropped from 127 in 2001 to just about 100 today.

Faced with the dilemma of either paying a tremendously increased premium or letting the policy lapse and wasting all the years of premium payments, savvy consumers and insurance agents have come up with some other alternatives.

Good News, Bad News

The good news is that, armed with a better understanding of the long-term care insurance market and better actuarial projections (remember, this baby is only about 20 years old), the premiums on new long-term care insurance policies are much less likely to see the sharp price increases that were experienced by people holding older policies. The bad news, however, is that the premiums are significantly larger than they formerly were.

Where Do You Start?

The first thing you have to do is understand some of the terms, options, and provisions found in long-term care insurance policies.

Length of Coverage

The average stay in a nursing home is about 2 1/2 years, although we are all familiar with people who have been there much longer. The most common period for long-term care insurance coverage is 3 to 4 years. To some extent, this is attributable to the Medicaid look-back period, which, until a recent change in the law, was 3 years; it now has been raised to 5 years. When you apply for Medicaid to cover the cost of long-term care in a nursing home, Medicaid looks back 5 years from the time of your application and will disqualify you from Medicaid coverage for a period that does not begin until you are in the nursing home and your assets have been spent down to no more than $2,000. The duration of the disqualification period depends on the value of the assets you gave away. However, presently Medicaid does not even inquire about gifts you made more than 5 years earlier. If you get a long-term care insurance policy that will cover the cost of 5 years of nursing home care, you could give away your assets when you first go into the nursing home, have the policy substantially pay for the cost of care during the next 5 years, and then apply for Medicaid at the end of 5 years.

But what if the look-back period changes? This is not an idle question: In the past, Congress increased the period from 2 years to 3 years and then, most recently, to 5 years. Getting a policy that provides lifetime coverage might not be necessary, but a policy with 6 years of coverage might be a good call.

Waiting Period

A waiting period is the provision in a long-term care insurance policy that delays the paying of benefits for a specific period, from the time you first enter the nursing home. During this waiting period, you are responsible for the cost of your own care. Or are you? If you are over 65 and are covered by Medicare, you could be eligible for Medicare coverage for the full cost of the first 20 days in the nursing home and all but a $119 per-day copayment (in 2006) for the next 80 days. Therefore, a 100-day waiting period might not pose much of a financial burden for someone covered by Medicare. As you would expect, the longer the period you choose for a waiting period, the lower your premium will be. The range of waiting periods from which you can choose are subject to the insurance regulations of your particular state, but they range from no waiting period to a year. Most people pick 90 to 100 days.

Waiver of Premium

A waiver of premium is the provision in a long-term care insurance policy that eliminates the need to continue to pay the premiums for the policy while you are in a nursing home and receiving benefit payments from the policy.

Nonforfeiture

Nonforfeiture is the provision in a long-term care insurance policy that allows you to cancel the policy but still receive some amount of reduced benefits if you need long-term care in the future. This is an expensive form of coverage because it greatly increases the potential payout by the insurance companies, who factor in their pricing a projected number of people who will buy a policy and then let it lapse without receiving benefit payments. If you choose to have a nonforfeiture provision in your policy, it can raise the amount of your premium a great deal. However, it still might be a good choice if you are concerned about whether you will have enough money in the future to continue to pay the premiums necessary to keep the policy in effect.

Renewability

Guaranteed renewability is a standard provision of most long-term care insurance policies that prohibits the insurance company from canceling your policy if you are late paying your premium, as long as you make your premium payment within a specified grace period. Having a guaranteed renewability provision protects you from losing the protection of your policy and wasting your earlier premium payments if you are late with a premium payment due to illness or a temporary lack of attentiveness.

Inflation Protection

Inflation is a fact of life. Things will cost more in the future. The trend of increasing costs for nursing home care makes it even more important that, if you are considering purchasing a long-term care insurance policy, you make sure the value of your policy is not diluted by failing to factor in inflation. Inflation protection through a policy provision for a 5 percent compound inflation rate protection will increase the cost of your premium, but it is worth it.

Inflation protection can be particularly important to the holder of a long-term care insurance policy because many people who buy these policies might not use them for 30 years or more. Protecting the policy benefits from inflation is a significant consideration. Three primary alternative provisions for inflation can be made a part of a long-term care policy: 5 percent compound interest, 5 percent simple interest, and benefits based upon inflation as determined by the Consumer Price Index. When you first pick your policy, you have the option of either the 5 percent compound-interest provision or a 5 percent simple-interest provision, which will be factored into your premium payments.

The difference between a simple-interest provision and a compound-interest provision can be quite large. A daily benefit of $150 will rise to $300 in just about 20 years using a 5 percent simple interest formula. That same initial daily benefit amount of $150 will reach $300 after only about 15 years using a 5 percent compound interest formula.

The Consumer Price Index, or CPI, inflation protection provision is offered to existing policyholders periodically by the insurance company for an additional premium. The bottom line is that although the effect on your premium could be significant, the dilution of the value of your policy without that provision makes it all but mandatory.

Examples

A 59-year-old married man buying a policy with 10-year coverage, a 180-day waiting period, and a 5 percent compound inflation provision would have a premium of $3,078 per year.

Without the inflation protection, his premium would be $1,386 annually.

A 50-year-old married woman buying the same policy with the 5 percent compound interest factor would pay a premium of $2,098. Without the inflation protection, her premium would be $761 per year.

Group Policies

It is always nice to be a member of a group. But when it comes to purchasing a group long-term care insurance policy, it is important to note that, for some reason apparent only to the politicians writing these rules, some states do not apply the same regulations to buyers of group policies. In Massachusetts, for instance, an individual policy may not be sold that excludes coverage for Alzheimer's disease. Unfortunately, group policies excluding this important coverage may be legally sold in Massachusetts. Obviously, it is very important to carefully scrutinize any group long-term care policy that you might consider buying.

Lowball Shopping

People who in the past picked a policy because the premiums were low are now often the people getting burned by the increases in policy premiums. This lesson should not be lost on people who are considering buying policies now. Certainly, price is a factor and prices will vary from company to company. However, the stability of the company and its track record in both paying on policies and maintaining stable premium levels are also of paramount importance. If there is a good spin to increased premiums, it is that they can be considered an indication that the company is paying its claims. One would think that no company would refuse to pay on a claim but some companies are more apt to contest payment on their policies. A good insurance agent can help you compare companies.

Long-term care insurance involves contemplating not only your own longevity, but also that of the company from which you might choose to buy a policy. If the company from which you buy a long-term care insurance policy goes bankrupt or otherwise finds itself in dire financial straits, you could find yourself having paid premiums for years for a policy that is worthless when you finally need it. Somewhat less devastating but still distressing is the possibility that the financial instability of your company could leave you facing large premium increases in later years of the policy. Consider the source, and buy your insurance from a well-established, highly rated company.

Buy It Early

It used to be that the argument for buying long-term care insurance at younger ages was that your annual premiums would be less—and that argument still holds. An even better argument for buying early is that, as insurance companies are looking at ways to control their costs, they are becoming much more stringent in the health standards of the people to whom they will sell insurance. They also have 20 years of actuarial experience that could make some companies less apt to sell their products to a type of client that it would have considered 20 years ago. A word to the wise: Get the insurance while you can.

Examples

A long-term care insurance policy for a 55-year-old married woman with a 5-year lifetime benefit of $360,000, a $200 per-day benefit, and a 90-day elimination period would cost her an annual premium of $1,680. That same policy at age 65 would cost her $3,552 annually.

If her husband bought the same policy at age 55, his annual premium would be $2,016. If he waited until age 70 to purchase the same policy, his premium would be $5,328 per year.

Putting It Off

As the old saying goes, when you are up to your ass in alligators, it is difficult to remember that your initial objective was to drain the swamp. Many of us know that we should prepare for long-term care—and the sooner, the better. But when you have more pressing needs, such as college expenses for your children or your own retirement plans, long-term care planning just seems too distant a need. The problem with this thinking is that the cost of delaying your purchase of a long-term care policy increases the policy costs dramatically.

More Examples

For a single male buying $100 per-day coverage with 5 percent compound interest and a 180-day wait, the annual premium for purchasing the identical policy at different ages would be:

Age 50: $1,581

Age 55: $1,674

Age 60: $2,066

Age 65: $2,669

Age 70: $3,872

Age 75: $5,806

Picking a Policy You Can Afford

Policy benefit periods can range anywhere from 2 years to life. Policies for a 4-year coverage period could be 50 percent less than a policy that covers you for 6 years, according to the Long Term Care Group. Because the average stay in a nursing home is now 2.4 years, it might make sense to get the less costly policy that covers you for the lesser period. However, under recently enacted changes in the Medicaid laws, a 4-year policy would no longer buy you the time to give away assets to family members and still qualify for Medicaid when the policy was exhausted. The new look-back period of 5 years essentially mandates a long-term care policy that covers you for at least 5 years, so you can make gifts to family members and still qualify for Medicaid when the policy has been fully paid out. You can also reduce your premium by moving back the date at which the policy will start paying benefits. Logically, the sooner you have the policy begin to make payments, the potentially more in payments the insurance company will have to pay—and the more the premium will cost you. Many people choose a 100-day waiting period before the policy benefits start to be paid. Currently, Medicare fully pays for the first 20 days in a nursing home and then pays for the next 80 days subject to a copayment that, in 2006, is $119 per day. It is important to note that, to be eligible for Medicare payments for the first 100 days, you must go to the nursing home from a hospital, not from your home.

Creative Solutions

If you cannot presently afford a policy at the benefit level you would prefer, buy a policy with a small amount of coverage and an inflation rider; then, after a few years, get another policy to supplement that initial policy. Overall, you will save considerable money. If a 50-year-old bought a policy with a $100 per-day coverage for 4 years and then 10 years later bought another policy with $100 per-day coverage, his premium would be less than if he bought a $200 policy at age 60. He also would have had some coverage for all the years between 50 and 60. The following table shows some examples of annual premiums.

Example Annual Policy Premiums

Policy Holder	Premium per Day	Compound Interest	Waiting Period	Annual Premium
50-year-old single male	$200	5 percent	180-day	$3,162
50-year-old single male	$100	5 percent	180-day	$1,581
60-year-old single male	$100	5 percent	180-day	$2,065
60-year-old single male	$200	5 percent	180-day	$4,131

Good News

Just as some thought *Star Trek, the Next Generation* was an improvement over the original *Star Trek* (think Captain Picard vs. Captain Kirk), the more recent generation of long-term care insurance policies are an improvement when it comes to consistency of the premiums. The insurance companies have learned from their experience in this relatively new form of insurance. Drastic premium increases for policyholders of the new policies are unlikely.

It Pays to Be Married

"When it comes to long-term care insurance and country club dues,
it pays to be married."
—Ron Nathan, financial planner

It pays to be married in many instances. In fact, some would say that it pays and it pays and it pays. But do not listen to those cynics. A recent development in long-term care insurance has been greatly reduced premium costs when married couples buy long-term care insurance together. When you think about it, it makes sense: Married people are more likely to be in a position to care for each other at home for some period of time before a nursing home stay would be required. Single people without such a devoted caregiver are more likely to need the services of a nursing home earlier.

A 59-year-old married man buying a long-term care insurance policy that covers 10 years in a nursing home with a 180-day waiting period and a 5 percent compound interest inflation factor would pay an annual premium of $3,078. If this same man had bought the same policy but was single instead of married, his premium would have been $4,397. See how much it pays to be married?

Another new development in policies for married couples is "shared benefits," a policy provision by which husbands and wives can share the total coverage years according to their needs. So, for example, if both the husband and wife purchased coverage for 4 years each and one of them goes into the nursing home while the other remains healthy and in the community, the healthy spouse can share some of the years of coverage from his or her policy to cover the institutionalized spouse who has exhausted his or her own benefits.

Who Is in Jeopardy of a Premium Increase?

The owners of older policies in general and those with shorter waiting periods and lifetime coverage periods are most likely to find themselves facing a premium increase. What do you do if you are notified of a policy premium increase and you do not want to lose your coverage, but you find it difficult to provide in your budget for the additional premium? Work with your insurance agent to see if you can reduce the amount of your daily benefit, reduce the policy coverage period, or extend the waiting period before the policy starts paying, as alternatives to either having to pay an increased premium or letting the policy lapse.

If you think the cost of long-term care is expensive today, think again. It is expected to be far more costly in the future, when many baby boomers might find themselves in nursing homes. In 2005, the average cost of a private room in a nursing home was $69,400. This was an increase of 6 percent over 2004 and 13 percent from 2003 to 2004. The costs vary tremendously in various parts of the country: Alaska has the most expensive nursing home costs, which, in 2005, was $201,000 a year, according to the *Genworth Financial 2005 Cost of Care Survey*. The views must be spectacular in the Alaskan nursing homes; I cannot imagine that the weather is much of a draw.

Let's Get Creative

The cost of nursing home care is constantly going up. Inflation protection should not be considered an option; it should be considered a necessity. Without inflation protection, the policy you buy today might serve you little at a time when you need the policy to start paying. But inflation protection is a long-term care insurance policy provision that can add tremendously to the cost of the policy. According to the old proverb (as contrasted with all of those new proverbs), "You can't have your cake and eat it, too." John Heywood first recorded this proverb in 1546 in a book of proverbs. I suppose, like many proverbs, it is not a job requirement to make much sense. After all, what good is a cake if you do not get to eat it? In any event, a good way to have your cake and eat it, too, when it comes to getting inflation protection without breaking the bank is to buy a policy now that will permit you to pay for inflation protection later. This will help keep your payments down in the early years of your ownership of the policy.

Before You Actually Apply for a Policy

After you have applied for a long-term care policy, the insurance company will obtain a copy of your medical records to evaluate your insurability. A random note on your medical record made by your physician, particularly one related to cognitive functioning, can have a significant effect on whether your application for long-term care insurance will be accepted. Your physician might not have even discussed the matter with you, but it can still come back to haunt you.

Fortunately, under the Health Insurance Portability and Accountability Act (HIPAA), you have the right to see your medical records. So check out your medical records before you apply for a long-term care insurance policy. If you find mistaken or inappropriate notations on your record, you can bring these matters to your physician's attention and ask him or her to correct the record.

Also check with your long-term care insurance agent about the position of the insurance company regarding any prescription drugs you are taking. The insurance company could consider an innocuous prescription to be a narcotic that can end up either disqualifying you for the policy or making the premiums much higher. When it comes to health conditions and prescriptions that concern the underwriters of long-term care insurance companies, the companies vary quite a bit about what they consider important; you might want to evaluate policies from a number of long-term care insurers to see which company matches you best.

Crime Doesn't Pay

Just a final word of caution: Deep within the fine print of all long-term care insurance policies is an exception to coverage that permits the insurance company to refuse to pay benefits if you end up having to go to a nursing home because of injuries you suffer while committing a felony or participating in a riot or an insurrection. Apparently, if you hurt yourself while committing a misdemeanor, you will still be covered, but I advise playing it safe and steering clear of all criminal and violent endeavors so you don't jeopardize your long-term care insurance benefits. No one asked, but I thought you should know.

10

ALTERNATIVES TO LONG-TERM CARE INSURANCE

"Everybody wants to live forever, but nobody wants to grow old."
—Jonathan Swift

W hat Swift neglected to say, perhaps because it goes without saying, is that even more undesirable than growing old is growing old in a nursing home. But unfortunately, it is a fact of life for many older Americans. The cost of long-term care in a nursing home is expensive. Finding the funds to pay for this care can be difficult.

For many people, deciding to how to fund long-term care needs is reminiscent of the old joke about the heavily accented Maine resident telling the tourist requesting directions, "You can't get there from here (pronounced 'heah')."

Many people who want to provide for long-term care have a significant amount of assets, but not necessarily sufficient income to allocate toward long-term care insurance premiums, particularly if they consider long-term care insurance as a product with which they win only if they lose: They get a financial payout from the policy only if they go into a nursing home.

More people are finding that, in their particular circumstances, neither private funding, reverse mortgages, nor long-term care insurance are workable solutions for meeting their realistic long-term care needs. In response to this problem, creative minds are coming up with new and inventive ways to meet the needs of aging baby boomers and their parents.

Many of these solutions involve life insurance. Life insurance sounds like a simple concept: You pay premiums to the insurance company, and when you die, they pay you money. But life insurance is quite a bit more complicated than that. To understand how it can be used to help meet long-term care needs, you need to know some of the basic concepts behind the different kinds of life insurance.

Life Insurance 101

The most basic kind of life insurance is term life insurance. It involves pure insurance coverage that is in effect for a particular period of time, such as 10 or 20 years. If you die while the policy is in force, you win (sort of) and the insurance company pays you money. However, there is no cash value to a term life insurance policy. If you plan to have the policy for a long time, the premiums generally will increase substantially as you get older. Particularly for young families that need the most insurance bang for the buck, term insurance makes some sense. However, it does not offer opportunities for long-term care planning.

Permanent Life Insurance

Four primary kinds of permanent life insurance are available: whole life, universal life, variable life, and variable universal life. All permanent life insurance policies are based on a portion of your regular policy premium payment being allocated to pay for your life insurance coverage. This is the policy's death benefit, which is the amount that is paid to your beneficiaries at your death. The rest of the premium, after taking out insurance company management fees, is applied to a cash value savings account for you.

Whole Life Insurance

Whole life insurance is a simple concept. The premium that you pay is always the same. Part of each premium payment is invested by the company and permits you to accumulate a cash value inside the policy that you can access through loans or by cashing in the policy. However, sometimes the premiums for plain-vanilla whole life insurance can be higher than policyholders want to pay. For this reason, the insurance industry came up with the concept of universal life insurance.

Universal Life Insurance

Universal life insurance is a hybrid of term insurance and a savings fund that earns interest at money market rates. With universal life insurance, you can change the amount of your life insurance as your insurance needs change. Your premium can change as well. Premiums are lower than for whole life insurance but more than the cost of term insurance for younger people.

Variable Life Insurance

Variable life insurance provides you with greater choices of where the insurance company will invest your cash-value dollars. You can choose from different stocks, bonds, or money market funds. If your investments do well, your death benefit and cash value go up. If your investments do not do well, your death benefit and cash value go down, although there generally is a guaranteed minimum death benefit. The amount of your premium remains the same throughout the policy's existence.

Variable Universal Life Insurance

Variable universal life insurance gives you the flexibility of adjusting the amount of your death benefit and premium, as with universal life insurance, and the ability to choose how your cash value is invested, as with variable life insurance.

Viatical Settlement Companies

A viatical settlement company can buy your life insurance while you are alive. The company becomes the beneficiary of your policy and continues to pay the premiums. You get a lump-sum payment while you are alive that you can choose to use for long-term care needs. *Viatical* comes from the Latin word *viaticum*, which means provisions for a journey.

The amount that you receive from a viatical settlement company ranges most often from 10 to 50 percent of the face value of the policy. The amount that you receive depends primarily on your life expectancy: The shorter your life expectancy is, the higher percentage of your policy's death benefit you are likely to receive. Since the enactment of the Health Insurance Portability and Accountability Act of 1996 (HIPAA), payments from qualifying viatical settlement companies are generally tax-free to people who are either terminally ill or chronically ill. For purposes of HIPAA, a person is considered to be terminally ill if he or she is reasonably expected to die within 2 years. A chronically ill person for HIPAA purposes is someone who is unable to perform at least two activities of daily living, such as eating and bathing, or who has a severe cognitive impairment. Payments to a chronically ill person that are used for long-term care in a nursing home provide tax-free income to the person selling his or her insurance policy.

As with many things that sound too good to be true, viatical settlements are not necessarily as good as they sound. Only about half of the states regulate viatical settlement companies. Like the unanswerable question of whether Certs is indeed a breath mint or a candy mint, many states are unable to determine whether viatical settlements should be regulated as insurance or as an investment. Even in states that regulate viatical settlement companies, there are numerous unscrupulous companies doing this work.

Talk to your insurance agent to get his or her advice about viatical settlement companies, but also see if your policy has provisions for accelerated death benefits. If your policy does have such a provision, you will receive more money from your own insurance company through this policy provision. A claim for accelerated benefits through your insurance policy will be quicker to process than obtaining money through a viatical settlement: You'll get your money faster from your own insurance company.

Finally, before you sell your policy to strangers, you should consider selling the policy to family members who have been named as the beneficiaries of your policy. In this way, you deal with someone you already trust. The family member could come up with the money to pay you through a home equity loan or other sources.

If you are concerned about whether you will have enough money in the future to continue to pay the premiums necessary to keep your life insurance policy in effect, and if you need the money now to pay for the cost of long-term care, selling your policy to a family member or, as a last resort, to a viatical settlement company could be a good choice.

Accelerated Death Benefits

The term *accelerated death benefits* does sound a bit like an oxymoron. It refers to a provision of many permanent life insurance policies that can assist in providing money to help pay for long-term care needs. Accelerated death benefit provisions or riders permit the policyholder to tap into a policy's substantial death benefit during his or her lifetime to meet costs of assisted living, at-home care, or nursing home care. A big advantage to using life insurance to meet long-term care needs is that, unlike the case with long-term care insurance, if you never need to use the policy to pay for long-term care, it is available as a conventional life insurance policy to provide death benefits to your family upon your death.

This contrasts favorably with long-term care insurance that generally provides no benefit to the policyholder other than the payment of long-term care needs. With long-term care insurance, if the policyholder never uses the policy to meet those needs, neither the policyholder nor his or her family receives any other payments from the policy. If you are lucky enough to never have to enter a nursing home, you end up losing the benefit of every dollar you paid in premiums for the insurance f or years. This is not to say that the money paid in premiums was wasted because what you bought was insurance protection in case you needed it. Still, many customers feel that after paying their premiums faithfully for many years, some financial benefit should go to them or their families.

With an accelerated death benefit rider, any amount that is withdrawn from the policy during the life of the insured to meet long-term care needs obviously reduces the amount of the death benefit available at death to pay the policy's beneficiaries. However, for many people, the belief that they are covering their potential need long-term care while also providing a legacy for their families is quite attractive.

These riders are generally offered in conjunction with the sale of whole life or universal life policies; as with whole life and universal life policies in general, the premiums are greater than those for a term policy. However, you could be getting more value because, just as the long-term care insurance policy offers protection for only potential long-term care needs, term life insurance offers only death benefits. With a whole life or universal life insurance policy, you can get a policy that provides for both death benefit needs and long-term care needs. In addition, such a policy can also be a source of money during your lifetime through a loan from the insurance company. Such a loan does not have to be repaid until your death. Even then, the repayment is merely deducted from the amount of the death benefit.

A common life insurance policy with a long-term care rider will have a universal life or variable universal life insurance policy as a base, with an accelerated death benefit rider that permits you to take 2 percent of the death benefit per month. Some policies set a base below which the death benefit may not be reduced. Some even include additional provisions that will extend the long-term care benefits after the policy limits have been met.

Example

A typical $300,000 universal life insurance policy for a 65-year-old woman would carry an annual premium of $6,447 without a long-term care rider. With a long-term care rider, the cost increases by only $302.

Theory vs. Reality

In theory, a frugal young consumer might consider buying a term life insurance policy for his or her young family to cover expenses if a parent died while children still depended on that parent for support. That same consumer might then let the term life insurance policy lapse when the children are self-sufficient and direct those premium dollars to a long-term care insurance policy to meet his or her own potential needs for long-term care. The total premiums for both insurance products would be less, making this, on the surface, an attractive alternative.

But what if, even in this best of all possible worlds, at the time you decide to purchase long-term care insurance, your health (or lack thereof) makes buying that policy too expensive? In the worst case, what if your health disqualifies you from coverage? Or what if the premiums for long-term care insurance itself have risen to an unacceptable level by the time you decide to buy it? These are the risks inherent in this choice. Ultimately, you face the real possibility of paying years of term life insurance premiums for a policy upon which you never make a claim, and then letting that policy lapse and transferring your premium dollars to payments on a long-term care insurance policy for which you pay premiums for years and never make a claim because you never require long term care. In that case, you would have paid and never received a nickel.

"Insurance is like marriage. You pay and pay, but you never get anything back."
—Al Bundy of the television show *Married with Children*

Contrast that choice with buying a whole life or universal life insurance policy that will pay you if you have long-term care needs or you die. Neither is a particularly fondly anticipated goal, but they are contingencies for which a prudent person should plan. In addition, in these days when people who bought long-term care insurance many years ago are facing unanticipated premium rate increases, buying life insurance to meet the dual needs of long-term care insurance and life insurance involves a premium that you can depend upon not to rise unexpectedly as time goes by. The cost for this extra protection is quite reasonable.

John Hancock LifeCare Benefit Rider

The John Hancock LifeCare Benefit Rider typifies the movement toward combining long-term care benefits with a life insurance policy. The policyholder can access some, all, or none of the life insurance benefit to meet long-term care needs. The cost of the policy is less than buying a permanent life insurance policy and a long-term care policy separately. The cost of the annual premium for such a rider with a $500,000 death benefit and a $10,000 monthly long-term care payment for a 45-year-old male is $3,914, which represents only a 5.2 percent increase in premium for the policy without the long-term care benefit rider (which would be $3,719).

The annual premium for the same policy for a man at age 65 would be $12,234. The cost of the premium for the policy without the long-term care rider would be $11,647, a difference of only 5 percent.

For a 45-year-old woman buying the same $500,000 death benefit and a $10,000 per month maximum payment for long-term care, the cost with the long-term care rider would be $3,146 per year for the premium. This represents an increased premium cost of only 4.9 percent for the same life insurance coverage without the long-term care rider. If she waited until age 65 to purchase the same insurance, the premium would be $9,775 per year with the long-term care rider, which is only 4.4 percent more than the policy without the rider, or $9,358.

Single Premium Life Insurance

Another option is a single premium life insurance policy with a provision allowing the policy proceeds to be used for long-term care. These policies might have specific provisions for the payment of long-term care costs either in a nursing home or at home. As the name implies, the policy is bought with a single payment that can be as little as $10,000 but more often is within the range of $50,000 to $100,000. The source of your single-premium payment can be your regular savings, or even an IRA or another insurance policy. As with all life insurance, the policy will have a death benefit that is double or even triple the amount of your single payment.

What is so useful about this type of insurance policy is that monthly you have the option of taking out 2 percent of the death benefit for nursing home care or 1 percent for home health care. This gives you money for 50 months of nursing home care or 100 months of care in your own home. As with other insurance products, another attractive feature is that your money in the policy accumulates on a tax-deferred basis. You pay no income taxes until you take the money out—and even then, you pay income tax only on the policy's earnings. In addition, the value of your policy should increase over time, as should the death benefit.

If you never need the money during your lifetime, at your death, the substantial death benefit will be paid to the beneficiaries of the policy totally income tax–free. If you do not need the money for other purposes during your lifetime, you always have the option of canceling the policy and getting back at a minimum what you paid for the policy. These policies are generally available to people no older than 80.

Finding the Money

People who reach the magic age of 70 1/2 when they are required to begin withdrawing from their retirement plans present another interesting possibility. In that instance, if the individual does not have an immediate need for those funds, he or she can use the funds that must be distributed to pay the premium for life insurance with a long-term care rider.

Another Thing to Think About

Less often stated, but a real-life consideration in the decision of whether to purchase long-term care insurance or life insurance with a long-term care rider, is the matter of whether the insurance company issuing the long term-care insurance policy might contest a claim made years later for long-term care benefits. This is of particular concern because anyone who makes a claim for long-term care benefits is, by definition, not in great shape to fight the insurance company on this matter. It could be that the insurance company has determined as a matter of policy to try to keep its costs lower by making the claims process difficult, or the initial application could contain incorrect medical information that the insurance company still can contest years later. Regardless of the motivation, the potential problem is the same: the risk of paying the premiums on the long-term care insurance policy for many years, only to find that when the policy is needed, it is not available. However, when the basic vehicle for long-term care planning is life insurance, the insurance company might be more apt to pay the long-term care claim because the company understands that, ultimately, it will be paying on the policy somehow; there would be no benefit to contesting it when it is tapped into for long-term care benefits.

Swap

What if you bought a life insurance policy many years ago without an accelerated death benefit rider? Instead of cashing in your policy and incurring potential income taxes on investment gains from years of accumulating significant cash value, you can choose to merely swap your policy for another insurance policy with the accelerated death benefit rider and avoid any income taxes when you acquire the new policy. Or maybe you have invested in conservative "let me sleep at night" investments such as certificates of deposit that offer little in the way of interest in an economy of low interest rates. You, too, might find that you can be well served by purchasing a life insurance policy that can provide you with long-term care benefits, life insurance benefits, and investment benefits.

But That's Not All

In even more instances, it makes sense to use a life insurance policy with an accelerated death benefit as a planning vehicle for long-term care needs. If one spouse, due to health reasons, is unable to qualify under increasingly stringent underwriting standards for long-term care insurance, the couple might consider buying a second-to-die universal life policy. As the name implies, with a second-to-die policy, the insurance company does not pay the insurance policy proceeds until both the husband and wife have died. Columbus Life offers such a policy for which the underwriting standards are less stringent. Such a policy could provide long-term care benefits if the surviving spouse requires nursing home care.

Other Considerations

Many considerations arise when buying a life insurance policy with the intention of making it available as a source of funds for long-term care needs. Does the policy restrict coverage to nursing homes, or will it pay for assisted living or at-home care? How is the amount of the long-term care benefit calculated? Is an inflation rider available? These are important considerations when comparing policies and choosing one to best meet your needs.

Creative minds in the insurance industry have also come up with life insurance products that provide a life insurance policy coupled with a right to purchase long-term care insurance at specific time periods in the future. This gives you the opportunity to evaluate your situation at various stages of your life.

Deferred Annuities

Another creative way to provide for the costs of possible long-term care is through a deferred annuity. Many people (including myself) have been critical of annuities as an appropriate investment for older people, but it is probably better to think of annuities like carbohydrates: They are not bad in and of themselves, but if used inappropriately, they could be bad for you. One criticism of annuities as an investment for older people is the penalties that are attached to premature withdrawal. However, some deferred annuities are available with a provision for a penalty-free withdrawal amount if the proceeds are used for long-term care needs. Generally, a deferred annuity does not allow the surrender or withdrawal of amounts from the annuity without a "surrender charge," but in this instance, that charge would be waived to permit money from the annuity to be used for long-term care needs.

Just as a long-distance runner benefits from loading up on carbohydrates, an older person might benefit from buying an annuity to be available for long-term care needs. This is true particularly when age and health considerations might make the option of buying life insurance for those needs either unavailable or too costly. People within the ages of 65 and 85 might find that annuities offer a better buy than life insurance.

People in their 50s and early 60s who are in good health might find that life insurance offers more coverage for their premium dollars and would opt for the low-carb alternative of life insurance instead of annuities to meet their long-term care needs.

Disability Insurance

Another option some companies offer permits people between the ages of 60 and 70 who have disability insurance to exchange their disability policy for a long-term care insurance policy. A particular advantage is that the policyholder is not required to meet any insurability standards at the time of the exchange.

Surf and Turf

People who have difficulty making up their minds at a restaurant can always choose the surf and turf. When it comes to long-term care planning, mixing long-term care insurance policies, life insurance policies, and annuities in varying degrees to meet your long-term care needs also can be a rather savory choice.

For example, a person might consider buying a long-term care insurance policy with a short benefit period that correspondingly has a lower premium. The need for more extensive long-term care coverage could be met by combining that long-term care insurance policy with a life insurance policy that has a long-term care rider. Another option would be to reverse the emphasis by having a life insurance policy with a long-term care rider cover the initial long-term care needs, and supplement that policy with a long-term care insurance policy.

As always, the mantra "Do the math" applies. Have your insurance agent compare the premiums by varying the products and coverage, with the ultimate goal of meeting your possible future needs for long-term care in a manner that is most cost-effective for you.

A Workable Solution

In a 2005 statement to the House Ways and Means Committee, Professor Yung-Ping Chen of the University of Massachusetts Boston, an eminent scholar in the field of gerontology, proposed an interesting three-prong approach to paying for long-term care services. Professor Chen's proposal, which he has labeled a "three-legged-stool" model, uses long-term care insurance along with public and private funding to meet the needs of Americans for long-term care services in an inventive and eminently workable solution.

Professor Chen starts with the recognition that many people both lack sufficient funds to privately pay for long-term care services and are unwilling to purchase long-term care insurance. He proposes diverting a small amount of a retiree's Social Security cash benefits, such as 5 percent, to fund a program that would pay for basic long-term care services. The trade-off, Professor Chen explains, is a small amount of retirement income for long-term care protection that, in turn, provides greater overall economic security for the retiree. Under the terms of his proposal, this Social Security–funded program would cover the costs of either a year in a nursing home or 2 years of home care. This coverage, in turn, would be supplemented by the purchase of long-term care insurance policies, the premiums for which would be reduced because of the benefits provided by the Social Security–funded prong of the three-legged stool, which would be used before the long-term care insurance policy would be required to pay any benefit.

The third leg of the stool would be private funding, which, in turn, would be substantially reduced because of the coverage provided by the other two elements of the program. Professor Chen's proposal is a realistic and innovative way of meeting long-term care needs for a growing segment of the population. To date, Congress has not taken action to follow up on this proposal, but hope springs eternal.

Planning for long-term care in a nursing home for you or a family member presents problems. For baby boomers, the planning is for an event that might or might not occur far off in the future. For the parents of baby boomers, the need is more imminent, but the costs to meet that need looming closer on the horizon can be staggering. Fortunately, through inventive uses of life insurance and other financial products, more choices are now available beyond long-term care insurance to help meet those needs.

Part III
GOVERNMENT PROGRAMS

11

SOCIAL SECURITY

*"If all the economists were laid end to end,
they'd never reach a conclusion."*
—George Bernard Shaw

A n old Indian legend tells of six blind men who each touched a different part of an elephant and came to conclusions of what it was like. One thought the elephant was like a wall, another a spear, another a snake, still another a tree, another a fan, and the last a rope. Of course, there was some truth in the observations of each of them, but all of them missed important details that would more accurately describe the elephant.

Social Security is an elephant. You will hear it described in many ways, and often there will be kernels of truth in the observations. But just as often, important information is missing that could have given you a better understanding of the true nature of Social Security.

I will tell you the truth.

Although I have a steadfast rule never to trust anyone who asks me to trust him, you can trust me: I'm a lawyer. Okay, maybe that did not convince you—perhaps you should just read what I say and make up your own mind.

Basic Coverage

The Social Security system provides basic coverage as good as a defense designed by coach Bill Bellichik of the New England Patriots. To be fully insured under the Social Security system, you need to have earned 40 credits over your working lifetime. This is not a particularly difficult condition to meet. You can get as many as 4 credits per year based upon your earnings. In 2006, you need to have earned only $970 to earn a credit, so even earning as little as $38,880 would provide you with the maximum number of credits to be fully insured. Presently, more than 96 percent of workers pay into the Social Security system.

Calculating Your Benefits

Not quite the same as counting your blessings, but perhaps equally important, the amount that a person receives for Social Security retirement benefits is based upon average earnings over the person's highest-earning 35 years. The number of credits earned above the qualifying 40 credits is irrelevant.

COLAs

One of the most refreshing acronyms is COLA, which stands for cost of living adjustment. Social Security retirement benefits are increased automatically each year based upon the increase in the Bureau of Labor Statistics' Consumer Price Index for Urban Wage Earners and Clerical Workers (CPI-W). In 2006, the increase was 4.1 percent.

Look for Your Annual Statement

Okay, it does not have the ring of "Look for the Union Label," which, despite our best intentions, some of us found ourselves singing in our minds back in 1975. But the annual statement that we get from the Social Security Administration is a key document that contains specific information on our earnings throughout our working lives. When you get your annual statement, review it carefully. Make sure that the information is correct, in general. In particular, make sure that you are properly credited for your highest-earning 35 years of wages because those years determine the amount of your benefit.

You should also carefully review the statement for not just your earnings history, but also your personal information, such as your name and birth date. If a mistake has been made, you can correct it in a timely fashion—it will become an emergency if you wait to correct mistakes until you are about to apply for Social Security benefits.

By the way, that catchy tune "Look for the Union Label" used in a commercial for the Ladies Garment Workers Union has an interesting history itself. Advertising guru Paula Green, who also came up with the slogan "We Try Harder" for Avis, wrote the words. Malcolm Dobbs wrote the music, and it became a hit with American consumers as part of a commercial intended to make consumers aware that cheap, non-union-made clothing was hurting American workers.

The Times They Are A-Changing

In 1965, about two-thirds of American workers waited until they were 65 or older to begin receiving benefits. Now more than half take early retirement payments at age 62. Three-quarters of workers choose to get their Social Security retirement benefits before they reach full retirement age (see Table 11.1).

Table 11.1   Full Retirement Age

Year of Birth	Retirement Age for Receiving Full Social Security Benefits
Before 1938	65
1938	65 and 2 months
1939	65 and 4 months

(continues)

Table 11.1   Full Retirement Age (continued)

Year of Birth	Retirement Age for Receiving Full Social Security Benefits
1940	65 and 6 months
1941	65 and 8 months
1942	65 and 10 months
1943–1954	66
1955	66 and 2 months
1956	66 and 4 months
1957	66 and 6 months
1958	66 and 8 months
1959	66 and 10 months
1960	67

Show Me the Money

Many Americans under full retirement age have taken up Cuba Gooding Jr.'s tagline in the 1996 movie *Jerry Maguire*. They choose to start receiving Social Security benefits as early as age 62 rather than wait until their full retirement age. The age for receiving early Social Security retirement benefits was set at 62 for men in 1961. It had previously been lowered in 1956 for women to age 62.

The problem with receiving early Social Security retirement benefits is that you receive less money. Or do you? If you elect to start receiving Social Security benefits before you reach the age of full retirement, your monthly benefit check is reduced a fraction of a percent for each month before your full retirement age. On average, if you retire at 62, your monthly check will be about 20 percent less than if you had waited until full retirement age. However, according to the Social Security Administration, based upon what some actuary in a cubicle is telling them, taking early retirement benefits will not actually decrease the amount you receive over your lifetime. The reduced monthly check is balanced out by the fact that you begin receiving the money years earlier.

Consider the Social Security Administration as a helpful friend when it comes to helping you determine when to retire. The Social Security Administration has interactive benefit calculators on its Web site, www.ssa.gov, that can provide tremendous assistance in making retirement decisions. These calculators enable you to compare the amounts that you would receive by retiring at different ages with other variables such as your projections of future earnings.

A Bird in the Hand

Some people believe it is best to get your money from Social Security as early as possible, at age 62, so that you can have more control over investing that money rather than leaving it up to Uncle Sam to invest. In addition, taking your Social Security benefits earlier could enable you to leave more of your money to compound in tax-deferred investments, such as IRAs, for a longer period of time.

Delayed Satisfaction

Workers who postpone applying for Social Security benefits till age 70 will receive a greater monthly payment for the rest of their lives. For each year people born in the years 1937 and 1938 put off claiming Social Security retirement benefits after they reach full retirement age and until age 70, they receive an increase of Social Security benefits of 6.5 percent. People born in 1939 and 1940 who delay claiming Social Security retirement benefits get a 7 percent annual increase in benefits, people born in 1941 and 1942 get an annual increase of 7.5 percent, and people born in 1943 or later get an 8 percent increase.

Over-Under

In sports betting, you can make a bet called the "over-under," in which you choose to bet on whether the total number of points amassed by both teams, such as in a football game, will either exceed or be less than the casino's "over-under" figure. In Social Security, your determination of whether to take your benefits early or later is a similar bet with the Social Security Administration.

In this case, the over-under figure set by the Social Security Administration is its calculation of your life expectancy. Increased benefit amounts for delaying retirement are intended to equalize the total amount that a person would receive if he or she postponed claiming Social Security benefits with someone who retired early and received a reduced amount if both lived to their Social Security Administration's actuarially computed life expectancies. However, the Social Security actuaries do not know you. They do not know your health or the likelihood that you will live shorter or longer than what they believe your life expectancy will be. Strictly looking at the morbid question of how long you expect to live, if you think you will live less than what Social Security projects as your life expectancy, you are better off taking the money early. If you think you will live longer than projected, you should delay retirement.

Take the Money and Run

So when does it make sense to take the money and run?

The initial no-brainer answer to that question is that if you need the money and do not have other sufficient sources of income, you should take the money early. If you come from a long line of short lines—that is, your family history is not one of longevity—you may want to take the money early. Similarly, if your health is already poor, go for the early money.

Conversely, if you are healthy and come from a family blessed with longevity, you might want to put off starting your Social Security retirement benefits until you can receive the larger benefit amount available to you if you put off receiving benefits until you are of full retirement age or beyond.

A Work in Progress

If you are still working, you might want to wait to claim Social Security retirement benefits. Once you reach full retirement age, however, the amount that you earn does not reduce the amount of your monthly benefit check; if you are still working and have not reached the age of full retirement, the amount of your monthly check is reduced. In 2006, for every $2 you earn over $12,480, your early retirement benefits are reduced by $1.

Until 2000, people who waited until their full retirement age but continued working were penalized by having their benefits reduced by $1 for every $3 they earned over $17,000. If this rule were still in effect today, someone earning around $75,000 would not receive any benefits before age 70.

Now that the earnings limitation has been removed for workers of full retirement age (which for people born in 1941 who are reaching full retirement age in 2006 is 65 years and 8 months), the question becomes whether to claim their Social Security retirement benefits now and continue to work, or delay claiming their benefits and get a larger check for each year delayed, up to age 70.

Getting a Larger Check Later

Putting off applying for Social Security retirement benefits and getting a bigger monthly check could be enticing if you have considerable longevity in your family or if you married a much younger person who will most likely outlive you and collect Social Security retirement survivor benefits.

A surviving spouse of full retirement age can receive his or her deceased spouse's full Social Security retirement benefits. The surviving spouse can receive reduced survivor benefits as early as age 60. A surviving spouse between the ages of 60 and his or her age of full retirement will get between 71 and 94 percent of the deceased spouse's benefits.

As in the classic *Seinfeld* episode in which George was humiliated when he was caught putting the same chip back into a dip after taking a bite out of the chip, "double dipping" is not allowed. If a surviving spouse is entitled to his or her own Social Security retirement benefits in an amount greater than what he or she would receive as a surviving spouse, the spouse is paid the larger of the two eligible benefits.

Loophole

A surviving spouse who is mathematically inclined might determine that he or she is better off taking an early surviving spouse benefit until he or she reaches full retirement age and then switching to his or her own Social Security retirement benefit. The law allows this. Whether this makes sense for a particular person depends on the age of the surviving spouse and his or her earnings, compared to the Social Security benefit derived from the deceased spouse. Fortunately, for those of us who are not mathematically inclined, the Social Security Administration Web site, www.ssa.gov, has interactive online calculators that can help you find the answer to this question.

Another Reason to Delay Taking Benefits

For many of us, procrastination is its own reward. However, putting off applying for Social Security benefits and continuing to work could be of some benefit to you if the added working years will make a considerable difference in your 35 highest wage-earning years and raise the amount of your benefit. Again, you can calculate this by going to the Social Security Web site, www.ssa.gov, and using the calculators there.

By the way, with logic only a government bureaucrat could possibly comprehend, if your birthday is on the first day of any month, the determination of your benefits is made as if you were born in the previous month.

Spousal Benefits

There are many benefits to being married. One that is easier to quantify is the right of a spouse to receive a spousal benefit equal to half of the other spouse's full Social Security retirement amount. If your spouse is eligible to receive Social Security retirement benefits based upon his or her own work history, he or she will receive whichever benefit payment is greater.

Loophole

Sometimes the math works out so that a married person can choose to take early benefits at age 62 based on his or her own work history, and then when the other spouse reaches full retirement age, switch back to take spousal benefits. In many instances, this results in an increase of total benefits. As always, do the math.

> *"Today it takes more brains and effort to make out the income-tax form than it does to make the income."*
> —Alfred E. Neuman of *MAD Magazine*

Then there is the question of income taxes. If you file as an individual and your gross income plus nontaxable interest (such as from tax-free bonds) and half of your Social Security benefits are between $25,000 and $34,000, you may have to pay income taxes on half of your Social Security benefits. If your income as just described is greater than $34,000, as much as 85 percent of your Social Security benefits is subject to income tax. When you start taking your Social Security benefits, whether it is early, at full retirement age, or later (up to age 70), you have to consider the money you might lose to income taxes when you figure what you can earn by investing the money that you receive.

A Myth Is as Good as a Mile

A lot of myths surround Social Security and only confuse and scare older Americans. The truth, while still serious, is not quite so bad.

Social Security Is Broke

Some doom-saying nay-sayers say that the Social Security system is as broken as Humpty Dumpty. Well, not exactly. In fact, Social Security is in considerably better shape now than it was in 1983 when President Ronald Reagan set up a commission to study it. At that time, the Social Security trust fund reserves were just about gone. Now they are about $1.6 trillion in the black.

Some have said that program will become insolvent as soon as 2018. So if the most pessimistic projections end up being true, in 2018 the money taken in will be insufficient to cover the benefits being paid out. However, because Social Security has been running at a surplus and is expected to do so for many more years, the system has billions of dollars of savings to pay for those rainy days. Even under the most dire of projections, Social Security will have enough money to pay all of its obligations until the year 2042—and even then it is projected to have enough money to pay for 70 percent of the benefits expected to be paid then by the Social Security system. Some recent projections from the Congressional Budget Office have even pushed the date back to 2052 before the present system would be unable to fully pay its obligations, and they raise the amount it will be able to pay even at that time to 80 percent of benefits.

It is also important to remember that these projections that the president and others are throwing out as facts are, in fact, just guesses. No one really knows how future life expectancy, population growth, immigration, economic growth, inflation, and interest rates will ultimately influence the efficacy of the Social Security system. One of the more curious underlying assumptions behind the negative projections for the future of Social Security is a sharp decline in immigration. This is even more startling when you consider that if the projected decline in our country's birthrate occurs, there will be an increased need and opportunity for foreign workers.

If past performance is an indication of the likelihood of making successful predictions, consider that the Social Security trustees were projecting in 1997 that the trust fund would be exhausted by 2029. A period of better-than-expected economic growth proved their predictions to be woefully inaccurate. As Mark Twain said, "Facts are stubborn, but statistics are more pliable."

End of the Universe

An astronomer was giving a speech about the end of the universe. He explained that the Big Bang had occurred 4.6 billion years ago and that 10 trillion, trillion, trillion years from now, our world will come to an end. Suddenly there was a scream from the back of the room. A student stood up and said, "Did you say the world would end in 10 trillion, trillion years?" The astronomer responded by saying, "No, I said 10 trillion, trillion, trillion years." "Oh," responded the student, "that is much better."

Social Security probably will not be around 10 trillion, trillion, trillion years from now, but it will be around and pretty damn solvent for the next 37 years. That will be true even if we do nothing, which sometimes is a pretty good thing to do when you are talking about politicians. Problems exist, but this is not a time for panic. I'll let you know when that time comes.

Lions and Tigers and Baby Boomers, Oh My!

If she were alive today, Cassandra, the prophet of doom in *The Iliad* (and reportedly a Boston Red Sox fan), would be decrying the fact that when the approximately 76 million baby boomers start retiring, the Social Security system will fall apart. Cassandra and others of her ilk point out that the Social Security system today is funded by the payments of three workers for every retiree receiving benefits—by the year 2040, there will be only two workers for each retiree.

Calm down, Cassandra. Things are not so bad. First of all, workers today are earning larger wages and paying more into the Social Security trust fund to build up those reserves. Perhaps more important, many baby boomers are planning to work much later in life than would have been previously expected. Some enjoy the challenge and stimulation of working; others flat out need the money. Regardless of the motivation for their continued employment, these baby boomers who are working past retirement age will continue to pay into the system.

Who Wins Under Private Accounts?

The cornerstone of President Bush's proposal to "reform" Social Security is to have private accounts through which younger workers could choose to set aside a small percentage of their payroll taxes. These funds would go into private accounts that could be invested in the stock market. Without belaboring the many advantages and disadvantages of private accounts, it is important during this time of budget deficits and tremendous strains on the national budget to note one key fact: Private accounts will not increase the solvency of the Social Security program, which was the problem that most people thought was the one that needed to be solved. Not only will private accounts not help reduce the drain on the Social Security trust fund, but the transition costs to put private accounts into effect would cost as little as 754 billion dollars and as much as a trillion dollars.

So who does win under private accounts? Take a guess. Politicians in favor of individual private accounts have always emphasized that "the people" will make out so much better. Yet the real winners will be the large brokerage houses, banks, and mutual funds that will be doing the investing. They will be making money whether the markets go up or down. The fees that will be generated from millions of private accounts will be astounding.

Since 1988, private accounts have been available to British workers. During that time, the management fees and marketing costs passed on to individual workers have reduced the return on their investments by 43 percent. If the goal is to get a better return on the Social Security trust fund than that provided by U.S. Treasury securities, permitting the federal government to invest in the stock market would be far more effective at far less cost.

Don't Throw the Baby out with the Bathwater

Did you ever notice how violent some old sayings are? Throwing babies out with bathwater. Killing multiple birds with a single stone. What were they thinking? However, the lesson of this proverb is helpful. It is not necessary to make wholesale, expensive changes to the Social Security system to extend its solvency. The car needs a tune-up. We do not need a new car.

Tweak One

The first change would raise the maximum wages upon which Social Security taxes are levied. Presently, income over $94,200 per year is not subject to Social Security tax. The Social Security Administration adjusts this figure annually. Raising that cap, which would affect only about 6 percent of American workers, would result in much additional money being paid into the system without unduly burdening taxpayers. It also would take little cost to put into effect.

Tweak Two

Presently, the Social Security trust fund is invested in low-earning U.S. Treasury bonds. If the proponents of private accounts think that it would be a good idea for Social Security funds to be invested in the stock market and other better-paying investments, why not invest a portion of the Social Security trust fund in those same investments without any of the monstrous start-up costs and downside risks of individual accounts? And what about short-term downturns in the stock market? They will happen. What do we do when individual private accounts have lost money? Individual investors are in the market for the relatively short run; Uncle Sam is in it for the long run. Private accounts will not work. But investing Social Security trust fund money in the stock market will work, at a tremendously lower cost to the taxpayers. You do the math.

Tweak Three

If you can't lower the water, raise the bridge. When the Social Security system first went into effect in 1935, the usual retirement age was 65, which made good business sense for Social Security because the average life expectancy was a mere 60 years. Facing a serious Social Security shortfall in 1983, a law was passed to gradually increase the age for full retirement to age 67 for people born in 1960 or later. For people born between the years of 1943 and 1954, a group that includes most baby boomers, the age for full retirement is 66 years.

Increasing the full retirement age to a more realistic 70 years would take little tax money to implement and could result in people paying into the system longer and taking money out later. Presently, life expectancy is 77 years, but if you make it to age 65, your life expectancy becomes 83 years. Of course, with so many workers choosing to take early retirement benefits, to bolster Social Security for the future, the ages of both early and full retirement would have to be extended. Unfortunately for society's most vulnerable people, raising the age of early retirement would be a particular hardship. Special provisions could be made for these people, however.

According to Ron Gebhardtsbauer, a senior pension fellow at the American Academy of Actuaries, even increasing the retirement age by 1 year would reduce the multitrillion-dollar projected deficit for Social Security over the next 75 years by one-third.

Tweak Four

A controversial proposal would involve a "means test" for Social Security so that wealthier individuals would get reduced benefits, depending upon their income or assets. Means testing has been considered by many to be a bit mean spirited. Perhaps even more important, it also is not very much within the realm of realistic politics. It is unlikely that Congressmen and Senators, who are perpetually campaigning, would be willing to anger a significant number of influential members of the electorate by passing laws that would reduce the Social Security benefits to be paid to wealthier Social Security recipients.

Blame It on the Bossa Nova

This song, sung by Eydie Gorme, rose to no. 7 on the charts in 1963. And to show how there really is nothing new under the sun, the words *bossa nova* in Portuguese mean "new wave," although it is hard to think of Eydie Gorme and the punk rock movement of the 1980s known as "New Wave" as having any similarities.

Blame is important for many people. If we have to point a finger at someone for problems with the Social Security system, perhaps we should consider the legislative and executive branches of the federal government, which have too often spent our tax money in a manner that would insult drunken sailors.

For many years, the Social Security trust fund has been running at an extreme surplus, taking in far more money than it has paid out. This excess money has been invested in U.S. Treasury securities. But unlike you or me when we have a debt, Congress seems to forget that it has to pay this money back to retiring American baby boomers in the not-so-distant future. In fact, using an accounting practice that would make an Enron accountant blush, the debt that the federal government owes to the Social Security trust fund is not even counted in the federal budget as a debt. Instead of planning ahead for debts it knows it will have to start repaying soon, Congress has been using money loaned by American workers to the government on programs, both necessary and unnecessary. Yet it still manages to operate at a deficit that will become worse when not only the Social Security trust fund money will have to be paid back, but when Congress has to find other sources to borrow from to finance government operations.

As Will Rogers said, "I don't make jokes. I just watch the government and report the facts."

12

MEDICARE

"Thanks to modern medicine we are no longer forced to endure prolonged pain, disease, discomfort and wealth."
—Robert Orben

Medicare, which is more formally known as Title XVIII of the Social Security Act (I don't know about you, but I think that Roman numerals should be reserved for really important things, like Super Bowls), is a national system of health insurance for all recipients of Social Security who are at least 65 years old or disabled. Medicare eligibility is not based upon either your assets or your income.

Alphabet Soup

Medicare is like alphabet soup: A, B, C, and now D. Medicare Part A primarily provides insurance coverage for hospital care. Part B focuses on coverage of doctor's bills and outpatient services. Part A does not require the Medicare recipient to pay any premiums. Part B is funded partly through monthly premium payments of Medicare beneficiaries; the federal government pays the rest of the cost. Both Medicare Part A and Medicare Part B also require Medicare recipients to make co-payments and cover the cost of deductibles for many of the services provided by Medicare A and B.

A *co-payment* is the amount that you must pay out of your own pocket for a service covered by your insurance. A *deductible* is the amount that you must pay annually before your insurance will begin to cover any of your needs.

Medicare Part C was formerly known as Medicare+Choice and now is known as Medicare Advantage. (Unlike the 1950s television show *Dragnet*, though, I do not think that the name was changed to protect the innocent.) Part C provides increased benefits for a fee through private health insurance programs such as health maintenance organizations (HMOs), and preferred provider organizations (PPOs), and provider-sponsored organizations (PSOs).

HMOs, which are the most familiar of the Medicare Advantage plans, include all Medicare Part A and Part B health care benefits. In most HMOs, however, you generally can use only doctors and hospitals that are a part of the HMO. In most HMOs, your primary care physician is the gatekeeper to further treatment: You must see him or her before you can receive more specialized services under your plan, and you need a referral from your primary care physician before you can see a specialist. The biggest advantage to the patient is that the cost of participating in an HMO is generally less than with traditional Medicare.

With a preferred provider organization (PPO), you can see any doctor who is in your plan without a referral. However, if you go outside of your plan to a doctor or hospital, you pay extra. A PPO is a health-care network established by the doctors and hospitals themselves.

It's as Simple as ABC

According to Frank Sinatra in the 1955 song "Love and Marriage," you can't have one without the other. And Frank should know: He was married four times.

Judging by Frank Sinatra, love and marriage might not always go together, but Medicare Parts A, B, and C do. You truly can't have one without the other. To be eligible to purchase Medicare C coverage, you must already be covered by Medicare A and B. The coverage provided by the various Medicare C policies can differ a great deal.

Important Little Detail

In most states, if you enroll in a Medicare Part C plan during the 7-month period beginning when you turn 65, you can qualify for the coverage without having to answer any medical questions on your application. If you delay enrolling in a Medicare Part C plan until after that time, you will be required to complete a medical questionnaire and can be denied coverage due to health reasons. It is wise not to follow the advice of Mark Twain, who said, "Never put off until tomorrow what you can put off until the day after tomorrow."

Extra Benefit

Some Medicare Advantage plans actually pay all or part of your Medicare Part B premium, which can be a real money saver.

Medicare Part B: Pay Me Now or Pay Me Later

If you are still working when you reach the age of 65, you could be covered by a health insurance plan at your place of employment and will not need to sign up for Medicare Part B. However, generally if you are not covered by a group health insurance policy at work and you fail to enroll in Medicare B during the initial window of opportunity—the 7-month period that begins 3 months before you reach the age of 65—the premium for Medicare Part B when you do enroll later increases by 10 percent for each month that you could have enrolled but chose not to. You will continue to pay this penalty for the rest of your life.

Medicare Part B Premium Increase

Traditionally, the federal government has subsidized the cost of Medicare Part B coverage. In 2006, the covered individual paid 25 percent of the cost of Medicare Part B coverage, and the federal government paid 75 percent. Starting in 2007, individuals with incomes of between $80,000 and $100,000, as well as married couples with annual incomes of between $160,000 and $200,000, will be responsible for 35 percent of the Part B coverage cost. Individuals with annual incomes of between $100,000 and $150,000, as well as married couples with annual incomes of between $200,000 and $300,000, will have to pay 50 percent of the Part B coverage cost. Finally, individuals with incomes above $200,000 and married couples with incomes above $400,000 will be required to pay 80 percent of the Part B coverage. These income amounts will be increased yearly in accordance with the Consumer Price Index.

Just as we all are aware that Santa Claus always knows whether you have been good or bad, the IRS may know even more about you than Santa Claus. And unlike Santa Claus, who will not tell your parents anything about you, the IRS will provide income information on you to the administrators of Medicare: Make sure you do not lie about your income. Be good, for goodness's sake.

Medicare Part B Deductible

In addition to a covered individual's responsibility for the monthly premium, Medicare Part B enrollees must pay an annual deductible. This is $124 in 2006 and will be indexed for inflation in later years. The person covered by Medicare Part B must pay this deductible amount before Medicare begins to pay for services.

Medicare Part B Preventive Services

A number of good preventive health services available to Medicare B subscribers can help identify problems early, when they are most correctible. These include cardiovascular screenings for cholesterol, lipid, and triglyceride levels every 5 years. Also included are colorectal cancer screenings, which are imperative for people over 50 years old.

I was a bit nervous before my first sigmoidoscopy test, in which a scope was sent up my nether regions. Before going to the hospital, in an attempt to provide a little humor to lessen the tension, I placed some heavy tape across my butt cheeks. Written on the tape were the words "One way, do not enter." The doctor and nurse found this amusing, as did I until the tape was removed. Apparently I had misjudged the fur factor on my cheeks. In any event, at age 50 (oh, alright, 55, I procrastinated), I had my first colonoscopy, and the test was nowhere near the ordeal I had feared. This is a simple test that can save your life. If you are over 50, do yourself and your family a favor, and have one done. Colon cancer caught early is highly curable. Caught late, it is not.

Medicare B also covers diabetes screening, flu shots, glaucoma tests, Pap smears, hepatitis B shots, prostate cancer screenings, annual mammograms, and a full physical exam within the first 6 months that you enroll in Medicare B.

Mind the Gap

This phrase was a mystery to me for many years until I learned that it referred to signs and warnings about the dangerous gaps between London's underground railway system subways and the station platforms. The phrase first was used at the Embankment Station of the Northern Line, where the gap was particularly big.

But subways and clothing stores are not the only places with gaps. Medicare also has gaps in its Medicare A and B coverage, as well as expensive deductibles and co-payment provisions. Meeting this need are private health insurance policies referred to as Medigap policies. Medicare has authorized 10 standard Medigap plans offering different benefits. In keeping with the alphabet soup nature of Medicare, the 10 Medicare-authorized Medigap policies are referred to as policies A through J. Again, as with Medicare Part C, you must be enrolled in Medicare Plans A and B to be eligible to purchase a Medigap policy.

Before the passage of Medicare Part D to cover prescription drug costs, Medigap plans H, I, and J covered prescription drugs. When Medicare Part D became effective on January 1, 2006, these Medigap plans that covered prescription drug benefits were no longer allowed to be sold. The exception is that a person who already had a Medigap policy H, I, or J covering prescription drugs could renew the policy if he or she chose not to enroll in Medicare Part D.

Anyone covered through a Medigap policy for prescription drug costs also can enroll in Medigap plans A, B, C, or F without a waiting period for coverage for pre-existing conditions and without a medical questionnaire, as long as they enrolled in Medicare Part D during the initial sign-up period and also applied for a new Medigap policy within 63 days of coverage under Medicare Part D.

Traditional Medicare or Medicare Advantage?

An important decision is whether to stay with traditional Medicare coverage or change to one of the new Medicare Advantage-managed care plans. Your Uncle Sam wants you to switch. How do we know that? It's easy. He is giving billions of dollars to insurance companies to set up these new plans and lure Americans to them in the hope of reducing the cost and increasing the efficiency of the health-care system. Seniors who want to stay with the traditional Medicare programs with which they have become comfortable will find themselves stacking health-care premiums upon health-care premiums. In 2006, the Medicare Plan B premium is $88.50 per month; it costs up to $200 per month for Medigap policies to cover the co-payment and deductible costs of Medicare Plan B. On top of these is the cost of the new Medicare D prescription drug benefit. However, in return, you get greater choice over physicians to use.

On the other hand, there are advantages to Medicare Advantage. Your prescription drugs might be covered, so you would not need a Medigap policy because your Medicare Advantage program would already cover those benefits. Again, the drawback is that your choices for medical care are limited to the physicians and hospitals that participate in your particular Medicare Advantage program.

As if you did not have enough to worry about, there is a distinct possibility that the subsidies of the Medicare Advantage programs will soon fade away, particularly in light of increasing federal budget deficits. Without those federal subsidies, the insurance companies sponsoring the Medicare Advantage programs will have little choice but to raise the premiums. Sure, if you find that you are not comfortable with your Medicare Advantage program after a year, you can switch back to traditional Medicare coverage, but (and this is a really big *but*) you might be unable to obtain a Medigap policy because of a pre-existing illness for which you need ongoing treatment: Medigap insurers then could deny coverage or raise your premium rate to the stratosphere.

Medicare Prescription Drug Coverage

"It was clear as mud but it covered the ground."

I remember this line from a Harry Belafonte 1954 song, "Man Piaba" that was on a live album of my sister's that I used to play over and over. Harry Belafonte did not write the song to describe the Medicare drug plan, but he could have. Trying to comprehend the Medicare prescription drug plan can give you such a headache that you need a prescription drug.

The first opportunity to sign up for the plan ran from November 15, 2005, until May 15, 2006. You can choose from national plans as well as regional and statewide plans. The first step is to educate yourself. Don't throw out letters from former employers or Medicare that you might think are junk mail: They could contain important information for you.

Picking vanilla or chocolate is a fairly simple choice. When the ice cream flavor choices start reaching 60 or more, the choices become more difficult to make. The more difficult it is to make the decision, the more likely it is that people will just freeze and not make one at all. Failing to make a decision becomes a decision itself. There is no harm in not being able to pick an ice cream flavor when you're dazzled by too many choices. Unfortunately, failing to make a choice when it comes to a Medicare prescription drug program can have serious consequences.

The Medicare prescription drug program initially involved more than 80 insurance companies with 10 different companies selling plans on a national basis. The 10 companies initially approved to provide national prescription drug coverage are Aetna Life Insurance, Connecticut General Life Insurance, Coventry Health and Life Insurance, Medco Containment Life Insurance, MemberHealth, PacifiCare Life and Health Insurance, SilverScript Insurance, Unicare, United HealthCare Insurance, and WellCare Health Plans. However, there are also a number of plans that are limited by region or state.

In 2006, Alaska had the fewest stand-alone prescription drug plans (27), while Pennsylvania and West Virginia had the most (52). Overall, in 2006, the first year of the Medicare prescription drug program, there are 3,000 stand-alone prescription drug programs. If you live in different states during the year, you do not necessarily need to sign up for one of the national plans, as long as the plan in which you enroll provides mail-order prescriptions.

Many of the plans differ significantly, with deductibles ranging from no deductible to almost $100. A deductible is the amount that you must pay out of your own funds before the insurance kicks in and starts paying. Co-payments also vary, as do the specific drugs covered. Co-payments are your share of the cost of a covered prescription. Each plan has it own particular list of drugs, called its formulary. You must pay out of pocket for any of your prescription drug needs that do not appear on your plan's formulary.

Fly in the Ointment

A fly in the ointment is a pretty disgusting image and phrase describing something that interferes with a desired outcome. However, the derivation of this phrase goes back to the Bible, specifically the Book of Ecclesiastes: "Dead flies cause the ointment of the apothecary to send forth a stinking savour."

Having a prescription drug program through Medicare would seem to be a tremendous benefit to older Americans, but the complexity of the program, not to mention its other shortcomings, significantly taints that benefit for many people. Choosing a Medicare prescription drug plan is fraught with problems. Not all plans cover all drugs; so some of your drugs might be covered by one plan, while another plan might cover the rest. And even though you are tied to a plan for a year, the plan can change the drugs it covers with as little as 60 days notice to you.

Comparing plans can be quite difficult. The premiums vary significantly from plan to plan. Some plans have deductibles; others do not. Some require co-payments; others do not. Even the drugs covered vary from plan to plan. It should be a simple matter to merely compare the total costs to you between the various plans that carry the prescription drugs that you use. If the total cost to you in a plan with a higher premium but lower or no deductibles projects is less than the total cost of a plan with a lower premium but higher deductibles, the answer should be apparent. I say "should" because there are so many other variables that make it tough to compare plans.

Insurance or Sex

Late in 2005, Humana, one of the companies offering a Medicare prescription drug program, sent out letters to older Americans explaining its prescription drug program. The letters also provided a telephone number for people who had questions about the company's prescription drug program. Unfortunately, the telephone number in the letter was off by a single digit and sent inquiring seniors to the "Intimate Encounters" sex line. The line did not provide prescription drug insurance, but it did provide services from 99¢ up to $2.99 per minute, depending on the services requested by the caller. Just what the confused callers needed—more choices.

Uncle Sam's Pen Pal

The federal government is notifying about 14 million people who its records indicate are eligible for the Medicare prescription drug program at no cost or for a very nominal payment. People with less than $10,000 of assets and annual incomes of less than $14,345 qualify for this special treatment. The notification from Medicare includes a seven-page application. This application is intended to be clearer than many other federal government forms; however, there are certain to be people whose minds will glaze over when they look at the form. People who receive these forms and who do not understand what is required of them can choose to merely fill in their name and phone number, and return the form. A Medicare representative will then contact the potential applicant by telephone to go over the form and assist in its completion.

Identity Theft

Among the most enterprising people in America today are identity thieves who see every news event as an opportunity to prey upon the unwary and the vulnerable. In an effort to educate people who will be eligible for the new Medicare prescription drug benefit, Social Security employees are calling older Americans to inform them about the program and to verify information on the drug plan applications. Identity thieves posing as government workers are also calling and seeking personal information that can be used for identity theft. An important thing to remember is that the real Social Security callers will not be asking for your Social Security number, birth date, mother's maiden name, or other identifying information. If you or your parent or grandparent is asked for this information, do not provide it. You can verify whether the call is legitimate by calling the Social Security Administration at 800-447-8477. You can get the Social Security Administration's public fraud reporting form at www.socialsecurity.gov/oig/guidelin.htm.

Other Scams

Although the companies approved to offer Medicare prescription drug coverage are permitted by law to solicit your business by telephone, it is a good practice not to trust anyone who requests personal information about you on the phone whom you have not personally called. The better procedure is to ask them to send you information. Door-to-door sales of Medicare prescription drug coverage is not allowed by law, so if someone comes to your home saying that he or she is involved with the Medicare prescription drug program, do not speak with that person.

You can also double-check whether a particular company is authorized to provide Medicare prescription drug coverage either by telephoning Medicare at 1-800-633-4227 or by going to the Medicare Web site, www.medicare.gov.

Drugs in a Nutshell

Private insurance companies that have been approved by Medicare are offering prescription drug plans that differ from plan to plan in the drugs they cover, as well as the deductibles and co-payments required. However, by law, the value of each plan must be at least equal to the standard Medicare prescription drug plan. Under the terms of the standard plan, people are required to pay for the first $250 of the costs for covered drugs each year; 25 percent of the cost of covered drugs between $251 and $2,250, up to a maximum of $500; all of the costs of covered drugs between $2,251 and $5,100; and 5 percent of the cost of covered drugs above $5,101, or a copayment of $2 for covered generic versions of prescription drugs and $5 for covered brand name prescription drugs, whichever is greater. Those enrolled also must pay 100 percent of the costs of prescription drugs that are not covered.

As confusing as that might seem, particularly as to the gap in insurance coverage that is being referred to as the "doughnut hole" of noncoverage for drug costs between $2,251 and $5,100, this is only the standard plan. It is important to remember that the insurance companies participating in the program can vary the standard plan to an actuarial equivalent. This makes sense only to an actuary, but for the rest of us, it means that as long as the overall value provided is equal to or better than the standard Medicare prescription drug plan, the insurance company can provide different coverage.

In an actuarially equivalent plan, the cost sharing can vary through such mechanisms as tiered co-payments. For example, a beneficiary's co-payment could be less for a generic drug than a brand-name drug.

Who Is Keeping Score?

According to Grantland Rice's famous quote, "For when the One Great Scorer comes to write against your name, He marks—not that you won or lost—but how you played the game." That might be true, but while you are alive on this Earth, winning and losing is important. If they were not, scores would not be kept.

Keeping track of your prescription drug purchases is also important because the amount of your insurance coverage depends upon the total cost of your prescription drug purchases over the year. If you buy your drugs through your plan, the company will maintain a running record of the cost of your drug purchases. If you buy your drugs somewhere else, you must make sure that you send the receipts for your purchases to your prescription drug plan provider.

Doughnut Hole or Hell Hole?

Some plans pay for a part of the doughnut hole. For a higher premium payment, some plans pay for the entire doughnut hole and there is no coverage gap. For example, the Humana Complete Plan provides for co-payments until the participant's total out-of-pocket costs reach $3,600. The co-payment cost of generic payments is $7; brand-name prescription drugs have a co-payment of $30. A generic drug is a prescription drug that has the same active ingredients as the more expensive and well-known brand-name drug. Generic drugs come to the marketplace when the patent protection on a particular brand-name drug has expired. As another example, the Aetna Medicare Rx Premier Plan has a $2 co-payment for preferred generic and a $40 co-payment for brand-name prescriptions for 30-day-supply prescriptions and no initial deductible. Further complicating the process of comparing different policies is the fact that some companies have different co-payments for 30- or 90-day supplies of prescriptions.

The standard benefit prototype of the prescription Part D program has you paying a deductible of $250 before coverage kicks in. Then you are responsible for 25 percent of the prescription costs from $251 to $2,250. The doughnut hole appears at that point, and your plan stops paying until your total covered prescription costs reach $5,100.

This unusual setup presents this possibility: If your prescription drug costs are $2,000 per year, the Medicare prescription drug program will pay 66 percent of your prescription costs. But if your prescription costs are $5,000 per year, the program will pay only 30 percent of your prescription drug costs. The people who need coverage most, get the least coverage. These doughnuts are bad for your health. There is some concern that an unintended result of the doughnut hole in coverage (I think, by the way that "goose egg" would have been a better metaphor) is that some seniors will neglect to get their prescription drugs while in the doughnut hole because they will not be able to afford their drugs. For this reason, if you already have a prescription drug program that covers drugs during what would be the doughnut hole period, you would be wise to stay with that coverage.

In another example of either effective lobbying or legislative indifference, the Medicare law prohibits people from being able to purchase supplemental insurance to fill the doughnut hole period.

Sticky Little Detail

Only prescription drugs that your plan covers count toward the $3,600 out-of-pocket prescription drug payments that you must make before the catastrophic coverage of 95 percent of your prescription drug costs of $5,101 or more kicks in. To make things even worse, the cost of any prescriptions that you bought in Canada or any other foreign country do not count toward your costs necessary to reach your catastrophic benefit coverage. This puts you in the unenviable position of paying less for your prescription drug needs by buying Canadian drugs, but never being able to reach your out-of-pocket maximum under the law that would trigger the catastrophic coverage to pay for 95 percent of your drug costs. Thank your congressmen and senators for that one.

Exceptions Process

Each drug plan must develop its own exceptions process under which you can ask the drug plan to cover a nonformulary drug or to reduce the cost sharing for a formulary drug. In other words, you can ask the drug plan to make a ruling that its formulary requirements apply to all plan enrollees except for you. An unfavorable determination can be appealed. The prescribing physician plays an important role in the exception process because an exception will be granted only if the plan agrees with your doctor's certification that no other drug on the plan's formulary would be as effective for you as the drug in question, or that the drugs contained in the plan's formulary would cause adverse consequences to you.

What Are Your Choices for Prescription Drugs?

Everyone who is already covered by Medicare has three options for prescription drug coverage. The first choice is to essentially do nothing and stay in the traditional Medicare program, HMO, or company-retiree plan and not sign up for any of the Medicare prescription drug programs. Whether it makes sense for you to enroll in a Medicare prescription drug plan depends on the premiums required by the plans offered in your area, whether the plans you are considering will cover your particular prescription drug needs, and, most important, whether you can get your prescription drugs more economically through other non-Medicare plans available to you or on your own, such as through Canadian pharmacies.

The second option involves maintaining your traditional Medicare coverage while enrolling in a separate Medicare-approved prescription drug program (PDP).

The third and final option is to enroll in a private health plan that provides Medicare-covered health services as well as prescription drug coverage.

However, it is very important to remember that if you did not enroll during the initial 6-month period when the benefit first became available to you, you could be subject to a premium penalty of at least 1 percent of the national average premium for each month after your initial enrollment period ended until the time of your later enrollment. Fortunately, if you already have prescription drug coverage that is at least as good as Medicare D, you will not be subject to a premium penalty if you enroll in Medicare's prescription drug program within 63 days of leaving your equal or better prescription drug coverage plan.

If you are covered for prescription drugs as a retiree under the health plan of a former employer, you can stay with that plan without having to pay the premium penalty even if your employer withdraws that benefit from your retiree health plan, as long as you promptly enroll in a Medicare D plan within 63 days of losing your prescription drug benefits through your group coverage at work.

The initial enrollment period for people already on Medicare ran from November 15, 2005, until May 15, 2006. Those people who were already covered by Medicare had to join a Medicare prescription drug plan during that time to avoid the potential 1 percent per-month premium penalty for late enrollment. For everyone else, to avoid the late-enrollment premium penalty, potential participants must enroll during the 6-month period that begins during the 3 months prior to the month they go on Medicare and extends until 3 months after the month they first become eligible for Medicare.

What If Your Medigap Policy Pays for Prescriptions?

If your present Medigap policy pays for prescriptions, you have two choices. First, you can choose another Medigap policy that does not cover prescription drugs and sign up for a stand-alone prescription drug plan. Second, you can drop your Medigap plan's prescription drug coverage and enroll in a prescription drug program through Medicare D. Third, you can stay with your present Medigap policy with its prescription coverage. However, ultimately, this will probably turn out to be an expensive choice because the premiums likely will rise for these plans, and few Medigap plans are considered to have creditable coverage to Medicare; you would probably have to pay the late-enrollment fee when you ultimately enroll in a Medicare prescription drug plan.

You cannot have a Medigap plan that covers prescriptions and a Medicare prescription drug plan: You must pick one. Beginning in 2006, no new Medigap policies were allowed to be sold with drug coverage. This means that no new participants can enroll in a Medigap plan's drug benefit. This most likely will cause the premiums to rise.

How Good Are You at Predicting the Future?

Complicating an already complicated decision-making process of whether to enroll in a Medicare prescription drug plan now is the fact that, with the 1 percent per-month penalty for late enrollment, it is not enough to compute the cost to you now for prescription drugs through various plans; you must also predict your future needs in making the decision of whether to enroll now. Even if your drug costs are low now and would not seem to warrant enrolling in a Medicare prescription drug plan, the late-enrollment penalty might influence you to enroll now as a hedge against your future prescription drug needs.

This quandary is one that Congress understood would affect relatively healthy older people because the ultimate success of the Medicare prescription drug program depends upon luring healthy seniors into the program. A basic tenet of health insurance is that premiums from healthy policyholders who do not often use their health insurance help pay for the cost of treating the less healthy policyholders who use their policies more frequently. According to a study by the Kaiser Family Foundation, if 80 percent of healthy seniors enroll in the Medicare prescription drug programs, the premiums will go up only 11 percent in the second year of the program. But if only 20% of these highly prized healthy seniors join the Medicare prescription drug programs, the premiums will rise 42 percent in the second year of the program.

Medicaid

Medicaid recipients must get their coverage through the new Medicare drug plan. If they do not choose a plan themselves, they will be assigned one randomly, which might not even cover the drugs they need.

TRICARE

Military retirees who are covered by the TRICARE for Life program have an easy choice: Do not join any of the prescription drug programs. Benefits negotiated by the federal government with the drug companies are better than any of the those in the Medicare prescription drug plans.

How Do You Tell If Your Present Coverage Is Creditable?

Finally, an easy answer. You should receive a letter from your employer sponsoring your prescription drug plan (or whomever else is sponsoring the plan) stating whether your coverage is creditable (which means it is at least as good as Medicare's). This is important because if it is creditable, you can join a Medicare D prescription drug program later without a penalty. Keep your letters for proof later.

You can also go to www.benefitscheckuprx.org, an easy-to-use interactive Web site that was set up by The National Council on Aging. It allows you to input information and determine whether your present insurance coverage is creditable. The Web site also helps you determine whether or not you qualify for premium subsidies or other programs to assist you with your prescription costs.

If an employer subsequently drops your creditable plan, for example, you can enroll in a Medicare prescription drug plan without a late penalty if your plan was creditable and you sign up for a new plan within 63 days of losing your former coverage.

Things to Consider When Choosing a Drug Plan

After you have determined that it is in your best interest to enroll in a Medicare prescription drug program, you should consider the following issues:

- The amount of the premium.
- The deductible. Will it be the standard $250 or lower? Does the total cost of the prescription drugs that you take at least equal

the deductible amount plus a year's worth of premium payments?

- Does the plan's formulary include the particular drugs you need? Also pay close attention to the strength and dosages of the drugs, and the number of days covered in each prescription.

- Are the pharmacies you presently use in the plan's network of pharmacies?

- Is mail order allowed or required? What are the prices for mail order? How many days' worth of your prescription can you get by mail at a time?

- Does the plan require step therapy, by which you must try other drugs before you are allowed to take the one prescribed by your physician?

- Does the plan use tiered cost sharing, requiring different co-payments for generics and brand-name drugs?

- Are there quantity limitations on the number of prescriptions in a month or the number of pills in a prescription?

- Who sponsors the plan? Are they reliable? Are they experienced?

- What are the plan's rules for temporarily providing you with prescription drugs that are not covered by the plan during a transition period? How long is the transition period?

- What is the plan's exception and appeals process?

- Finally, do you have creditable coverage through employment or the VA so that you do not need to consider a Medicare prescription drug plan?

If You Take a Lot of Drugs

If you take a great deal of prescription drugs, you could be better off with a low-premium plan with few bells and whistles. You might have to pay for $3,600 worth of prescriptions in a year before you qualify for the greater catastrophic care coverage, in which the plan pays 95 percent of your prescription costs. This could compare favorably with a plan that provides for greater coverage, but with a higher premium, and delays qualifying you for catastrophic coverage.

Using the Medicare Plan Finder

Go to www.medicare.gov and click on "Compare Medicare Drug Plans." Then enter your Medicare member number, or click the Search button to find all the plans in your area by inputting your ZIP code. This gives you the many plans that serve your geographical area. You can then narrow down the number of plans by putting in the names of the prescription drugs that you take. You should also enter the dosages you take. Then compare the cost, deductible premiums, and other factors by comparing up to three plans at a time. Print this list. Unfortunately, this list will not necessarily tell you whether all of the drugs are listed and what restrictions are placed on the drugs.

Go to the Formulary finder and enter your state and drug names. This gives you two lists of plans. The list at the top of the page gives you plans that cover all of your selected drugs. This list at the bottom gives you plans that cover only some of the drugs.

For more information, you can also go the Landscape of Local Plans on the Medicare Web site, with print so tiny that no senior can read it. You can make it larger on your computer, but once again, computer skills are at a premium when it comes to comparing plans.

Don't Give Up the Ship

Medicaid recipients who don't have a computer are at a distinct disadvantage when choosing among the available programs. But don't give up the ship: Throughout the country there are more than a thousand State Health Insurance and Assistance Program offices known by the acronym SHIP (finally, a good acronym) that can help people compare plans. The SHIP program sometimes goes by different names. In

Massachusetts, the SHIP program is called SHINE, another good acronym that stands for Serving Health Information Needs for Elders. If you need to access one of the ships so it does not pass you in the night, go to www.medicareoutreach.org or call 800-243-4636.

Sign Me Up

When you have made the difficult decision as to which Medicare prescription drug program is right for you, enrolling in that plan is a simple matter. You can do it by phone by calling Medicare at 1-800-633-4227, or you can show off your computer savvy and enroll online at www.medicare.gov. You can also call the plan directly to enroll.

When you have joined a plan, you generally can switch only once a year, between November 15 and December 31.

"I'm just getting warmed up."
—Al Pacino in *Scent of a Woman*

The only role for which legendary actor Al Pacino won an Academy Award was as Col. Frank Slade in the 1992 movie *Scent of a Woman.* In the movie, he gives a climactic, impassioned speech in which he says, "I'm just getting warmed up," when school officials attempt to silence him at a prep-school disciplinary hearing. Unfortunately for people going through the awful process of picking a Medicare Part D prescription drug plan, they should all get ready to do this again soon: There probably will be premium increases next year as well as other significant changes to the various plans. Federal subsidies are keeping the costs down for the companies offering these plans. It would be naïve to think that these subsidies would continue much longer. These programs will continue to morph over the next few years, in both cost and coverage. Some plans also will be driven out of existence through competition. The bottom line is, the one thing you can expect is that your Medicare prescription drug plan costs will increase in the next few years.

Who Benefits Most from Medicare Part D?

"No matter how cynical you get, it is impossible to keep up."
—Lily Tomlin

Sometimes it seems as if the pharmaceutical companies operate under their own version of the Golden Rule: "If you have the gold, you make the rules." When it became clear that a prescription drug bill was going to become law, they exerted their lobbying influence on Congress to make sure that Medicare would be prohibited under the prescription drug law from negotiating directly with the pharmaceutical companies for lower prices for Medicare recipients as the Veterans Administration does for the five million American veterans receiving prescription drugs through the VA. The promise Congress made to the American public was that competition among private insurance companies would result in lower prices for consumers. If you believe that one, the salesman of the Brooklyn Bridge wants to speak with you. The fact of the matter is that, using its large group-buying clout, the VA is able to negotiate drastically lower prices for veterans. There is absolutely no reason to think that Medicare could not have done the exact same thing and saved American consumers tremendous amounts of money.

Noting the absurdity of the provision of the law prohibiting Medicare from negotiating reduced bulk prices for prescription drugs, Michigan Sen. Debbie Stabenow said, "Fortune 500 companies, the individual states, large pharmacy chains, and even the Veterans Administration can use the bargaining clout of big bulk purchases to get lower drug prices, but HHS (The Department of Health and Human Services, which oversees Medicare) is barred from using the strength of its 41 million Medicare recipients."

A 2005 study done by Families USA, a health-care consumer advocacy group, compared the cost of the 50 most commonly prescribed drugs for older Americans through the VA with the cost of those drugs under the Medicare transitional drug discount cards that were used from June 1, 2004, until 2006, when the regular Medicare prescription drug coverage took over. Not surprisingly, the lowest prices for drugs were found through the VA plan. The median price difference for the 50 prescription drugs was $220.44 annually.

Specifically, Plavix, the most prescribed prescription drug for older Americans, had a lowest Medicare drug discount card cost of $1,230 a year, whereas the VA cost was only $887 for a year's supply. The greatest difference in cost was found in the sale of the generic drug isosorbide mononitrate, which dilates blood vessels, making it easier for the heart to pump. The VA cost was 713 percent less than the best Medicare drug discount card price.

Despite assurances by Health and Human Services Secretary Mike Leavitt that "the costs of drugs under the prescription drug plan shows the competitive marketplace is reducing the price of prescription drugs for consumers and taxpayers," an analysis of prescription drug costs during the first seven weeks of the program indicates the opposite is true. According to the House Committee on Government Reform,[1] Medicare drug plans increased their prices by more than 4% during the first two months of the Medicare prescription drug program. The average price of Plavix went up 11 percent during this time; the average price of Aricept, an Alzheimer's medication, rose 10.8 percent and the average price of Celebrex increased by 7 percent during this time period. These price increases are almost 80 percent greater than increases in the prices of the same drugs from Canadian pharmacies during the same period. Even more startling is the increase in Medicare prescription drug plan costs when compared to the online pharmacy Drugstore.com. During the same two month period, the price increases under Medicare prescription drug programs were more than fourteen times greater than the increases in prescription drug costs at Drugstore.com. These price increases combined with the fact that the greatest increases were found in the plans that offered the lowest drug prices in December 2005 have brought concerns that some Medicare prescription drug plans were engaging in "bait and switch" tactics, luring customers to their plans with lower prices and then rapidly raising the prices of their prescription drugs.

Oh, Canada

Baby boomers had their recreational drugs in the 1960s and their Lipitor in the twenty-first century. Doug Stephan, the host of the nationally syndicated *Doug Stephan's Good Day* radio show, recently attended a wedding in the U.K. where he was seated at the reception with a number of 1960s rockers. After a while, Doug noticed that the conversations of these cultural icons had evolved over the last 40 years from sex, drugs, and rock 'n roll to aches, pains, and prescription drugs. Baby boomers have joined their parents, and both are taking an array of high-cost prescription drugs. However, the prices for prescription drugs have soared in recent years. More people have become aware that they can get these same prescription drugs from Canadian pharmacies for around 40 percent less than they pay for their prescription drugs here in the states.

Unfortunately, often the savvy consumers who buy their needed prescription drugs from Canadian pharmacies are breaking a 1987 federal law that forbids the importation of prescription drugs except in small amounts under a "personal use exemption." This law was strengthened when Congress removed a provision from the Medicare Prescription Drug bill when it was being debated in 2003 that would have permitted the importing of drugs from Canadian pharmacies with appropriate safeguards to ensure the quality of the drugs. Money talks, and the lobbyists for the pharmaceutical companies were shouting to get this provision removed from the bill that eventually became law. According to Donald L. Bartlett and James B. Steele, the authors of an article entitled "Why We Pay So Much for Drugs" in the February 2, 2004, edition of *Time* magazine, the pharmaceutical companies have more than 600 lobbyists in Washington; between 1996 and 2003, $435 million was spent to influence favorable legislation. In addition, between 1991 and 2002, the pharmaceutical industry made campaign contributions of $57.9 million.

The argument made by the large pharmaceutical companies in support of prohibiting the importation of Canadian drugs has always been that the American consumer needed to be protected from drugs made in Canada that somehow might not be of sufficient quality for Americans. This argument is absurd enough when you consider the lack of protection that the American consumer has received from the combination of the FDA and the American pharmaceutical companies. It is even more outrageous when you realize, as was pointed out in the *Time* magazine article, that more of our "American-made" prescription drugs are actually made in foreign countries where there is little FDA oversight. Primarily due to tax incentives, Ireland is a hub for prescription drug manufacturing. Lipitor, the biggest-selling anticholesterol drug, is made in Ireland, as is the little blue pill, Viagra. Prescription drugs that many Americans think are made here in the USA also come from Sweden, France, Japan, and Singapore. Although the FDA inspects pharmaceutical-manufacturing plants abroad before they open, its oversight after opening is, as Bartlett and Steele noted, quite limited.

According to Ron Pollack, the executive director of Families USA, "A big reason why the new Medicare program is so costly is because Congress and the President chose to support the pharmaceutical lobby over the interests of America's seniors and taxpayers. At a time when drug costs continue to skyrocket and the federal budget is in deep deficit, this needs to change."

Another interesting provision that was inserted into the Senate Medicare bill but was removed before final passage of the legislation was one that would have made the prescription drug coverage provided to senators and congressmen through their health-care plan the same as what Medicare recipients would get. This provision was dropped so fast that it never even made it to the joint House-Senate conference committee for consideration.

Generics

Greater use of generic drugs could save consumers $20 billion over brand-name drugs, according to a report from Express Scripts, a St. Louis–based company that administers employers' prescription drug benefits.[2] Generics are not the answer to every prescription drug need, but they probably are the answer much of the time. Generic switching of drugs with the same components presents few issues. However, therapeutic switching, which occurs when a drug with a slightly different makeup is used, could bring some difficulties.

Yet for many people, the therapeutic switched drug might be entirely sufficient. This study by Express Scripts is even more important because it is expected that $38 billion worth of brand-name drug sales are expected to lose patent protection by 2008. The greatest savings in generics are projected in the area of gastrointestinal drugs, where savings could be $5 billion per year.

Health Savings Accounts

The Medicare Act of 2003 also created a new way for people to manage their health costs: health savings accounts. Through these accounts, qualifying individuals can put tax-free money into a special account and withdraw the money (also tax-free) when needed to pay for health-care expenses. If you stay really, really healthy, ultimately you can take out the money at retirement, after having deferred income taxes on the account and its earnings for all of those years. Unlike the previously authorized flexible savings accounts, the funds put into a health savings account may be invested and, most important, do not have to be used in the same year in which they are deposited; they can be accumulated for later use. An employer can also choose to contribute to an employee's health savings account, and the payments made by the employer are not considered taxable income to the employee.

To qualify for a health savings account, the individual must be covered under a high-deductible health plan (at least $1,000 for individuals and $2,000 for family plans) and not be covered under any other form of health plan except for dental insurance, disability insurance, accident insurance, vision care, or long-term care insurance. Qualified people may contribute the lesser of the annual deductible under the high-deductible health plan, or $2,250 for an individual insuring only himself, or $4,500 for a person paying for family coverage. These amounts are indexed for inflation and are expected to increase annually.

A healthy person who has paid more in health insurance premiums than he or she incurs in medical costs over the year could find the health savings account appropriate. On the other bandaged hand, a person who does not have the readily available cash to pay for an annual high-deductible amount before his or her health insurance would kick in or who generally spends much more than his or her annual deductible on health-care expenses should probably not consider this option. When it comes to health care, one size definitely does not fit all.

Health Care Program

Unfortunately, by and large we do not have a health-care system in this country: We have a sick care system. By this, I mean that we spend much of our time, efforts, and money to fight diseases rather than prevent them. A health-care system would emphasize more healthful lifestyle choices and earlier detection of diseases instead of dealing with illnesses after they have reached critical stages. The benefits of a true health-care system could be enormous. People would live longer, healthier, more active lives. An extra bonus is that the cost of maintaining health is less than combating disease. Fortunately, some unabashedly good news was found in the new Medicare law: As I indicated earlier, it now provides new preventive benefits to all Medicare Part B participants. A greater emphasis on health care could save not just lives, but also money for Medicare, a program that sorely needs cost savings. It would be money well spent.

The Future of Medicare

"Forget about it" was one of the great lines in movie history, spoken by Johnny Depp as undercover FBI agent Joe Pistone in the 1997 movie *Donnie Brasco*. Here, though, it refers to the fact that so many people are upset over the projected deficits in the Social Security program—yet Social Security pales next to the potential financial ruin the country is facing in regard to Medicare in the future. Social Security? Forget about it!

Just how deep is the quagmire of Medicare? Presently, Medicare has an unfunded liability of $30 trillion for the needs of people who are now in the system or are projected to be receiving benefits over the next 75 years. This assumes that the present levels of benefits, tax rates, and premiums are maintained. The new prescription drug benefit alone accounts for $6.9 trillion of this liability. When President Bush first proposed the prescription drug coverage to Congress, the 10-year cost estimate was $395 billion. Two years later, the President's cost estimate rose to $700 billion. To put the overall Medicare debt of $30 trillion into perspective, the gross domestic product (GDP), which measures the total value of all goods and services produced in America, was $11.75 trillion in 2004.

Cures Worse Than the Disease

Some have suggested that raising the age of eligibility would reduce the costs of Medicare. Although this proposal seems to have a logical simplicity, upon further consideration, it appears to be flawed in significant aspects. If the age of eligibility were raised, a large segment of the population would be unable to meet their health care needs. By contrast, lowering the age of Medicare eligibility might do just the opposite by putting younger and healthier people into the risk pool of Medicare enrollees. Those people would be less likely to use the system as much but would still provide money to keep the system afloat through their premiums.

Beware of Insurance Companies Bearing Band-Aids

The battle between those who believe that the private sector can always provide better, more efficient service than the public sector and those who believe that some essentials can be provided in a less costly manner and more efficiently through the government is a battle that we can expect to continue for a long time.

According to Robert M. Hayes, the president of the Medicare Rights Center, government-operated Medicare is able to keep administrative costs down to about 2 percent. Private HMOs and managed-care companies have administrative costs of between 12 and 18 percent because of higher executive salaries, lobbying costs, and advertising. So if cost savings is as important as we all believe it is, perhaps we should reconsider before throwing the Medicare baby out with the bathwater by turning over to private interests the responsibilities for providing health-care coverage.

Ethical Issues

Medicare does not pay for every possible medical treatment. Medicare rules require that the treatments be medically reasonable and necessary; experimental treatments are not authorized. Times have changed, however. What was experimental 40 years ago when Medicare was first implemented is often just standard practice today. Artificial hearts and liver transplants are two treatments that were hardly imagined 40 years ago, let alone authorized to be paid for by Medicare.

The ethical dilemma is, when should Medicare pay for the costs of experimental treatments that might not offer a significant chance of success if, without such treatment, the patient has little or no chance of survival? Obviously, from the patient's perspective, anything that offers even a slight chance of increased health and survival is worth doing. From a larger perspective, however (sort of a national triage), does the cost of experimental treatments divert limited funds from the patients who could more readily be treated effectively? I certainly do not have the answer, but it is a question that must be considered.

A 2005 study by the Rand Corporation dealt with the issue of Medicare costs dramatically increasing in the future as further advances in medical technology occur. Defibrillators that are surgically implanted into a patient with heart disease could add an additional $21 billion in costs if only half of the patients with new cases of heart disease received these devices. Other developing technologies could be even more expensive. According to the Rand study, "A preventive treatment for Alzheimer's disease or new cancer-fighting drugs could each increase elderly spending 8 percent and anti-aging compounds—an area of active research in biomedicine—could drive up costs from 14 to 70 percent."

The study projected spending on health care for the elderly to grow to $600 billion by 2030. Interestingly, the study also pointed out that the health-care costs brought about by obesity are very significant. More Americans are becoming aware that obesity represents a serious public health risk and are acting to reduce this problem.

A more optimistic view of improved health-care technology focuses on reducing disability rates among older Americans and prolonging productivity at work. In addition, the possibility exists that the costs of future technological advances might go down as they become more common, a scenario already seen in the costs of cell phones and computers. In addition, less expensive medical procedures could be developed that might serve the same purpose as the predicted technological advances.

In any event, it probably is wise to remember the words of Danish physicist Neils Bohr, who said, "Prediction is very difficult, especially about the future." The words of renowned philosopher and baseball player Yogi Berra also come into play: "The future ain't what it used to be."

Endnotes

1. House of Representatives Committee on Government Reform, Minority Staff, "Medicare Drug Plan Prices Are Increasing Rapidly" (February 2006).

2. Emily Cox, Andy Behm, Doug Mager, and Steve Miller, *Generic Drug Usage Report 2004.*

13

MEDICAID

*"Life would be infinitely happier if we could only be born at the age of
eighty and gradually approach eighteen."*
—Mark Twain

nfortunately, advancing aging generally brings with it advancing disability. When those disabilities reach a stage at which an elderly person can no longer care for him- or herself at home, and when bringing in assistance to the elder in his or her own home becomes either impractical or unaffordable, moving to a nursing home becomes the primary alternative. The expense of living in a nursing home is significant. For many people who have not financially planned sufficiently for this possibility, paying for that cost from their own assets becomes impossible, so they turn to Medicaid. Understanding the complicated Medicaid system is important for any baby boomer with aging parents, as well as those aging seniors themselves.

Medicaid is the joint state and federal program that constitutes the only government program that pays for the cost of long-term care in a nursing home. With the cost of nursing home care as much as $70,000 or more per year, many people do not have the income or assets to pay for an extended stay in a nursing home and find themselves and their families turning to Medicaid for help. According to federal statistics,

Medicaid presently pays for about half of the country's costs for nursing home care.[1] These statistics showed that Medicaid paid 49.3 percent of nursing home costs, personal funds paid 25.1 percent, Medicare paid 12.5 percent, private insurance paid 7.5 percent, and various other sources paid 5.6 percent.

According to a September 2005 study by the United States Government Accountability Office (GAO), of the total $295-billion Medicaid expenditures in 2004, payments for long-term care needs made up $93 billion of that amount. According to this same report, which referred to Congressional Budget Office projections, an aging population will result in an increased need for long-term care services that the Congressional Budget Office anticipates will double the cost of Medicaid over the next 10 years. Despite recent Congressional efforts to reduce the cost of Medicaid, it is a program that will only be getting bigger in future years.

Medicaid Planning

Medicaid planning is the name for the legal and financial planning done by lawyers experienced in Medicaid laws. These lawyers help arrange the finances of their older clients to make them eligible for Medicaid. An essential element of Medicaid planning often involves transferring assets of older clients to younger family members. Medicaid planning often has a dual purpose: first, to provide for the nursing home costs incurred, and second, to preserve assets so they can be passed on as a legacy to the next generation.

There is nothing illegal, immoral, unethical, or fattening about Medicaid planning, but the decision of whether to take advantage of the laws that permit such planning is one that each family must make for itself.

Many in Congress and the state legislatures are concerned about the effect of Medicaid planning on the costs incurred by both the federal and state governments. Their emphasis seems to be on doing what is necessary to reduce the number of people who are receiving Medicaid assistance for their long-term care needs. However, others have focused their interest less on reducing the number of people who must impoverish themselves to qualify for Medicaid and more on the larger question of how to deal in a societal way with the growing long-term care needs of an aging population.

Looking for Loopholes

Early movie comedian and atheist W. C. Fields was in the hospital dying when a friend came to visit and noticed that Fields was reading the Bible. When the friend inquired why, Fields replied that he was "looking for loopholes." Fields died on Christmas day 1946, a holiday this pre-Grinch Grinch was said to despise. But looking for loopholes is a long and honored tradition for lawyers. Medicaid planning is an area of the law in which lawyers, myself included, have managed to find many legal methods that allow clients to avoid some of the more Draconian Medicaid rules and protect a small legacy for their children.

Changing Rules

It has been said that change is the only constant. Nowhere is that proverb more true than in the case of Medicaid. The rules regulating Medicaid continue to change approximately every 7 to 10 years. In 1986, 1993, and 2006, major changes were made in the Medicaid laws, making Medicaid planning by individuals a difficult task.

On December 19, 2005, the House of Representatives voted 212–206 to approve a budget bill that made drastic changes to Medicaid. Two days later, the Senate approved the bill by a vote of 51 to 50; Vice President Dick Cheney casting the tie-breaking vote. At that time, however, senators who opposed the bill managed to make minor changes to the bill that sent it back to the House for another vote before it could become law; that gave opponents of the bill time to lobby against its passage. On the second go-round through the House of Representatives, the vote was even closer, 216–214, but the result was the same. The vote was primarily along party lines, with Republicans supporting the bill and Democrats opposing the bill. However, 13 Republicans voted against the bill in its second vote in the House. On February 8, 2006, President Bush signed the Deficit Reduction Act of 2005 into law. However, even though the President signed the bill, it did not become immediately effective in all of the states. Some states had to enact legislation on their own in order to bring their laws into compliance with the Deficit Reduction Act. With typical confusing bureaucratic precision, the effective date of the new Medicaid rules in some states will not be until the first day of the first calendar quarter beginning after the completion of the next regular session of the state legislature. For example, if a particular state's next legislative session was to begin in September of 2006 and end in January 2007, the effective date for the new Medicaid rules in that particular state would not be until March 1, 2007.

The Rules

> "The mind demands rules; the facts demand exceptions."
> —Mason Cooley

Before you can deal with the particular facts that might demand an exception, you have to know the rules. The rules of Medicaid are complex, sometimes changing, and often confusing. This is why it is so important to be familiar with them.

Spousal Impoverishment

When one member of a married couple requires nursing home care, the other spouse, who is referred to in the Medicaid regulations as the "community spouse," is permitted under special rules to retain some assets and income over and above the usual limitations for a single person.

The community spouse is permitted to keep half of the couple's combined countable assets, up to a specific amount set by the state. Under federal law, this may not exceed a figure that is inflation adjusted each year. In 2006, the maximum amount that a community spouse can keep is $99,540. In addition, if that amount is less than the state-mandated minimum, the community spouse may keep all of the combined countable assets, up to a federally set amount that also is adjusted annually for inflation. This stands at $19,908 in 2006.

Countable Assets

Just as there were good witches and bad witches in *The Wizard of Oz*, there are countable assets and noncountable assets in determining Medicaid eligibility. It is also important to remember that if a person is married, the assets of both the husband and the wife are considered, even if only one of them is going into the nursing home. In general, noncountable assets include personal property such as clothing, furniture, and jewelry. But don't try to be cute and use your cash to buy Oriental rugs and call them furnishings, or buy a large diamond, as one Massachusetts Medicaid applicant foolishly did. That tactic will not work—nor should it.

Also noncountable is the value of a car that may not be worth more than $4,500 for an unmarried Medicaid applicant. However, there is no limit on the value of a car for the community spouse.

Prepaid funeral plans are also noncountable. The cost of a funeral can be prepaid with a funeral home for not only the nursing home resident, but also his or her spouse, if any, without incurring a financial penalty for Medicaid. Special bank accounts for funeral costs, trusts to hold money for a funeral, and life insurance designated to be used for funeral purposes are also allowed.

Your Home

"There's no place like home."
—Dorothy from *The Wizard of Oz*

For you trivia fans, according to Munchkin Jerry Maren, the short actors who played the Munchkins in the movie were treated like dogs, at least as far as wages were concerned. They were paid $50 per week for a 6-day workweek. By contrast, Toto, the dog, got $125. Maybe he had a better lawyer.

Apparently, Medicaid officials were children once, too, and remember fondly the movie *The Wizard of Oz* because the Medicaid rules give special treatment to the home. Until the passage of the Deficit Reduction Act of 2005, the home was generally considered a noncountable asset. In some states, the home was not counted as long as the nursing home resident intended to return home, regardless of how reasonable that likelihood was. In other states, the nursing home resident had to prove that there was a likelihood of his or her returning home to maintain the home as a noncountable asset. In any event, under the laws prior to the Deficit Reduction Act of 2005, the states put a lien on the home of Medicaid recipients. Now, through the estate-recovery program, they seek to retrieve every penny that was expended for long-term nursing home care on behalf of the owner of the home. It should be noted, however, that even when the state has a lien requiring that it be reimbursed upon the death of the Medicaid-receiving homeowner, the lien is for what the state has paid the nursing home, which is considerably lower than the amount the nursing home resident would have paid the nursing home if he or she had been a private patient.

Under the provisions of the Deficit Reduction Act of 2005, equity that exceeds $500,000 in the homes of residents in nursing homes that receive Medicaid is countable in determining Medicaid eligibility. This means that someone with a home with equity greater than $500,000 must spend that excess equity on his or her nursing home care to qualify for Medicaid. This figure will increase with inflation each year beginning in 2011. The law also permits the individual states to presently increase the permitted equity amount to as much as $750,000. As always, however, there are exceptions to the rule. If the nursing home resident has a spouse living in the home, excessive equity will not disqualify the homeowner from Medicaid benefits.

Tip

When a husband and wife own their home together and one goes into a nursing home, the excessive home equity problem can be avoided by simply changing ownership of the home to just the community spouse.

In addition, the state lien is not levied until the surviving community spouse dies, if he or she survives the spouse in the nursing home. An easy way to avoid the lien when a husband and wife own their home jointly is to have the nursing home resident give his or her ownership interest in the home to the spouse before applying for Medicaid. There is no transfer penalty for this gift, and this simple technique will totally avoid the state's lien on the home. In this instance, it is important for the community spouse to remember to change his or her will so that assets do not pass to the spouse in the nursing home if the community spouse predeceases the spouse in the nursing home. Any assets inherited by the spouse in the nursing home would immediately disqualify him or her from receiving further Medicaid payments until the money inherited had been spent.

Similarly, if the home is owned by a nursing home resident jointly with a sibling who lived in the home for at least a year before the other sibling entered the nursing home, it can be transferred without any penalty to the sibling living in the home.

Free Advice and Worth Every Penny

The preceding tip can be extremely helpful, but what if the institutionalized person cannot make such a transfer of ownership because of mental incapacity? To avoid this problem, it is very important for everyone, but particularly elderly people, to have a durable power of attorney. This legal document enables you to appoint someone to act on your behalf in financial matters if you are unable to do so. This is an inexpensive document that your lawyer can draft for you; do not be penny-wise and pound-foolish by trying to write your own durable power of attorney. Particularly in the context of Medicaid planning and real-estate transfers of ownership, the durable power of attorney must be carefully worded to comply with applicable laws and regulations.

More Tips

When there is no community spouse to give a home to, the nursing home resident can take out a reverse mortgage in whatever amount is necessary to bring down his or her equity to the $500,000 permitted level. Money taken out through the reverse mortgage can be used for daily needs, to buy long-term care insurance, or to purchase a life insurance policy that can be used to provide inheritance for children or others if the home eventually will be subject to the state's Medicaid recovery program when the older person dies.

Another win-win way to reduce the equity in the home to the Medicaid allowable level is to have the elderly homeowner sell a partial interest in the home to his or her children. The children can become joint owners of the property by purchasing a percentage interest in the home. Using this technique not only can help make the elderly homeowner eligible for Medicaid, but also protect the home from the state's recovery program when the elderly homeowner dies.

Yet another alternative involves having the elderly homeowner sell the home to his or her children for its assessed value. The assessed value of the city or town is generally considerably lower than the fair market value of the property, yet Medicaid will accept such a sale as valid. In this situation, the children can save a considerable amount of the equity in the home.

Snapshot

Determining assets for purposes of a Medicaid application is not done, as you might expect, when first applying for Medicaid. Instead, the determination is based upon the value of the assets at the time that the nursing home resident first enters the nursing home. The date of this determination is commonly called the snapshot date. Therefore, particularly in states that allow a community spouse to keep only half of the maximum community spouse resource allowance, you will want to make sure that you do not reduce your assets before going into a nursing home to a level that will restrict the amount of assets you will be able to keep. Although spending down your assets to reach a level that makes one member of a couple eligible for Medicaid benefits is advantageous, it is advantageous only if those assets are spent down after the snapshot date.

Spend-Down

People who have more assets than they are allowed to keep are faced with a decision of what to do to reduce or spend down their assets in a manner that serves them best. Homeowners should consider prepaying their real-estate taxes when a community spouse will continue to live in the home. Paying a full year's real-estate taxes ahead of time will reduce the amount of your assets. This will aid in Medicaid eligibility and also apply those excess assets to a cost that will ultimately become due.

If you have been putting off buying things for the house, such as a new television or a new stove, now is the time to buy it. Spending down excess assets on personal items or things for the home of the community spouse is allowed, within reason. A new television set is fine; Oriental rugs are not.

While you are at it, you should consider paying off outstanding bills. With logic that only a politician or a bureaucrat would understand, in evaluating your financial position, Medicaid considers only the total amount of your countable assets; it totally avoids any consideration of your debts. Unfortunately, when you consider your financial position, your debts constitute a significant part of that. If you need to spend down assets to qualify for Medicaid, consider paying off or at least paying down your mortgage, if you have one. Pay off your credit card debts. Now there is a novel idea. Prepay your income taxes through estimated payments. Your mantra should be, "If you owe it, pay it."

Look-Back Period

Under Medicaid law, there is a period of ineligibility for a person who gives away assets to reduce holdings to a Medicaid-eligible level. Before the enactment of the Deficit Reduction Act of 2005, when a person applied for Medicaid, the state determined whether that person made gifts or other transfers of assets within the previous 36 months and then set the appropriate disqualification. For certain kinds of trusts, the look-back period was 60 months, as a further disincentive to using these trusts that in the past had been used successfully to shelter substantial assets.

The specific period of Medicaid disqualification prior to the enactment of the Deficit Reduction Act of 2005 was determined by going back to the date of the gift and dividing the amount of the gift by the particular state's average monthly private-pay rate, as determined by the Medicaid authority in that particular state. For instance, in Massachusetts, where the private pay rate was $6,960 in 2005, if a person gave away $69,600, he or she would have had a 10-month disqualification period that would start at the time of the gift before he or she would be eligible for Medicaid benefits.

But this changed dramatically following the enactment of the Deficit Reduction Act of 2005. Now the look-back period has been made a consistent 5 years instead of the rule of 3 years for some transfers and 5 years for others. But more significantly is the change in the start of the penalty period resulting from any transfers. Now the penalty period does not even start to run until the Medicaid applicant is in a nursing home and has run out of money and is eligible for Medicaid.

Extending the look-back period to 5 years and changing the date of the start of the disqualification period for gifts carries a potentially devastating effect for older people who made normal gifts to children or grandchildren for tuition, birthdays, or weddings as long as 5 years ago when they were healthy, but who now find themselves having to go to a nursing home at a time when the law may characterize those gifts as being impermissible transfers. Even gifts made 5 years earlier to charities or religious institutions could be considered impermissible transfers for a person now entering a nursing home who needs Medicaid coverage. The Deficit Reduction Act of 2005, in effect, seems to require older Americans to be sure that they have funds to cover the cost of 5 years in a nursing home before making any kinds of gifts. With the average cost of a nursing home at $70,000 per year, this is a tremendous burden for most people.

More Exceptions

There are some exceptions to the gift-disqualification rules. Most notably, a spouse going into a nursing home may transfer without penalty his or her ownership interest in the home to his or her spouse without a penalty. A parent is allowed to give his or her home to an adult child who has lived in the home and cared for them for 2 years.

People who think they are being amazingly clever sometimes attempt to get around the transfer disqualification by trying to "sell" their home to their children for a dollar. This, they argue with a straight face, is a sale and not a gift. This kind of thinking reminds me of the old saying, "Never try to teach a pig to sing. It is a waste of your time, and it really annoys the pig." Frankly, to attempt to disguise such a gift as a sale is futile and probably insulting to the state Medicaid workers. Credit them with more intelligence. Anyone who would attempt to characterize such a gift as a sale would find that a disqualification period would be calculated by determining the fair market value of the property, deducting the amount of money paid ($1, in this example), and calculate the disqualification period based upon the difference.

Home Improvement

Home Improvement is not just the name of Tim Allen's popular sitcom that, between 1991 and 1999, never ranked out of the top 10 shows. It also represents another opportunity for spending down money in a way that can have a direct benefit to the community spouse and, ultimately, the rest of the family of the institutionalized senior seeking Medicaid coverage for nursing home costs. Many older people have lived in their homes for a long time; often those homes are in dire need of repairs, updates, or improvements. Home improvements are a good way to spend down money to make the senior eligible for Medicaid while improving the value of a noncountable asset, the home.

Home Sweet Home

If there is no community spouse, it still might make sense to keep the home and use the money to make necessary repairs so that the home can be rented during the time that the elder is in a nursing home. This results in a win-win situation because the profit that is derived from renting the home will be applied to the elder's nursing home costs and will correspondingly reduce the amount that Medicaid has to pay for the elder's nursing home costs. On the other hand, if, through proper planning, ownership of the home is done in a manner that avoids the state's estate-recovery lien upon the death of the Medicaid recipient, the home will most likely be an asset that increases in value over time and is available as a legacy to the next generation.

Keeping a life estate interest in the home and transferring a remainder interest in the home can enable a senior to avoid having the home subject to estate-recovery upon his or her death. It also can provide a stepped-up tax basis in the property when it passes at death to the adult children of the senior. This would reduce or even eliminate the income tax impact if the adult children sold the home following the death of the senior. In addition, a life estate can avoid probate and, during the lifetime of the nursing home resident, provide income that can be used to pay a portion of the nursing home costs; this would reduce the amount Medicaid pays to the nursing home.

At its essence, a life estate is an arrangement by which the elderly homeowner keeps the right to use and control his or her home throughout his or her lifetime. At death, the property passes automatically and outside of probate to the named individuals, who are called remaindermen. The value of the remaindermen interest in the property when the life estate is set up is not considered for transfer penalty purposes as a transfer of the entire fair market value of the property. Instead, the value of the amount transferred is based upon IRS and Medicaid charts. This might significantly reduce the value of the interest transferred by recognizing that the remainderman does not really receive anything until the death of the life tenant. This can result in a shorter period required to protect the home from estate recovery.

So, for example, a 60-year-old whose house is valued at $200,000 could give away a remainder interest in the home, which would be valued, according to IRS tables, at $68,100. Using the previous law prior to the enactment of the Deficit Reduction Act of 2005, and with Massachusetts transfer-disqualification figures, the disqualification period would have been only 10 months from the time the gift of the remainder interest in the home was made. Now, however, the disqualification does not begin to run until the elder is in the nursing home and out of money. Therefore, to utilize the life estate technique, it is imperative that the family be able to provide for payments to the nursing home for the period of disqualification—in this example, it is 10 months.

Another creative way to use a life estate for Medicaid planning involves having an elderly parent buy a life estate in the home of one of his or her children. In this instance, the parent would pay for the right to live with the child in the child's home for the rest of his or her life. This technique will permit the elderly parent to shelter from Medicaid consideration the money used to pay the child for the life estate. An important condition of such an arrangement is that to be fully effective for Medicaid asset sheltering purposes, the parent must live in the home for at least a year.

The Medicaid rules for life estates vary from state to state, so make sure you consult with an experienced elder law attorney to see whether this might be right for you or your parent or grandparent. A good place to find an elder law attorney is the Web site of the National Academy of Elder Law Attorneys, www.naela.org.

Every Rule Has an Exception, Including This One

In Chapter 3, "Annuities," I expressed my general displeasure for annuities as investments. However, there are exceptions to that rule. One of those exceptions arises when a married person is going into a nursing home and wants to shelter assets to help provide for the needs of the community spouse, while still maintaining eligibility for Medicaid. Again, although the rules differ significantly from state to state, the last-minute purchase of an annuity is an effective way for a couple to protect assets for the community spouse without jeopardizing Medicaid eligibility for the spouse in the nursing home.

Here's how this works: Other assets that are countable for determining Medicaid eligibility, such as stocks, bonds, or bank accounts, are cashed in. The money is used to purchase an annuity for the benefit of the community spouse that meets specific Medicaid requirements. When done properly, excess assets that would be countable and disqualifying for Medicaid purposes are converted into a stream of income for the community spouse that is not counted in determining the eligibility of the institutionalized spouse. Because converting the otherwise excess disqualifying assets into an annuity for the community spouse is properly considered the exchange of countable assets for a noncountable asset of equal value (the annuity), no gift is involved; therefore, there is no transfer penalty. For this reason, the purchase of an annuity for Medicaid purposes is not something that need be done, or should be done, long before applying for Medicaid.

Not all annuities qualify for Medicaid purposes. Specifically, such an annuity must be actuarially sound; that is, its payout must be based upon the age of the community spouse. In addition, the annuity must be irrevocable and cannot have a life insurance component.

Much has been made in the media of the provision of the Deficit Reduction Act of 2005 that requires the state to be named as a beneficiary of the annuity, to be reimbursed at the death of the nursing home resident for whatever the state has paid on his or her behalf. However, many in the media have overlooked the fact that if the annuity is purchased for the benefit of the community spouse and not the spouse in the nursing home, the state is eligible only for reimbursement if the community spouse later requires Medicaid to cover his or her own nursing home costs. So annuities can still work to save money, particularly for a community spouse.

As with all legislation, the Deficit Reduction Act appears to have loopholes. These loopholes might be able to be exploited to save assets for elderly Medicaid applicants. However, anyone using the more aggressive techniques runs the risk of having the courts interpret the law in a way that closes the loophole. With that being said, it would appear that the law would permit a person to give a portion of their money to their children and buy an annuity with their remaining money to cover their costs in a nursing home for the period of disqualification brought about by the gift, thereby saving money for their family that would otherwise have to be spent on their care.

Half-a-Loaf Giving

The federal and state governments would prefer that people who need nursing homes use or spend down all of their assets on their own care until they reach the level of countable assets for Medicaid eligibility. For an individual, that is $2,000. However, there was a loophole that, until the enactment of the Deficit Reduction Act of 2005, was perfectly legal: People were allowed to use a simple formula that considered the amount of their income, the amount of their assets, the cost of their care, and their state's monthly disqualification amount to arrive at an amount that they could give to family members, while keeping sufficient assets that, along with their income, would have covered their costs in the nursing home during the period of disqualification. This technique was called half-a-loaf giving because quite often people safely gave away around half of their assets to family members without jeopardizing their Medicaid eligibility when they ran out of ready cash to pay for their nursing home needs.

Under the Deficit Reduction Act of 2005, however, half-a-loaf giving has been reduced to just crumbs because of the later mandated starting date for the disqualification period. However, in a twist on the old half-a-loaf technique, a nursing home resident can give away assets that will, for example, cause him or her to be ineligible for Medicaid benefits for 2 years. However, he or she can also buy a noncountable annuity that will cover the costs in the nursing home for the 2 years of ineligibility. In this way, annuities can be used to effect significant gifts to family members.

Another possible tactic that might be available to help protect family assets is a new spin on half-a-loaf giving that is being called reverse half-a-loaf giving. An example of reverse half-a-loaf giving is where an elderly person with $100,000 of countable assets gives those assets away to his or her children and then applies for Medicaid. In a state where the state's monthly disqualification amount is $5,000, a 20-month disqualification would be declared. A part of the Medicaid laws that was not changed by the Deficit Reduction Act provides for a disqualification period to be reduced if the people who received the gifts, return the gifts. The amount of the reduction of the disqualification depends upon the amount of the gift returned to the elderly giver. This is called a cure of a disqualifying transfer. In my example, if the children returned $50,000, there would be a partial cure that would reduce the disqualification period to 10 months. The money returned would be used to pay for the cost of the elderly person's nursing home costs. After ten months and the spending down of the returned $50,000, the elderly nursing home resident would be eligible for Medicaid and the family would have saved $50,000, the amount of the gift that the children were able to keep. Under the new rules, if the elderly nursing home resident had initially given away $50,000 and kept $50,000, he or she would have lost it all because he still would have had a ten month disqualification, but it would not have begun to run until after he had already spent down the $50,000 that he kept. Therefore the reverse half-a-loaf giving would appear to present an opportunity for significant asset protection by elderly nursing home residents. It should be emphasized again, however, that this kind of aggressive exploitation of loopholes in the law sometimes backfires if the law is interpreted so as not to allow this tactic, even though it appears to comport with all requirements of the new law. Always consult with an experienced elder law attorney before considering any aggressive Medicaid planning.

A possibly less aggressive half-a-loaf tactic that appears to be available under the new law involves giving away money and buying an annuity to cover the costs during the disqualification period. For example, if an elderly nursing home resident with countable assets worth $200,000 gave away $100,000 to family members in a state with a $5,000 monthly disqualification figure, he or she would have a 20 month disqualification period. If the elderly nursing home resident then used his or her remaining $100,000 to purchase an annuity that met Medicaid standards, the annuity would not be considered a countable asset, so the disqualification period would begin immediately. The funds received from the annuity could then be used to pay for the cost of the nursing home during the 20 month disqualification period. Once again, the bottom line would be that the elderly nursing home resident would have saved considerable money for his or her family.

How Much Do You Pay?

A nursing home resident who has been approved for Medicaid coverage still must contribute most of his own income toward the cost of his care in the nursing home. Any pension, Social Security retirement payments, or other income must be paid to the nursing home after deducting a small amount as a monthly personal needs allowance (around $60 per month, in most states), the cost of any uncovered medical costs (including medical insurance premiums), and, for married nursing home residents, an allowance for at-home spouses if they need the money.

Increasing the Spousal Resource Allowance

If a community spouse does not have enough money to meet his or her support needs, the law also provides in certain circumstances for increased financial assistance to the community spouse in two ways: First, the community spouse could receive some of the income of the institutionalized spouse, such as Social Security or pension benefits that would otherwise be a part of the institutionalized spouse's patient pay amount (PPA) that would go to the nursing home. Second, as an alternative, the community spouse could keep a greater amount of countable assets to generate the additional income necessary to meet his or her living expenses.

Consider this example the GAO gave in its 2005 report entitled *Medicaid—Transfer of Assets by Elderly Individuals to Obtain Long Term Care Coverage*. A community spouse may be permitted to keep a savings account with $300,000 that earns 2 percent interest annually, resulting in an additional $500 of income that can be used for the community spouse's living expenses. Under the present law, a Medicaid recipient's income must be used first to meet the community spouse's increased needs before a community spouse is permitted to keep more assets than otherwise would be allowed by law.

Personal Care Agreements

Another technique used to reduce the assets of a Medicaid applicant is the personal care agreement, which has become less popular as states employ increased scrutiny. Through a personal care agreement, an aging family member hires another member of the family, often an adult child, to perform home care for the older family member. Being paid for these services, which many care-giving family members do for free, makes some family members uncomfortable, but it is a legitimate way to be paid for the considerable work done in caring for a relative. It is also a legal way to shelter assets that would have to be spent down before that person would become eligible for Medicaid. The money to pay for a personal care agreement can come from either the ready assets of the aging family member or through a reverse mortgage or home equity loan.

Although Medicaid certainly will initially look upon any personal care agreement with some amount of skepticism, Medicaid also will accept and recognize them in appropriate circumstances. It is critical that such an agreement be in the form of a written contract and that the contract be executed fully before the caretaker child performs the services. Tax rules should also be adhered to strictly. Again, consulting an experienced elder law attorney is essential.

Life Insurance

Life insurance presents special considerations for families facing a Medicaid nursing home stay. Cash value life insurance is a countable asset. For policies insuring the life of a nursing home resident, it often makes sense to cash in the policy and give that money to the community spouse or spend it down. For life insurance on the life of the community spouse, it is important to remember to change the beneficiary of the policy so that if the community spouse dies before the spouse in the nursing home, the policy proceeds are not paid to the spouse in the nursing home. Failing to change the beneficiary to other family members, for example, would give the spouse in the nursing home the life insurance proceeds from the policy and make him or her ineligible for further Medicaid coverage until the full amount of the life insurance proceeds were spent on the care of the spouse in the nursing home.

Often it is not advantageous to cash in the policy, so another option is to borrow the cash value of the policy from the life insurance company so that the cash value of the policy for Medicaid purposes is small or even reduced to nothing. This strategy enables the family to save the difference between the cash value of the policy and the death benefit.

Another possible use of a small life insurance policy is to have it designated for use to cover payments for funeral costs.

Retirement Plans

As with life insurance, making sure that the beneficiary designations are in order is of prime importance. This saves funds from being lost if the spouse in the nursing home inherits the retirement account of the community spouse, and it provides for future tax deferral under the minimum distribution rules described in Chapter 1, "IRAs and 401(k)s."

Trusts

Never trust anyone who says "Trust me." Of course, you can trust *me* on this one: The effectiveness of trusts, which were at one time a widely used method for sheltering assets and preserving Medicaid eligibility, is now greatly diminished. Congress perceived that trusts were being more frequently used to shelter assets from Medicaid eligibility consideration, so it enacted laws dramatically restricting the use of trusts for Medicaid purposes. Even trusts that had met all of the requirements of the laws at the time they were created were affected by later changes in the laws made after the trusts were drafted but before their makers applied for Medicaid benefits.

A good indication of Congress's distaste for trusts used for Medicaid planning is that the look-back period used to be longer for assets placed into a trust. Assets directly given away formerly carried 36-month look-back period; transfers accomplished through the use of a trust had a

60-month look-back period, a further disincentive from using this technique. Now, however, the Deficit Reduction Act of 2005 has made all manner of transfers subject to a 60-month look-back period. In this time of uncertainty with Medicaid planning, the formerly less advantageous technique of using trusts for Medicaid planning might actually see a bit of a resurgence, particularly when used to protect the home of the Medicaid recipient.

Do Nothing

The primary choice of procrastinators everywhere is to do nothing. However, for exceptionally old or terminally ill homeowners facing a nursing home, it might be the better option when compared to selling the home. As I indicated earlier in this chapter, Medicaid pays nursing homes at a rate that is significantly less than the private pay rate throughout the states. The lien that Medicaid has upon the home is for the cost of the care for which it has paid on behalf of the nursing home resident. Therefore, if faced with the choice of selling a home to get money to pay directly to the nursing home at the higher private pay rate, or keeping the home and applying for Medicaid and letting a lien be placed on the home for the lesser amount of the state's monthly Medicaid payments, the option of not doing anything and paying the state back through the sale of the home after the death of the home-owning Medicaid recipient may be the choice that preserves the most assets for the family. The more likely that the nursing home resident will not be in the nursing home for many years, the better this option becomes.

Hard Choice for Hard Times

When an elderly married couple is faced with one of them going into a nursing home and the other not being able to keep enough of their assets through conventional Medicaid planning to get by on, some couples may consider getting a divorce. A divorce court judge can order the transfer of assets to the community spouse such that the assets cannot be considered by Medicaid when determining the eligibility of the person going into a nursing home. It is a sad situation when aging couples are faced with the decision to divorce in order to have enough money for the community spouse to survive, but unfortunately this may occur more often under the new more restrictive Medicaid laws.

As If You Don't Have Enough to Worry About

Sometimes, what you don't know can hurt you. Many people are unaware that 30 states presently have laws that permit adult children to be held financially responsible for the support of their aging parents. It is not beyond the realm of possibility for the states to look toward the children of nursing home residents to pay for the cost of their care when new, more restrictive Medicaid laws act to disqualify indigent elderly people from Medicaid coverage. These laws have been rarely, if ever, enforced and are of questionable constitutionality, but the bottom line is, in desperate times the states might take desperate measures.

Estate Recovery—or, the State Giveth and the State Taketh Away

From the time Medicaid was introduced in 1965, the individual states have been given the option of taking back from the estates of deceased Medicaid recipients all the money expended by Medicaid for the recipient's care in a nursing home. The law also authorized states to put a lien on the property of Medicaid recipients to ensure that the state would be repaid before children or other heirs received anything from the estate. Because a person applying for Medicaid must essentially be impoverished—with the notable exception of being able to own a home with no more than $500,000 worth of equity—the target for estate recovery and Medicaid liens has generally been the home of the deceased Medicaid recipient. Although the states were permitted by federal law to enact their own legislation to recover the cost of Medicaid payments made on behalf of home-owning Medicaid recipients, most states found this to be distasteful and chose not to enact such laws.

In the 1993 overhaul of the Medicaid laws that was done as part of the Omnibus Budget Reconciliation Act of 1993 (OBRA), in an effort to offset some of the cost of Medicaid, Congress required the individual states to implement Medicaid estate-recovery programs. Congress gave the states some leeway in establishing their own estate-recovery programs, but they were required to have some program in effect. The individual states were also allowed to limit the assets from which they would seek payback to the assets contained within the probate estate of the deceased Medicaid recipient. The probate estate of a deceased person consists solely of things that were owned in his or her own name alone. Joint property and property with beneficiaries, such as insurance policies and trusts, are not considered probate assets. The estate-recovery programs of states that limit their recovery efforts to probate property permit Medicaid recipients and their families to avoid estate recovery by using planning techniques such as life estates. Alternatively, states have the option to enact laws that expand the definition of the estate from which they may exact estate recovery to include such non-probate assets as joint tenancies, trusts, and life estates.

According to the *2002 Medicaid Estate Recovery Work Group Report to the Pennsylvania Intra-Governmental Council on Long-Term Care,* 30 of 48 states surveyed used the less intrusive probate estate standard for estate recovery. Florida and Texas, in particular, have laws that are quite protective of the home from estate recovery.

Exceptions

Federal and state laws do, however, permit the estates of some Medicaid recipients to avoid estate recovery. Surviving children of the long-term care Medicaid recipient who are disabled are not subject to estate recovery. Nor are brothers and sisters of the long-term care Medicaid recipient who are living in the home, were co-owners of the home with the Medicaid recipient, and had lived in the home for at least a year before the Medicaid recipient was institutionalized. Also exempt are adult children of the Medicaid recipient who had lived in the home with the Medicaid recipient and who took care of the Medicaid recipient for at least the 2 years before he or she entered a nursing home.

If a surviving spouse still lives in the home and was a joint owner of the home with the spouse who was in a nursing home receiving Medicaid coverage for the costs of long-term care, the states do not attempt to recover the cost of the Medicaid funds for that person's care from the value of the home. However, some states place a lien on the home and merely defer their right to be repaid until the surviving spouse has died.

An easy way to avoid any estate-recovery complications when the long-term-care Medicaid recipient is a homeowner is merely to have the Medicaid recipient give his or her interest in the home to the spouse. In this way, at the time of the person's death, the home is entirely in the name of the surviving spouse who is still living in the home. This is a real no-brainer, with no downside because there is no Medicaid disqualification for gifts between husband and wife. The only significant asset of most married couples that is not countable when determining initial Medicaid eligibility is the house; thus, it is the only significant asset that can be successfully sheltered from estate recovery by merely giving it to the community spouse.

States are also required to not pursue estate recovery when to do so would result in an undue hardship. The definition of "undue hardship" is left up to the individual states to determine for themselves. Generally, though, this rule applies to homes of particularly modest value and income-producing property, such as a farm that is necessary for the support of surviving family members.

From the onset, estate recovery has been a controversial policy that appears to many people to be a mean-spirited attempt by the government to steal often-meager inheritances. Many people consider a home, in particular, to be more than just bricks and mortar and wood: It takes on a greater emotional meaning. The ability to pass on this legacy is very important to many older people and their families. In addition, the perception exists that the estate-recovery laws are applied inordinately to the poorer citizens of our country. Finally, much evidence suggests that estate recovery just does not bring in sufficient money to make it worth the human toll.

Partnership for Long-Term Care

An innovative program that, prior to the recent enactment of the Deficit Reduction Act of 2005, was available only in California, Connecticut, Indiana, and New York is the Partnership for Long-Term Care. This is a joint program between the private and public sectors that helps pay the costs of long-term care while preserving some of the person's assets as a legacy to children and others. Until recently, due to federal legislation passed in 1993, other states were not permitted to enact Partnership for Long-Term Care laws without adopting an estate-recovery provision that effectively removes the attractiveness of the program. In the hope that Congress would change its mind on this valuable program, 16 states passed laws to set up Partnership for Long-Term Care programs if and when the federal laws were changed.

These efforts were rewarded when expansion of the Partnership for Long-Term Care was made a part of the Deficit Reduction Act of 2005. A key provision of the Deficit Reduction Act of 2005 requires long-term care insurance policies to contain compound inflation protection for policyholders up to age 75 to qualify for the Partnership for Long-Term Care program. As discussed in Chapter 9, "Long-Term Care Insurance," inflation protection is a very important option in a long-term care insurance policy.

Although the specific provisions in the states that do have Partnership for Long-Term Care programs vary, under the Partnership for Long-Term Care, people involved in the plan can increase the amount of the assets they are allowed to keep and still qualify for Medicaid. Usually, the amount that they are allowed to keep is equal to the amount of coverage provided by a long-term care insurance policy they purchase privately; the New York program allows a participating individual to keep all of his or her assets if the person purchases a qualifying long-term care policy. While an individual in a state that is not involved in the Partnership for Long-Term Care program is allowed to have only $2,000 worth of countable assets (not including the value of a home that has equity of no more than $500,000 or $750,000 in those states choosing to raise their exemption to this federally mandated limit) and still qualify for Medicaid, under the Partnership for Long-Term care program, an individual buying a long-term care policy that provides

$100,000 worth of benefits would be able to keep $100,000 of assets and still qualify for Medicaid. This provides a tremendous incentive to purchase long-term care policies. It also reduces that amount of taxpayer money that would be needed for Medicaid to pay for long-term care.

Obviously, this is not a solution for everyone. Some people will not be able to afford a long-term care policy, and others might not qualify for long-term care policies because of health problems. However, for significant numbers of the middle class seeking to find a way to pay for long-term care without going broke, while preserving some sort of legacy for the next generation, this is an option worth considering.

Long-Term Care Insurance Tip

Prior to the enactment of the Deficit Reduction Act of 2005, when the look-back period was generally three years, many people purchased long-term care insurance that would cover their needs in a nursing home for three years. This was good thinking at the time because it provided a person with the opportunity to transfer assets to family members when he or she entered a nursing home, have the long-term care insurance pay for the cost of the nursing home for three years, and then be in a position to apply for Medicaid three years later without a penalty. But now that the look-back period has been changed to five years, what do people do about needing two more years of long-term care insurance coverage to maintain their plan? Adding additional years of coverage to an already existing long-term care insurance policy is not an option the insurance companies offer. However, for people who still qualify, buying a new policy for two years of long-term care coverage is well worth considering.

Congressional Assumptions

"When you assume, you make an ass out of u and me."
—Neil Simon

Felix Unger spoke this line in Neil Simon's classic comedy *The Odd Couple.*

Many politicians seeking to reduce Medicaid costs have assumed that wealthy people are consistently giving away large amounts of money to qualify for Medicaid benefits for long-term care in a nursing home. As a consequence of this perception, the Deficit Reduction Act of 2005 extended the look-back period and placed greater restrictions on the ability of people to transfer assets and qualify for Medicaid. The facts, however, do not support the assumptions of these politicians. Their opinion is based on anecdotal evidence and assumptions. According to a GAO 2002 Health and Retirement Study, elderly households with household income and resources above the national median most often gave away only $4,000. The average amount of cash given away by this group amounted to only $12,010.

It is also important to note that, according to the report of the "Kaiser Commission on Medicaid and the Uninsured" released in June 2005, most elderly people do not have sufficient assets (excluding their home) to pay for the cost of a year or more in a nursing home. And of those older Americans who do have sufficient assets to pay for stays in a nursing home for more than 3 years, according to the Kaiser report, few of them are likely to need nursing home care. The typical nursing home resident is a person without a spouse, over the age of 85, and with functional or cognitive limitations. Unfortunately, these people generally have few assets to either give away or use for their own care. Extending the look-back periods and making more Draconian asset-transfer rules might sound good to politicians, but the facts do not support the likelihood of substantial savings by enacting the Deficit Reduction Act of 2005.

Congress Solves a Problem That Doesn't Exist

"Never assume the obvious is true."
—William Safire

It might seem obvious that because the cost of long-term care is great and, for Medicaid to pay for a person's long-term care needs, his or her assets must be few, many people of substantial means would choose to make themselves eligible for Medicaid by giving away their assets. It might seem obvious, but it is not true.

In their study *The Economic Status of the Elderly, Medicare Brief no. 4,*[2] Robert L. Clark and Joseph F. Quinn found that older Americans in excellent health were three times richer than their counterparts in poor health. Healthy married older couples were 10 times wealthier than the older couples in poor health. Far from having to give away assets to make themselves eligible for Medicaid coverage for their long-term care needs, studies have shown that most disabled older people still living in the community have few assets beyond their home and are already financially eligible for Medicaid—or would be in as little as 6 months of institutionalization.[3] Despite the perception that older people are in large numbers giving away their assets to qualify for long-term care through Medicaid, the facts indicated in a study done by Brenda Spillman and Peter Kemper show that 44 percent of the elderly in nursing homes paid for their care using their own funds exclusively. Another 16 percent entered nursing homes and paid privately until they went through their funds and then turned to Medicaid. Twenty-seven percent used Medicaid from the start to pay for their nursing home costs. The remaining 13 percent of nursing home residents had their costs paid by other sources, including Medicare, which pays for the first 100 days of care in some instances.[4] Those people who first entered the nursing home on Medicaid generally qualified for Medicaid because they did not have many assets, not because they had given their assets away.

Instead of trying to qualify earlier for Medicaid by giving away assets to their children, the exact opposite could be happening. Edward Norton describes in an article that considering the amount of their income and assets, many nursing home residents were actually applying for

Medicaid later than would be expected. Norton concluded that many nursing home residents were, in fact, receiving money from their family or dipping into the equity in their homes to postpone having to apply for Medicaid.[5] As for trusts being used to enhance Medicaid eligibility, economists Donald Taylor, Frank Sloan, and Edward Norton found that although about 40 percent of older Americans could enhance their Medicaid eligibility by way of a trust, only about 8 percent of these people actually had trusts, and most of those trusts were done for the more common purposes of avoiding estate tax and probate.[6]

Another study confirmed that when wealthier individuals most often create trusts, the trusts are focused on avoiding estate tax rather than planning for Medicaid.[7] And as Jerry Seinfeld would say, "Not that there is anything wrong with that." Reducing potential estate taxes through trusts is considered legitimate and intelligent tax planning. When it comes to tax planning, it is wise to remember the words of Judge Learned Hand: "Over and over again, courts have said that there is nothing sinister in so arranging one's affairs so as to keep taxes as low as possible. Everybody does so, rich or poor; and all do right, for nobody owes any public duty to pay more than the law demands. Taxes are enforced exactions, not voluntary contributions."

Controlling the cost of Medicaid is an important fiscal goal. However, Congress should not lose sight of the fact that the greater goal is to tend to the needs of our country's older, vulnerable citizens at the ends of their lives. Harsh laws and greater bureaucratic requirements for Medicaid eligibility do little to save money but much to make life difficult for many Americans whose lives are already difficult enough. More effort should be expended on finding fiscally sound ways to meet the long-term care needs of all of our citizens. Until the time that Congress acts to effectively deal with the growing problem of financing long-term care for all of our citizens, many older people will have little choice but to do Medicaid planning. The rules for Medicaid planning have changed drastically with the enactment of the Deficit Reduction Act. It will take time before we know better how the new Medicaid laws will work and what Medicaid planning techniques will be the most effective. During this period of uncertainty it is more important than ever to make sure that you are getting good advice. Make sure that your lawyer and other financial advisors are knowledgeable and current when it comes to the new world of Medicaid planning.

Endnotes

1. 2002 National Health Expenditure data, at http://cms.hhs.gov/staqtistics/nhe/historical/t7.asp, Table 7.

2. Robert L. Clark and Joseph F. Quinn, *The Economic Status of the Elderly, Medicare Brief no. 4,* National Academy of Social Insurance (Washington, DC: 1999).

3. Frank Sloan and Mae Shayne, "Long-Term Care, Medicaid, and the Impoverishment of the Elderly," *Milbank Quarterly* 71, no. 4 (1993): 575–599.

4. Brenda Spillman and Peter Kemper, "Lifetime Patterns of Payment for Nursing Home Care," *Medical Care* 33, no. 3 (1995) 280–296.

5. Edward C. Norton, "Elderly Assets, Medicaid Policy, and Spend-Down in Nursing Homes," *Review of Income and Wealth* 41, no. 3 (1995): 309–329.

6. Donald Taylor, Frank Sloan, and Edward Norton, "Formation of Trusts and Spend Down to Medicaid," *Journal of Gerontology: Social Sciences* 54B, no. 4 (1999): S194–201.

7. Jonathan Feinstein and Chih-Chin Ho, "Elderly Asset Management and Health," in *Rethinking Estate and Gift Tax Taxation,* ed. William G. Gale, James R. Hines, and Joel Slemrod (Washington, DC: Brookings Institution Press, 2001).

Part IV

HEALTH CARE DECISION MAKING

14

ADVANCE-CARE HEALTH DIRECTIVES

"Dying is a very dull, dreary affair. And my advice to you is to have nothing whatever to do with it."
—W. Somerset Maugham

ood advice, but hard to follow. Still, it might explain the reluctance of many people to have an *advance-care health directive*. This important document does not have a snappy name like a living will, but it is perhaps the best way to deal with planning for a serious illness.

Following the long, lingering death of Terri Schiavo and the media circus that surrounded the tragedy that became her final years, many people resolved to look into what they needed to do to avoid her fate. But time has a way of dulling our sense of immediacy when dealing with difficult and complex issues. Either because they feel overwhelmed by dealing with such a complicated matter or simply because it is, as Maugham said, such a dreary affair, many people have failed to take the steps necessary to avoid ending life as Terri Schiavo did. There is no more burning personal issue than end-of-life care. You owe it to yourself and your family to determine what level of care you want and do not want. Everyone should have an advance-care directive. The first step is learning how they work.

Living Wills vs. Advance-Care Directives

A living will is a document through which you are able to indicate the kinds of health-care treatments you do and do not want under particular circumstances. An advance-care directive, which is also sometimes called an advance-care health directive, health-care proxy, or durable power of attorney for health care, is another kind of legal document that permits you to choose the person you want to make health-care decisions on your behalf if you are unable, for whatever reason, to make those decisions on your own. An advance-care directive is based upon the premise that you have the right to choose or refuse health-care treatments. You do not lose that right if you become incapacitated; you merely lose the ability to make your wishes known. Your health-care agent or proxy acts like a stock proxy at a stockholders' meeting and makes decisions on your behalf.

Living wills can cause more problems than they solve. If they are too specific, they might not apply to the precise health issue at hand. This leaves the document open to interpretation and that is an invitation for the courts to get involved. If the document is not specific enough, it might be too vague, once again opening the door for judicial intervention. So, like Goldilocks who searched in the home of the three bears for the perfect porridge that was neither too hot nor too cold, people trying to craft a document that deals not only with every possible medical situation but also the specifics of treatment to deal with those contingencies are doomed to failure. In addition, medical workers in the midst of an emergency could misinterpret the document. Far better is the advance-care directive that appoints someone to step into your shoes—or those silly hospital slippers, as the case may be—and make medical decisions on your behalf guided by your principles that hopefully have been communicated to him or her.

Indeed, both the living will and advance-care directives are flawed. They are not perfect. But that is no reason for not having one. When I taught in the state prison system in Massachusetts, I had a student who was serving two consecutive life sentences. I was curious about the ability of someone to do this, so I asked him about it. He replied that he'd had the same thoughts at his sentencing hearing and angrily posed the question to the judge, "How do you expect me to do two consecutive life sentences?" The judge calmly responded, "Just do the best you can." An advance-care directive might not be perfect, but it could be the best we can do in this situation.

Many states do not specifically authorize living wills by law, but the document may still be of value in helping to determine the intentions and wishes of the individual making it. An advance-care directive does more than a living will: A living will speaks only to the situation of a terminal illness, while an advance-care directive appoints someone to step into a person's shoes and make any health-care decisions on his or her behalf, even if they are not life-and-death decisions. Sometimes people have both a living will and an advance-care directive. In that instance, the living will serves as a nonbinding guide for the health-care agent.

All 50 states recognize some form of advance-care directive. Through the full faith and credit clause of the Constitution, states are required, at least in theory, to honor advance-care directives written in other states. That being said, if you regularly spend time in more than one state, it is prudent to consider having an advance-care directive written to comply with the laws of each state in which you live. The standards for advance-care directives vary from state to state regarding the specific language required, witnessing, and notarization. Specific requirements might involve who can and cannot act as a witness, whether witnesses are even necessary, and whether the document must be notarized. Similar to the requirements for a will, many states require two witnesses. Many states also require notarization, and some declare the advance-care directive to be invalid if the person is pregnant while a patient. New Mexico advance-care directives do not require witnessing or notarization. Under the Federal Patient Self-Determination Act, any hospital or other health-care facility that receives Medicaid or Medicare funds is required to inform patients of their rights to an advance-care directive.

How Do You Start?

One size does not fit all. The optimum situation is to prepare an advance-care directive after consulting with your physician and lawyer so that the document represents a true and accurate understanding of the situation by all concerned. In particular, you should discuss your health history with your physician regarding what likely medical problems will confront you in the future. In addition, various religious denominations provide guidance for advance-care directives consistent with their religious principles.

Unfortunately, few people take the time and effort to carefully prepare an advance-care directive. Many people spend more time preparing to buy a refrigerator than they do preparing for a medical emergency. Often people download living wills or advance-care directive forms from the Internet. The danger here is that they do not understand what they are doing. Another risk is that the form does not conform to the law of the state in which they reside. However, even if one size does not fit all, something is better than nothing (at least most of the time). According to a survey by the National Academy of Elder Law Attorneys, only a third of Americans between the ages of 35 and 49 have advance-care directives. Many young people never even think of these matters. But they should. Karen Ann Quinlan, Nancy Cruzan, and Terri Schiavo were all young people when the paths of their lives were suddenly and permanently altered.

Whom Do You Trust?

The biggest decision in any advance-care directive is the person you choose to actually make the decisions on your behalf. You want someone who understands your wishes and is willing to follow them. (Come to think of it, many of us spend our lives trying to find someone who understands our wishes and is willing to follow them, but that is another story.) It is important not to have your advance-care directive complicate the decision by putting unreasonable limitations on your health-care agent. As with a living will, too much specificity in your advance-care directive can result in confusion. Medical science is constantly evolving. Specifically indicating the medical procedures that you do or do not want and under what circumstances you do or do not want them puts you in jeopardy of not being in tune with medical science at the time that your advance-care directive becomes operative. Too much specificity could actually result in confusion and court battles, which is one of the main things that people seek to avoid when making an advance care directive. A better choice is to have your advance-care directive generally indicate your desires and leave the specifics up to your health-care agent, acting in concert with your wishes at the time that your advance-care directive may be required.

Difficult Choices

If you were in a coma or persistent vegetative state, or if you were terminally ill or suffering from Alzheimer's disease or dementia, would you want to receive ventilator assistance, artificial hydration, or artificial nutrition? These are questions that are much more difficult than whether you want the steak or chicken at a wedding reception, but they are nevertheless important to consider.

How much medical care would you desire to receive if there was little or no hope of living independently? A respirator might be more acceptable to a person who is suffering from a treatable disease that makes breathing on one's own difficult, but it might not be acceptable if there is no reasonable hope of recovery. Artificial nutrition and hydration might be acceptable to a person who, on a temporary basis, needs these services as a part of his or her recovery process, but not as a method of merely prolonging an existence without hope of returning to a desired quality of life.

Many questions should be considered when drawing up an advance-care directive. Would you want to make an anatomical gift? How important to you is being self-sufficient? If your physical or mental abilities were severely impaired, would you want your life to be maintained? Where would you prefer to die? In 1950, half of Americans died at their homes. Now, with improvements in medical science over the last half-century, 85 percent of Americans die in a hospital, a nursing home, or some other health care facility. What are your religious feelings about death? Consider all of these questions when writing an advance-care directive.

Words

Words are important. I don't mean the song "Words" by the Bee Gees that was a hit song in 1968—although, to some people, the Bee Gees are pretty important. But words, their meanings, and their connotations are important. To some people, artificial nutrition and hydration are extraordinary medical procedures to be used when they are part of a recovery process, but not if they merely prolong suffering or a lifestyle at a level unacceptable to the patient. However, when artificial nutrition and hydration are referred to as "feeding tube and water," and when removal of these treatments is referred to as "starvation," the connotation is such that some people prefer to indicate in their advance-care directives that they do not want these treatments to be discontinued, regardless of the circumstances. There is no right or wrong in this matter; you must decide what you believe is best for you.

Details

Make sure that your primary physician has a copy of the advance-care directive. Also carry with you a wallet size card that indicates that you have an advance-care directive. You might want to register your advance-care directive as well. A number of places serve as registries; perhaps the most noteworthy is the U.S. Living Will Registry. There is no charge for registering an advance-care directive here.

The registry deals with more than just living wills. Health-care providers pay a small fee for access to its files, and the documents are stored electronically. If a health-care facility requires an advance-care directive, the registry will fax it.

HIPAA

It is also important to have HIPAA provisions within your advance-care directive. HIPAA is the acronym for the Health Insurance Portability and Accountability Act, which does not fall as trippingly off the tongue as "HIPAA." One of the purposes of HIPAA is to protect the privacy of medical information. Without specific HIPAA authorization in your advance-care directive, you run the risk that a hospital will not provide medical information or an insurance company will not provide medical billing information to your health-care agent The prudent thing to do is to include such language in your advance-care directive and durable power of attorney.

Do Not Resuscitate

Another important health-care document is a Do Not Resuscitate order. This refers to cardiopulmonary resuscitation and the situation in which a person stops breathing or the person's heart stops beating. In that event, unless this order is in effect, medical personnel will take the steps necessary to restore breathing and heart function. If you choose, and it is wise to do so, you can leave it up to your health-care proxy agent to determine whether to resuscitate, based upon your condition at the time.

Party On, Dude

With good old American ingenuity, many Americans who perhaps are looking just a bit too hard for an excuse to have a party are now having living will parties, at which people get together and talk about dying and final medical care. Generally, such a party consists of people getting together with a supply of generic advance-care directives. An expert discusses advance-care directives and takes questions from the attendees. After a question-and-answer period, people who attend the "party" can execute their documents and then have their signatures witnessed and notarized in accordance with their own state law.

I'm from the Government, and I Am Here to Help You

According to a study published in the *Archives of Internal Medicine*, the medical care costs for dying patients who did not have advance-care directives were approximately three times more than the medical costs of patients who had advance-care directives in effect. According to the American Medical Association, more than 70 percent of Americans will find themselves in situations in which an advance-care directive would apply, yet less than 15 percent of Americans have an advance-care directive, living will, or other similar document.

Cynics might think that Congress was more interested in saving money than patients' rights when it passed the Patient Self Determination Act of 1990 to increase public awareness of advance-care directives. A number of states have even considered requiring an advance-care directive as a condition of receiving Medicaid. According to Wisconsin state representative Curt Gielow, as much as 75 percent of a person's lifetime health-care costs are spent during the last 2 months of that person's life, often at a significant cost to Medicaid and taxpayers. Gielow does not believe that requiring advance-care directives would unduly pressure people to request that heroic measures not be employed to prolong their lives or, as some would say, prolong their deaths. Rather, he likened such a requirement to asking someone if they want to be an organ donor, as is commonly done when a person obtains a driver's license. The cost of maintaining the existence of patients who are in persistent vegetative states can be significant. According to the Wisconsin Department of Health and Family Services, in 2004, Wisconsin paid $6.3 million through Medicaid to maintain the existence of 116 patients in 2004. That breaks down to a cost of approximately $54,500 per patient.

History

Luis Kutner, a lawyer, first proposed living wills in 1967 to provide dying people with the power to direct and control their medical treatment at a time when they would be unable to directly make those decisions. The first living will legislation was passed in California in 1976. Seven more states passed living will laws within a year. By 1992, all of the states had passed some form of advance-care directive law.

In a number of landmark cases, the courts became involved in life-and-death decisions on behalf of people without advance-care directives. Each time, the public interest was captured, but a fickle public also quite often let its interest wander without learning the lesson and drawing up an advance-care directive.

The first major "right to die" case that captured the attention of the public was the case of Karen Ann Quinlan. Through her case in 1976, the New Jersey Supreme Court affirmed the rights of individuals to have someone else act on their behalf to make medical decisions if they are unable to do so. The court also recognized that the decision to terminate treatment, a decision that would likely lead to death, was one best made by families following consultations with their physicians rather than by courts. The court further recognized the principle that such decisions concerning life-or-death treatments should take into account the invasiveness of the treatment as well as the likelihood of recovery. Finally, the court recognized that patients have a right to refuse treatments even if such refusal would hasten their death. Following the New Jersey Supreme Court decision, Karen Ann Quinlan's father was authorized to make the decision to remove his daughter from the ventilator that maintained her existence.

In 1990, the United States Supreme Court in the case of Nancy Cruzan dealt with the question of advance-care directives and affirmed the right of patients to make advance-care directives that could authorize the refusal or termination of treatment.

Terri Schiavo

Nowhere did public attention become quite so riveted in a right-to-die case as in the case of Terri Schiavo. Much was written during the final days, months, and years of her life about her and her plight. Unfortunately, much of the extensive media coverage was biased and faulty.

Terri lived for more than 13 years after the accident that put her into a persistent vegetative state. The last 10 years of her life were filled with litigation. The wheels of justice can sometimes move excruciatingly slowly.

Terri Schiavo was born on December 3, 1963. She was an overweight child, but at age 18 she went on a physician-directed weight-loss program and reduced her weight from 250 pounds to 150 pounds; that was her weight when she first met Michael Schiavo, whom she married in 1984. Two years later, Terri and Michael moved to Florida, where Terri worked for a life insurance company and Michael managed a restaurant. Terri continued to drop weight and reached her goal of 110 pounds. According to court records in her case, she was "very proud of her fabulous figure and her stunning appearance, wearing bikini bathing suits for the first time and taking great pride in her improved good looks."

Then on February 25, 1990, her world fell apart when she collapsed at her apartment and suffered cardiac arrest. Her husband summoned emergency medical assistance. During the few minutes it took for the paramedics to arrive, Terri suffered a loss of oxygen to the brain that caused a permanent loss of brain function. She fell into unconsciousness and then into a coma. Emergency medical treatment was performed; without it, she would have died.

At the time, the cause of her cardiac arrest was attributed to a substantial reduction in her potassium level. The balance between sodium and potassium in the body is of critical importance. It was reported that Terri's chemical imbalance was connected with her diet, which included drinking 10 to 15 glasses of iced tea each day. According to court records, Terri's "aggressive weight loss, diet control and excessive hydration raised questions about Theresa suffering from Bulimia, an eating disorder, more common among women then men, in which purging through vomiting, laxatives and other methods of diet control become obsessive." However, later her autopsy indicated that the reduced potassium in her blood might have been affected by the emergency treatment she received following her cardiac arrest and could have been unrelated to any eating disorder.

Although after a couple of months Terri came out of her coma, she never regained consciousness. Both Michael and Terri's parents, Robert and Mary Schindler, were devoted to her care. By late 1990, despite continual medical care, Terri remained in what was diagnosed as a persistent vegetative state, with no evidence of any improvement. With conventional medical care proving fruitless, Michael took Terri to California to receive an experimental thalamic stimulator implant in her brain. Michael stayed in California, where he cared for her for months before returning with her to Florida in January 1991. Unfortunately, the experimental treatment did nothing to improve her situation. Her clinical assessments, according to court records, "consistently revealed no functional abilities, only reflexive rather than cognitive movements, random eye opening, no communication system and little change cognitively or functionally."

A *persistent vegetative state* is the medical term describing the condition of people who have had brain damage to their cerebral cortex and thalamus such that they are unaware of themselves or their environment. Although certain reflexive actions allow them to breathe on their own without the aid of a ventilator, and although they actually have waking and sleeping cycles, they are not aware of themselves or their surroundings. Reflexive responses such as crying or smiling could give the illusion that they are aware or reacting to specific stimuli, but they are not. When this condition persists for a period of at least a month without improvement, the vegetative state is considered a persistent vegetative state.

In 1993, a medical malpractice lawsuit was settled against the physician who had been treating Terri for fertility issues at the time of her collapse. The settlement provided for a payment to Terri of $750,000 and a separate payment for loss of consortium to Michael in the amount of $300,000. A payment on a claim of loss of consortium is done to compensate a spouse on the loss of the companionship of an injured spouse. A trust was established for Terri's money. The trust was managed by SouthTrust Bank as her guardian in this matter, along with an independent trustee. Michael had no control over the money or its use. It was at the time the malpractice case was settled that enmity first arose between Terri's parents and Michael. The Schindlers petitioned the courts to have Michael removed as her guardian, alleging for the first time that he had not properly cared for Terri and that his actions were disruptive to her treatment and condition. The court concluded that there was no basis for these allegations. The judge ruled "that he had been very aggressive and attentive in his care of Theresa. His demanding concern for her well-being and meticulous care by the nursing home earned him the characterization by the administrator as a 'nursing home administrator's nightmare.' It is notable that through more than 13 years after Theresa's collapse, she has never had a bedsore."

Despite continual and consistent medical reports indicating that there was little or no likelihood for any improvement in her condition, Michael clung to the hope that she could and would improve. Finally in 1994, four years after her collapse, Michael faced the reality of her condition. After consulting with Terri's treating physician, Michael, as guardian, created a "do not resuscitate" order for Terri if she had another cardiac arrest. He later lifted the order in the face of opposition by the nursing home housing Terri. However, from then on, his focus became one of permitting his wife to die naturally rather than prolonging her existence in a persistent vegetative state.

Then in 1997, Schiavo began court proceedings to withdraw the artificial life support that maintained his wife's continued existence. A guardian *ad litem*, Richard Pearse, a Florida lawyer appointed by the court to represent Terri's interests, reviewed the petition. Late in 1998, Pearse issued his report, which concluded that the medical records indicated that Terri's condition was a persistent vegetative state with no chance of improvement. He noted in his report that Terri's mother had said that Terri was able to respond to her. However, he also noted that such responses were neither documented nor seen by anyone else.

Pearse also noted that Michael's testimony that Terri had told him that she did not want life support if she was ever in such a position was not "clear and convincing." Pearse was concerned about the possibility that Michael's opinion was being affected by the money he would stand to inherit if Terri died. At the time of the report, more than $700,000 remained from Terri's medical malpractice settlement.

Michael challenged a number of Pearse's findings, perhaps most significantly in the report's failure to note that Michael had "formally offered to divest himself entirely of his financial interest" in Terri's estate. In February 1999, Pearse requested either additional authority or his removal as guardian *ad litem*. The court discharged him in June 1999.

After long and detailed hearings, on February 11, 2000, Judge Greer ordered the removal of Terri's artificial life-support system. Her parents opposed this decision and flooded the court with numerous motions and legal efforts to have the decision changed. Judge Greer gave the Schindlers every opportunity to be heard and to present evidence. However, it was also during these hearings that Judge Greer allowed testimony regarding conversations Terri was alleged to have had with Michael's brother and his wife at the time of funerals of close family members who had been sustained by artificial life support. In these conversations, they testified, Terri had indicated that she did not want such care if she herself were in such a position. This testimony was important to Judge Greer in confirming his decision to allow the removal of life support.

Perhaps most telling were the testimony and statements made at depositions by members of the Schindler family in which they indicated that their desire was to keep Terri alive regardless of the circumstances. When asked hypothetically if they would agree to amputate limbs if she contracted diabetes, they indicated that they would agree to amputate all of her limbs. The Schindlers indicated that they still derived joy from having her alive, even if Terri was in a persistent vegetative state and was in no way aware. Ultimately, the Schindlers stated for the record that even if Terri had told them that it was her desire to have artificial nutrition removed, that they would not do so. They also acknowledged, at that time, that she was indeed in a persistent vegetative state.

Following more hearings regarding the Schindlers' motions to have Michael removed as Terri's guardian, a date for removing her artificial life support was set for April 24, 2001. On that date, her feeding tube was clamped and she received no nutrition or hydration. It was expected that she would die within 10 days. However, 2 days later the Schindlers filed another lawsuit and were granted a temporary injunction ordering the feeding tube to be unclamped. The case worked its way through the courts until it reached the Florida 2nd District Court of Appeals where in October 2001 the court concluded that the Schindlers "presented no credible evidence suggesting new treatment can restore Mrs. Schiavo." Consequently, the court ordered the discontinuation of the artificial feeding.

The Schindlers did not give up. They filed new motions with affidavits from physicians that indicated that Terri's condition could be improved. The quality of these affidavits was later referred to by Terri's guardian *ad litem* as "marginal," but the court continued to provide the Schindlers with every opportunity to make their case. It was ordered that each side would select two expert physicians and also agree on a fifth physician to evaluate the situation. If they could not agree on the fifth doctor, the judge would pick one.

As might be expected, they could not agree on the fifth physician, so the judge appointed an impartial physician. Following extensive examinations and review of the medical records, all five physicians prepared reports. The court found that the neurologists Michael chose provided strong, scientifically supported, and clear and convincing evidence. In contrast, the testimony of the neurologist and radiologist the Schindlers chose was deemed to be substantially anecdotal and not clear and convincing. The impartial physician appointed by the court provided clear, scientifically grounded evidence that concurred with the two doctors Michael appointed. Their conclusion was that Terri was in a persistent vegetative state with no hope of recovering.

The court's decision to accept these medical opinions became the basis for another appeal by the Schindlers; they also renewed their efforts to have Michael removed as guardian. Once again, the 2nd District Court of Appeals upheld the trial judge and ordered him to set a hearing to determine when to remove the artificial life support. October 15, 2003, was the date set to once again remove her life support.

It's Politics As Usual

> "We're not doctors. We just play them on C-SPAN."
> —Congressman Barney Frank

By 2003, however, the case was no longer merely being fought in the courtrooms. The battle extended to the national media and the political arena. On October 6, 2003, Florida Gov. Jeb Bush filed a friend of the court brief in support of the Schindlers' continued legal efforts to prevent the removal of artificial nutrition.

On October 21, 2003, the Florida legislature got involved and, in a special session, passed a law specifically limited to Terri Schiavo authorizing the governor to intervene and requiring her artificial feeding tube be maintained. The legislature also required that a guardian *ad litem* report be produced to represent Terri's interest in this matter. Jay Wolfson, the appointed guardian *ad litem*, visited Terri personally, interviewed all of the parties involved, met with her doctors, and reviewed more than 30,000 pages of court records.

He noted that the withdrawal of artificial life support provided through nutrition and hydration was a sensitive issue to many people and had brought about much debate and discussion. However, he concluded that there was a consensus that artificial feeding could be withdrawn from a terminally ill patient or one in a persistent vegetative state.

He noted, "If persons unable to speak for themselves have decisions made on their behalf by guardians or family members, the potential for abuse, barring clear protections could lead to a 'slippery slope' of actions to terminate the lives of disabled and incompetent persons. And it is not difficult to imagine bad decisions being made in order to make life easier for a family or to avoid spending funds remaining in the estate on the maintenance of a person."

However, he also noted, "There is, of course the other side of that slippery slope, which would be to keep people in a situation they would never dream of: unable to die, unable to communicate, dependent for everything, and unaware, being maintained principally or entirely through state resources—and for reasons that may relate to guilt, fear, needs, or wants of family members rather than what the person's best wishes might otherwise have been."

Then, of course, there was the aspect of the case referred to by the guardian *ad litem* as "chillingly practical," the "cost of maintaining persons diagnosed in persistent vegetative states and terminal conditions alive for potentially indefinite periods of time—at what inevitably becomes public expense."

The guardian *ad litem* also dealt with an aspect of Terri's case that was particularly troubling to many: the videos taken by the Schindlers that some people interpreted to show a woman with a level of consciousness. Unfortunately, this conclusion was illusory, as the guardian *ad litem* indicated:

"A particularly disarming aspect of persons diagnosed with persistent vegetative state is that they have waking and sleeping cycles. When awake, their eyes are often open, they make noises, they appear to track movement, they respond to deep pain and appear startled by loud noises. Further, because of the autonomic nervous system, those brain related functions are not affected, they can often breathe (without a respirator) and swallow (saliva). But there is no purposeful, reproducible, interactive awareness. There is some controversy within the scientific medical literature regarding the characterization and diagnosis of persons in a persistent vegetative state. Highly competent, scientifically based physicians using recognized measures and standards have deduced within a high degree of medical certainty that Theresa is in a persistent vegetative state. This evidence is compelling. Terri is a living, breathing human being. When awake, she sometimes groans, makes noises that emulate laughter or crying, and may appear to track movement. But the scientific medical literature and the reports this GAL (Guardian Ad Litem) obtained from highly respected neuro-science researchers indicate that these activities are common and characteristics of persons in a persistent vegetative state."

The term *persistent vegetative state* was tossed around a great deal in the press and by many people with great conviction, although their knowledge of this medical term was limited to parroting whatever was being said by the "experts" whom they wanted to believe.

As I indicated earlier, a persistent vegetative state is the condition of people who have had brain damage to their cerebral cortex and thalamus so that they are unaware of themselves or their environment. Reflexive responses such as crying or smiling can give the illusion that they are aware or are reacting to specific stimuli, but they are not. When this condition persists for a period of at least a month without improvement, the vegetative state is considered a persistent vegetative state.

Although some supporters of the Schindlers tried to argue that Terri Schiavo was not in a persistent vegetative state, the objective medical evidence was to the contrary. Since the time of the severe anoxic trauma she had suffered in 1990, CT scans and other neurological tests confirmed that her cerebral cortex had shrunken and become principally liquid in nature. The damage to her brain due to the oxygen deprivation was irreparable. Despite the proclamations of well-meaning people that there were therapies and treatments that could actually regrow her brain tissue, there was no scientifically recognized evidence of this being possible.

Terri actually beat the odds of continuing her existence while in a persistent vegetative state. According to the American Academy of Neurology, few people in such a state live more than 10 years.

Ultimately, the GAL who was appointed to stand in Terri's shoes concluded that her situation provided no hope of recovery or improvement, and that the law provides for the removal of artificial nutrition in such circumstances where the intent of the patient is deemed by the court to be clear and convincing.

Terri died on March 31, 2005, although her life had ended 15 years earlier. In the end, as many as 40 judges in six separate courts had considered her plight at some time. Six times the case was appealed to the United States Supreme Court, and six times the court refused to hear the case. Terri was the subject of both specific state and federal legislation. All because she did not have an advance-care directive.

At the time of her death, the controversy continued as the Schindlers and others insisted that, despite all evidence to the contrary, Terri was not in a persistent vegetative state and that she could improve with therapy. An exhaustive autopsy was performed based on 274 external and internal body images and a review of her medical records, police reports, and social services agency records. The results of the autopsy completely confirmed the position of Michael Schiavo that, indeed, Terri had been in a persistent vegetative state with massive and irreversible brain damage. According to medical examiner Jon Thogmartin, half of her brain had been destroyed. In his report, he concluded, "This damage was irreversible and no amount of therapy or treatment would have regenerated the massive loss of neurons." In addition, the part of the brain that controlled sight was found to have been destroyed, indicating that Terri had also been blind at the time of her death. The medical examiner also found no evidence that she had been abused or strangled, allegations the Schindlers had made repeatedly against Michael Schiavo. Despite this conclusive evidence, the Schindlers refused to accept the report and clung to their position that Terri could have improved with care.

Terri's cremated remains were buried underneath a gravestone that lists February 25, 1990, as the date she "departed this Earth" and March 31, 2005, as the date she was "at peace."

Hopefully, the life and death of Terri Schiavo will come to be more than just an unfortunate personal tragedy that was played out as a media event. Her story should inspire people to confront the reality of their own mortality and take the steps necessary to ensure that their final days will be dignified and lived out in the manner they desire.

POSTSCRIPT

*"Never put off till tomorrow what you can do
the day after tomorrow."*
—Mark Twain

U nfortunately for those of us who have taken those words to
heart and managed to turn procrastination into an art form,
the day after tomorrow has arrived.

Denial is not just a river in Egypt, and as much as many of us baby
boomers might want to pretend that our parents are not aging, they are
getting older and they need our help. Our parents need our help now
dealing with the Medicare prescription drug program. They also need
our help navigating through the worlds of finance, taxes, and possibly
nursing homes.

And as we help our parents, we might notice that their present situation
possibly mirrors ours in the future. Maybe that will provide the incentive we need to start acting now to take care of the many aspects of
planning for our own later years. The earlier you plan, the more options
available to you. People do not plan to fail. All too often, however, they
do fail to plan.

Hopefully, this book will help you in your own planning. For those of you who are members of what has been called the "Greatest Generation," I hope you find this book helpful in planning for your immediate needs. For my fellow baby boomers, I hope this book will give you some guidance in how you can assist your parents, while at the same time helping you to recognize your own needs and give you some information so you can plan more effectively for yourself.

I have tried to make this book entertaining as well as informative because, frankly, no one really gets anything from a boring lecture (at least, I don't). If you learned something helpful, if I provoked you to think about some new things, or if I gave you a chuckle, I have succeeded. If not, well, as my wife has been known to say, "Steve, sometimes you are just not funny."

INDEX

401(k) retirement accounts
borrowing from, 11
company matches, 5-7
diversification, 12-13
early withdrawals, 11-12
from previous employers,
finding, 22-23
ignorance about, 13-14
rollovers, 10-11
Roth 401(k) accounts, 6-9
4 percent solution, 18
529 Plans, 28-29

A

accelerated death benefits, 149-150
taxability of, 57
accident insurance benefits,
taxability of, 56
accreditation
choosing assisted-living
facilities, 120
choosing nursing homes, 117
activities
choosing assisted-living
facilities, 124
choosing nursing homes, 114
ADEA (Age Discrimination in
Employment Act) 64-65
adjusted gross income (AGI). *See*
income limitations
administrative costs of
Medicare, 203
adult children, as financially
responsible for nursing home
care, 227
adult day-care centers, 106

advance-care health directives,
103-104, 239
Do Not Resuscitate order, 245
HIPAA, 245
history of, 247
living wills versus, 240-241
medical costs without, 246
parties for, 245
planning for, 241-242
registering, 244
specificity in, 242-243
Terri Schiavo case, 248-256
wording, importance of, 244
age discrimination, 63-64
ADEA (Age Discrimination in
Employment Act) 64-65
burden of proof in, 65
court cases, 65-74
disparate impact as, 67-69
disparate treatment as, 66
filing suit, 74-76
health insurance benefits and,
73-74
in layoffs, 65-66
reverse age discrimination, 71
state laws, 74
statistics in determining, 66
Age Discrimination in Employment
Act (ADEA) 64-65
AGI (adjusted gross income). *See*
income limitations
Alternative Mortgage Transaction
Parity Act, 80
annual statement of Social Security
benefits, 162-163
annuities, 31
deferred annuities, 34-36
estate planning and, 37

fees, 39-40
fixed immediate annuities, 32-33
IRAs and, 38
M&E (mortality and expense risk charge) 36
Medicaid eligibility and, 219-221
reverse mortgages and, 83
taxes and, 37
variable annuities, 40-43
variable immediate annuities, 33-34
appraisal fees for reverse mortgages, 88
Arnett, Ron, 73
artificial hydration, addressing in advance-care health directives, 243-244
artificial nutrition, addressing in advance-care health directives, 243-244
assets, spending down for Medicaid eligibility, 214-217
annuities, 219-221
Congressional assumptions about, 232-235
half-a-loaf giving, 221-222
life estates, 218-219
life insurance, 224-225
personal care agreements, 224
retirement plans, 225
trusts, 225-226
assisted-living facilities, choosing, 119-126
assumptions about spending down assets for Medicaid eligibility, 232-235
at-home care, reverse mortgages for, 94-95

B

baby boomers, as sandwich generation, 100
balanced portfolio, 25
Bank of America, 40

Barg, Gary, 100, 108
Bartlett, Donald L. 199
beneficiaries
contingent beneficiaries for IRAs, 4
rollover IRAs, 5
stretch IRAs, 4-5
BFOQ (bona fide occupational qualification), 64
bonds, ratio to stocks, 25
borrowing
from 401(k) retirement accounts, 11
from Social Security trust fund, 175
burden of proof in age discrimination, 65
Burger v. New York Institute of Technology, 66
Bush, George W. 210
Bush, Jeb, 253

C

calculating Social Security benefits, 162
calculators for retirement planning, 18
California, age discrimination cases in, 73
Canadian prescription drugs, 198-200
capital gains taxes, 57-59
capital improvements, as medical expense deductions, 49-50
care plans, choosing nursing homes, 115
Caregiver.com Web site, 108
caregivers
advance-care health directives, 103-104
Caregiver.com Web site, 108
facts needed, 105
fulfilling needs of, 107-108
geriatric care managers, 107

D

death. *See* funeral industry
deductibles, 178
   Medicare Part B, 180
deductions. *See* taxes
deferred annuities, 34-36
   as long-term care insurance,
   155-156
Deficit Reduction Act of 2005,
   210, 212, 215-216, 220-221, 226,
   230-232
defined-benefit pension plans from
   previous employers, finding, 22-23
delayed retirement versus early
   retirement, effect on Social
   Security benefits, 164-168
dependent care credit, taxes and, 48
dependents, taxes and, 45-48
disability insurance, as long-term
   care insurance, 156
disability insurance benefits,
   taxability of, 56
discrimination. *See* age
   discrimination
disparate impact, as age
   discrimination, 67-69
disparate treatment, as age
   discrimination, 66
distributions from IRAs. *See* IRAs
diversification, 401(k) retirement
   accounts, 12-13
divorce, Medicaid and, 226
Do Not Resuscitate order, 245
doctors, choosing nursing
   homes, 115
document-preparation fees for
   reverse mortgages, 88
"doughnut hole" of prescription
   drug coverage, 187-189
downsizing. *See* layoffs
durable power of attorney,
   importance of, 213

durable power of attorney for
   health care. *See* advance-care
   health directives

E

early retirement versus delayed
   retirement, effect on Social
   Security benefits, 164-168
early withdrawals, 401(k)
   retirement accounts, 11-12
education, 529 Plans, 28-29
EEOC (Equal Employment
   Opportunity Commission), age
   discrimination lawsuits, 75-76
Eldercare Locator, 104, 106
eligibility age, effect on
   Medicare, 203
employer contributions. *See*
   company matches
enrollment period for prescription
   drug plans, 190-192
Enron, 13
Equal Employment Opportunity
   Commission (EEOC), age
   discrimination lawsuits, 75-76
equity index annuities, 34-35
estate planning, annuities and, 37
estate recovery, Medicaid and,
   227-229
estate taxes, federal estate tax law, 9
estates, IRAs and, 5
ethical issues, Medicare, 204-205
eviction policy, choosing
   assisted-living facilities, 125-126
exceptions process, Medicare
   Part D, 189
experimental treatments, Medicare
   and, 204-205

F

family caregivers. *See* caregivers
Fannie Mae, Home Keeper
   mortgage, 85
federal estate tax law, 9

income taxes. *See* taxes
Individual Retirement Accounts.
  See IRAs
inflation, 16
inflation protection, long-term care
  insurance, 136, 142
insurance. *See also* health
  insurance; life insurance;
  long-term care insurance
  accelerated death benefits,
    taxability of, 57
  accident or health insurance
    benefits, taxability of, 56
  disability insurance benefits,
    taxability of, 56
  mortgage insurance, 87
interest rates
  laddering investments, 28
  locking for reverse mortgages,
    84-85
intervivos trusts, 58
investments. *See also* annuities;
  401(k) retirement accounts; IRAs;
  mutual funds; stocks
  529 Plans, 28-29
  in baby boomer-related
    companies, 23-24
  balanced portfolio, 25
  fees, 26
  laddering, 28
  long-term growth, 27
  risk, 27
  target funds, 25-26
IRAs (Individual Retirement
  Accounts) 4-5
  annuities and, 38
  rollovers from 401(k)
    accounts, 10
  Roth IRAs, income limitations, 7
  taxes on distributions, 52-54
IRS, life expectancy tables, 4. *See
  also* taxes
itemized deductions. *See* taxes

J–K

JCAHO (Joint Commission on
  Accreditation of Healthcare
  Organizations), 117, 120
John Hancock LifeCare Benefit
  Rider, 152
Johnson, Dr. Robert, 69

Kemper, Peter, 233
Klingaman, Leroy J. 55

L

laddering investments, 28
lawsuits, age discrimination, filing,
  74-76
layoffs, age discrimination in, 65-66
Leavitt, Mike, 198
legacy, home as, 93-94
lender-insured reverse mortgages,
  82-83
length of coverage, long-term care
  insurance, 134
licensing, choosing nursing
  homes, 116
liens on homes, Medicaid and, 226
life estates, Medicaid eligibility and,
  218-219
life expectancy, 17, 129
  IRS tables, 4
  Social Security benefits and, 166
life insurance, 19
  accelerated death benefits, 57,
    149-150
  combining with long-term care
    insurance, 156-157
  contesting long-term care
    claims, 153
  John Hancock LifeCare Benefit
    Rider, 152
  long-term care insurance
    versus, 151
  Medicaid eligibility and, 224-225
  paying premiums with
    retirement funds, 153

permanent life insurance, 146-147

second-to-die policies, 154

single premium life insurance, 152-153

swapping policies, 154

taxability of, 56

term life insurance, 146

viatical settlement companies, 148-149

living revocable trusts, 58

living will parties, 245

living wills, advance-care health directives versus, 240-241

loans, reverse mortgages. *See* reverse mortgages

location

choosing assisted-living facilities, 123

choosing nursing homes, 114

locking interest rates for reverse mortgages, 84-85

long-distance caregiving, 104-105

long-term care claims, contesting, 153

long-term care insurance, 129. *See also* Medicaid

accelerated death benefits versus, 149

affordability, 139-141

alternatives to. *See* life insurance

combining life insurance with, 156-157

comparing companies, 137-138

criminal acts and, 144

deferred annuities as, 155-156

disability insurance as, 156

group policies, 137

history of, 131-133

inflation protection, 142

life insurance versus, 151

marriage and, 141-142

Medicaid look-back period and, 231

medical records and, 143

Partnership for Long-Term Care, 230-231

premium increases, 142

provisions in policies, 133-137

reasons for buying, 131

reverse mortgages and, 81

self-insuring, 130

as tax deduction, 51

taxability of, 56

"three-legged-stool" model, 157-158

when to buy, 138-139

long-term growth investments, 27

longevity. *See* life expectancy

look-back period (Medicaid), 215-217, 231

M

M&E (mortality and expense risk charge), 36

marriage, long-term care insurance and, 141-142

matching contributions. *See* company matches

MDS (Minimum Data Set) Repository, 112

Meals on Wheels program, 106

means testing for Social Security benefits, 174

Medicaid, 207

adult children and, 227

at-home care and, 94-95

costs of, 208

countable and noncountable assets, 211-214

Deficit Reduction Act of 2005, 230-232

divorce and, 226

estate recovery and, 227-229

liens on homes, 226

and long-term care insurance, 139

look-back period, 215-217, 231

nursing homes
  adult children as financially
    responsible for, 227
  average stay statistics, 130
  choosing, 111-117
  long-term care insurance. *See*
    long-term care insurance
  Medicaid. *See* Medicaid

O

OBRA (Omnibus Budget
  Reconciliation Act of, 1993), 228
ombudsman, choosing
  assisted-living facilities, 123
open-end reverse mortgages, 84
oral contracts, choosing
  assisted-living facilities, 121
origination fees, 87
OSCAR (Online Survey,
  Certification, and Reporting
  database), 112

P

parents, as dependents on taxes,
  45-48
parties for advance-care health
  directives, 245
Partnership for Long-Term Care,
  230-231
Patient Self Determination Act
  of 1990, 246
payment plan options for reverse
  mortgages, 86
Pearse, Richard, 250-251
pensions from previous employers,
  finding, 22-23
permanent life insurance, 146-147
persistent vegetative state, 249, 255
personal care agreements, Medicaid
  eligibility and, 224
personal information, security in
  nursing homes, 117
pet policy, choosing assisted-living
  facilities, 124

pharmaceutical companies,
  lobbying efforts by, 199
planning, Medicaid planning,
  208-209
points (on loans) 87-89
Pollack, Ron, 200
PPOs (preferred provider
  organizations) 178
predictions about stock market,
  29-30
premiums. *See also* costs; fees
  long-term care insurance,
    132-133, 137-143
  Medicare Part B, 179-180
  prescription drug plans, 192
prescription drugs
  creditable plans, 193
  enrollment period for
    prescription drug plans,
    190-192
  generic prescription drugs,
    200-201
  Medicaid and, 192
  Medicare Part D, 183-190
    *Canadian prescription drugs
    and,* 198-200
    comparing plans, 195-196
    considerations when choosing,
    193-195
    enrolling, 196
    price increases under, 197-198
  Medigap plans and, 182, 191-192
  TRICARE for Life program, 193
preventive services, Medicare
  Part B, 180-181, 202
private accounts, Social Security
  benefits and, 171-173
private insurance companies,
  Medicare Part D offered by, 187
probate estates, Medicaid estate
  recovery and, 228
provisional income, 54
PSOs (provider-sponsored
  organizations) 178

Q–R

Quinlan, Karen Ann, 247
Quinn, Joseph F. 233

Reasonable Factors Other Than Age
(RFOA), 69
record-keeping for tax purposes,
59-60
recording fees for reverse
mortgages, 88
reducing Social Security
benefits, 166
reduction in force. *See* layoffs
registering advance-care health
directives, 244
regulations, choosing assisted-living
facilities, 119-120
remainder interest, 94
renewability, long-term care
insurance, 135
repayment of reverse mortgages, 90
requirements. *See* regulations
rescinding reverse mortgages, 93
respirators, addressing in
advance-care health directives, 243
retirement, delaying, 20-21
retirement age, raising for Social
Security benefits, 173-174
retirement age chart for Social
Security benefits, 163
retirement plans. *See also* financial
considerations
Medicaid eligibility and, 225
paying life insurance premiums
with, 153
reverse age discrimination, 71
reverse half-a-loaf giving, Medicaid
eligibility and, 221
reverse mortgages, 79-80
for at-home care, 94-95
conditions of, 91
conventional mortgages versus,
81-82
counseling regarding, 92

fees for, 87-89
FHA-insured reverse
mortgages, 82
Home Keeper mortgage
(Fannie Mae) 85
lender-insured reverse
mortgages, 82-83
locking interest rates for, 84-85
long-term care insurance and, 81
open-end reverse mortgages, 84
payment plan options, 86
reducing home equity for
Medicaid eligibility, 214
repayment, 90
rescinding, 93
scams concerning, 95
shared equity and shared
appreciation fees, 95-96
Social Security benefits and, 90
taxes and, 89
uninsured reverse mortgages,
83-84
when to use, 91-92
RFOA (Reasonable Factors Other
Than Age) 69
right to die. *See* advance-care health
directives
risk
in investments, 27
in variable annuities, 41
rollover IRAs, 5
rollovers, 401(k) retirement
accounts, 10-11
roommates, choosing nursing
homes, 115
Roth 401(k) retirement
accounts, 6-9
Roth IRAs
income limitations, 7
taxes on distributions, 52
rules changes in Medicaid, 209-210

S

sale of home, capital gains taxes and, 57-59

sandwich generation, baby boomers as, 100

scams
Medicare Part D and, 186
reverse mortgages and, 95

Schiavo, Michael, 248-252, 256

Schiavo, Terri, 248-256

Schiff, Irwin, 60

Schindler, Robert and Mary, 249-252, 256

second-to-die life insurance, 154

security
choosing nursing homes, 113
identity theft, 117

segment mutual funds, 23

self-insuring for long-term care, 130

selling
home, for Medicaid eligibility, 214, 217, 229
life insurance policies, 148-149

Senior Citizen's Freedom to Work Act, 50-51

service fees. *See* fees

services available, choosing assisted-living facilities, 122

Serving Health Information Needs for Elders (SHINE), 196

shared appreciation fees, reverse mortgages and, 95-96

shared equity fees, reverse mortgages and, 95-96

shared responsibility of family caregivers, 103

sheltering assets. *See* spending down assets

SHINE (Serving Health Information Needs for Elders), 196

SHIP (State Health Insurance and Assitance Program), 195

Shonts, Mildred, 117

single premium life insurance, 152-153

Sloan, Frank, 234

smell test, choosing nursing homes, 114

smoking policy, choosing nursing homes, 116

snapshot date (Medicaid) 214

Social Security
borrowing from trust fund, 175
proposed changes to system, 172-174
solvency of, 169-171

Social Security Administration, reporting identity theft, 186

Social Security benefits, 19-20
annual statement of, 162-163
calculating, 162
COLA, 162
coverage requirements, 162
early retirement versus delayed retirement, 164-168
life expectancy and, 166
means testing for, 174
myths about, 169-171
private accounts and, 171-173
raising retirement age for, 173-174
reducing, 50-51, 166
retirement age chart, 163
reverse mortgages and, 90
for surviving spouse, 167-168
taxability of, 54-55, 169

solvency of Social Security, 169-171

specificity in advance-care health directives, 242-242

spending down assets for Medicaid eligibility, 214-217
annuities, 219-221
Congressional assumptions about, 232-235
half-a-loaf giving, 221-222
life estates, 218-219
life insurance, 224-225

Age Smart
Discovering the Fountain of Youth at Midlife and Beyond
BY JEFFREY ROSENSWEIG
AND BETTY LIU
FOREWORD BY DR. KENNETH H. COOPER, M.D.

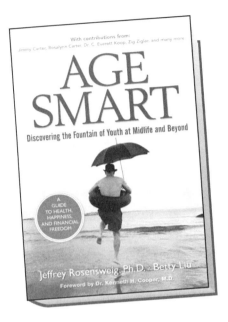

Age Smart is your entertaining, easy-to-use guide to p
paring for a longer, better, happier life. CNN commenta
Jeffrey Rosensweig and top journalist Betty Liu offer •
vice on topics ranging from money and health, work a
love, even spirituality…plus practical tools and checkli
you can start using right now, no matter how old you a
With contributions from Jimmy Carter, Helen Gurley Brov
Dr. C Everett Koop, Dave Oreck, Robert Mondavi, and ma
more. You'll discover what science has revealed ab•
protecting your long-term health…uncover financial realit
your advisors haven't told you…and learn how to strength
the human connections at the heart of a fulfilling life. Agi
well isn't dumb luck. *Age Smart* will help you take control
your aging: mind and money, body and soul!

ISBN 0131867628, © 2006, 256 pp., $24.99

Deal with Your Debt
The Right Way to Manage Your Bills and Pay Off What You Owe
LIZ PULLIAM WESTON

In *Deal with Your Debt*, award-winning personal finance
columnist Liz Weston explains the rules and explodes
the myths surrounding debt. You'll discover the crucial
role debt can play in your portfolio, identifying debts that
actually contribute to your wealth and flexibility, and managing those better-as you avoid or eliminate "toxic" debts.
Weston presents effective strategies for evaluating, moni-
toring, and paying every form of debt, from credit cards and
mortgages to student and auto loans. She offers practical
guidelines for how much debt you should take on and early
warning signs that tell you you're getting in too deep. You'll
find realistic (and often surprising) guidance on everything
from home equity loans and 401K borrowing to small business loans. Follow these strategies, and debt can work for
you-instead of the other way around!

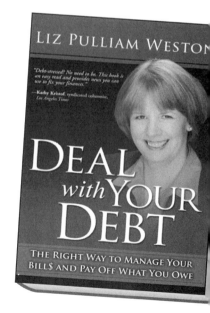

ISBN 0131856758, © 2006, 240 pp., $17.99